Soccer and Disaster

A sending off; the conceding of a vital goal; an untimely defeat – disaster is a much used term in sport. Yet soccer has also been the victim of real disasters: events where people lost their lives. But when compared to tragedies such as the Munich air disaster and Heysel Stadium disaster, of course the results of games become insignificant. Football is not more important than life or death.

This book looks at soccer disasters from across the globe. From the loss of talented young players in air crashes in Munich and Zambia, to fatal overcrowding in Johannesburg and Sheffield – the game, its fans and players have been the victims of negligence, complacency and misfortune. The causes, consequences and legacies of these and other disasters are explored here in a book that reveals frightening parallels and important lessons.

This was first published as a special issue of journal *Soccer and Society* which was entitled '*Soccer and Disaster*'.

Paul Darby is a lecturer in the Sociology of Sport at the University of Ulster at Jordanstown. He has written widely on Africa's place in FIFA'S global order. He was Academic Editor of the International Journal, *Soccer and Society* between 2000–2005 and is currently a member of the journals editorial board.

Martin Johnes is a lecturer at St Martin's College, Lancaster. He has written widely on both sports history and disasters.

Gavin Mellor is a lecturer at Coventry University and the University of Central Lancashire, and currently lectures at Liverpool Hope University College in the Sociology of Sport. He is currently Senior Reviews Editor for the International Journal, *Soccer and Society*.

SPORT IN THE GLOBAL SOCIETY

General Editors: J.A. Mangan and Boria Majumdar

The interest in sports studies around the world is growing and will continue to do so. This unique series combines aspects of the expanding study of *sport in the global society*, providing comprehensiveness and comparison under one editorial umbrella. It is particularly timely, with studies in the aesthetic elements of sport proliferating in institutions of higher education.

Eric Hobsbawm once called sport one of the most significant practices of the late nineteenth century. Its significance was even more marked in the late twentieth century and will continue to grow in importance into the new millennium as the world develops into a 'global village' sharing the English language, technology and sport.

Other Titles in the Series

Disreputable Pleasures
Less Virtuous Victorians at Play
Edited by Mike Huggins and J.A. Mangan

Italian Fascism and the Female Body
Sport, Submissive Women and Strong Mothers
Gigliola Gori

Rugby's Great Split
Class, Culture and the Origins of Rugby League Football
Tony Collins

Terrace Heroes
The Life and Times of the 1930s Professional Footballer
Graham Kelly

Barbarians, Gentlemen and Players
A Sociological Study of the Development of Rugby Football
Second Edition
Eric Dunning and Kenneth Sheard

Capoeira
The History of an Afro-Brazilian Martial Art
Matthias Röhrig Assunção

British Football and Social Exclusion
Edited by Stephen Wagg

The First Black Footballer
Arthur Wharton 1865–1930: An Absence of Memory
Phil Vasili

Soccer and Disaster

Paul Darby, Martin Johnes & Gavin Mellor

Routledge
Taylor & Francis Group

London and New York

This book is dedicated to all those who have lost their lives in football disasters around the world.

First published 2005 by Routledge, an imprint of Taylor & Francis
2 Park Square, Milton Park, Abingdon, Oxon, OX14 4RN

Simultaneously published in the USA and Canada
by Routledge
270 Madison Ave, New York, NY 10016

Routledge is an imprint of the Taylor & Francis Group

Typeset in Ehrhardt by Genesis Typesetting Limited, Rochester, Kent
Printed and bound in Great Britain by Antony Rowe Ltd Chippenham, Wilts

British Library Cataloguing in Publication Data
A catalogue record for this book is available from the British Library

Library of Congress Cataloging in Publication Data
a catalog record for this book has been requested

ISBN 0-714-65352-7 (hbk)
ISBN 0-714-68289-6 (pbk)

CONTENTS

Notes on the Contributors

Yiğit Akın is a research assistant at the Ataturk Institute for Modern Turkish History at the Bogazici University (Istanbul/Turkey). His main interest is in the social and cultural history of the late Ottoman and early Republican Turkey. He is currently undertaking research on the development of sports and physical education in Turkey during the first half of the twentieth century.

Peter Alegi is Assistant Professor of History and Co-Director of the African/African-American Studies Program at Eastern Kentucky University, USA. He has lectured in African history at Harvard University and Boston University, and in sport history at Tufts University. He is the author of *Laduma! Soccer, Politics and Society in South Africa* (University of KwaZulu-Natal Press, 2004).

Fabio Chisari, MA in Sports History and Culture, is a PhD student at De Montfort University of Leicester, working on a research project on a comparative history of football on TV in Britain and Italy. He has published various articles in specialized journals studying the relationship between sport and the media.

Paul Darby is a lecturer in the sociology of sport at the University of Ulster (Jordanstown). He has written broadly on the relationship between Europe and Africa as mediated by football. He is the author of *Africa, Football and FIFA: Politics, Colonialism and Resistance* (London and Portland: Frank Cass, 2002), and was Academic Editor of the International Journal *Soccer and Society* between 2000–2005. He is currently a member of the journals editorial board and sits on the Advisory Board of 'Impumelelo': The Interdisciplinary Electronic Journal of African Sport. He received his doctorate from the University of Ulster in 1997.

Paul Dietschy is Lecturer at the Franche-Comté University (Besançon, France). After his Ph.D. thesis on football and society in Turin, he has published articles on football history in France and in Italy during the fascist period. He has participated in the research and book for the FIFA Centennial with Tony Mason and Pierre Lanfranchi. He also co-manages the research seminar on sport, European societies and cultures at the Centre d'histoire de l'Europe du Vingtième Siècle (CHEVS) of the Institut d'Etudes Politiques (Paris).

Jeff Hill is Professor of Historical and Cultural Studies at de Montfort University. His *Sport, Leisure and Culture in Twentieth-Century Britain* (Palgrave/

Macmillan) came out in 2002, and he is currently working on a study of the representation of sport in twentieth-century novel writing.

Martin Johnes is a lecturer at St Martin's College, Lancaster. He has written widely on both sports history and disasters. His publications include *Aberfan: Government and Disasters* (with Iain McLean, Welsh Academic Press, 2000) and *Soccer and Society: South Wales, 1900–39* (University of Wales Press, 2002).

Gavin Mellor has taught the sociology of sport at Coventry University, the University of Central Lancashire and Liverpool Hope University College. He is currently working at Manchester Metropolitan University. His research interests include football and differing levels of identity, including local, regional and national. He has published in a number of sports and non-sports academic journals and is currently Senior Reviews Editor for the international journal *Soccer and Society*.

Aldo Panfichi has a Ph.D. in Sociology from the New School for Social Research, New York (USA). He is currently associate professor and researcher in the Department of Social Science and the Graduate School at the Universidad Catolica del Peru. His fields of research are football and popular culture, civil society and democracy in Latin America. Among his recent publications in the field of sports are co-authored with Jorge Thieroldt, 'Identity and Rivalry: The Football Clubs and Barras Bravas of Perú', in *Futbol, Futebol, Soccer: Football in the Americas* (ILAS, University of London, UK, forthcoming); co-authored with Jorge Thieroldt, 'Barras Bravas: Representation and Crowd Violence in Peruvian Football', in Eric Dunning, Patrick Murphy and Ivan Waddington (eds), *Fighting Fans: Football Hooliganism as a World Problem* (Dublin: University College Dublin Press, 2002); co-authored with Luis Millones and Victor Vich, *En el Corazón del Pueblo: Pasión y gloria de Alianza Lima 1901-2001*, Essays and Photographs (Fondo Editorial del Congreso del Perú, 2002).

Phil Scraton is Professor of Criminology in the Institute of Criminology and Criminal Justice, School of Law, Queen's University, Belfast. Until recently he was Professor and Director of the Centre for Studies in Crime and Social Justice at Edge Hill University College. His primary research includes: the regulation and criminalization of children and young people; controversial deaths and the state; the rights of the bereaved and survivors in the aftermath of disasters; the politics of truth and official inquiry; critical analysis and its application. He is author of *The State of the Police* (Pluto, 1985) and *Hillsborough: The Truth* (Mainstream, 2000), co-author of *In the Arms of the Law: Coroners' Inquests and Deaths in Custody* (Pluto, 1987), *Prisons Under Protest* (Open University Press, 1991) and *No Last Rights: The Promotion of Myth and the Denial of Justice in the Aftermath of the Hillsborough Disaster* (LCC/Alden Press, 1985), and editor of *Causes for Concern:*

Criminal Justice on Trial (Penguin, 1984), *Law, Order and the Authoritarian State: Readings in Critical Criminology* (Open University Press, 1987), *'Childhood' in 'Crisis'?* (UCL Press, 1997) and *Beyond September 11: An Anthology of Dissent* (Pluto, 2002). He has written extensively on a range of human rights and social justice issues and his current research is into women's imprisonment in Northern Ireland for the Human Rights Commission and into the welfare and rights of children and young people for the NI Children's Commissioner.

Victor Vich has a Ph.D. in Latin American Literature from Georgetown University, USA. He is currently associate professor at the Catholic University of Perú and researcher at the Instituto de Estudios Peruanos (IEP). He has published *El discurso de la calle: los comicos ambulantes y las tensiones de la modernidad en el Perú*, 2001, and *El canibal es el otro: violencia y cultura en el Peru contemporáneo*, 2002.

Graham Walker was born, raised and educated in Glasgow. He is currently Reader in Politics at the Queen's University of Belfast. He has published widely in the subject areas of sport, politics and sectarianism in Scotland and Northern Ireland; modern Irish and Scottish history; and Irish and British contemporary politics. He attended the 1971 Ibrox disaster match.

Foreword

The worship of Dionysus in the classical world witnessed the replacement of prudence by passion, and in its initial form, was savage and repulsive.[1]

The follower of Dionysius recovered in intoxication, physical and spiritual, an intensity of feeling which prudence had destroyed; he found a world of escapist delight; his imagination was liberated from the prison of every-day tedium.[2]

Prudence versus passion, Bertrand Russell once remarked, was a conflict that ran through history,[3] and it might be added, has run through the history of association football contributing not a little but by no means wholly, to the tragedies retold in *Soccer and Disaster*.

In the closed world of association football, as in other sports, the word 'disaster' has parochial, partisan, overheated connotations. Mostly, it relates to matches lost, cups unwon and leagues unconquered: glory unattained, humiliation encountered.

Soccer and Disaster, in fact, deals poignantly in tragedy; with lost lives, crushed limbs, mutilated bodies and traumatised emotions in stadii as disparate as Ibrox and Ellis Park and places as disparate as Lima and Munich. However, it describes not simply loss but also gain.

Soccer and Disaster uncovers English protective national mythology – the famous policeman on the white horse, and reveals the power of catastrophe to unite, albeit momentarily, bitterly protagonistic fans.

Dionysian passion also triumphs over physical pain:

In a League match in 1970s Calcutta, India, Mohun Bagan, the local favourites, won by a big margin. After the match the jubilant crowd rushed towards Esplanade, the central junction, to board buses and trams on the way home. A few bare-chested young lads stood on the rod of the tram's wheel because of the overcrowding, hanging on to the windows of the tram with one hand. They were waiving their shirts like Mohun Bagan flags. As the tram abruptly stopped at a road signal, one of the lads got thrown onto the street and his feet were run over by the wheels of the tram. However, as the tram started to move, the lad ran and jumped into the tram. After the tram had left, a severed toe was found amidst a few drops of blood while a thin red line stretched along the tramline. The pain got lost in the euphoria of victory.

Incidents such as these receive thoughtful attention in *Soccer and Disaster*.'

Finally, *Soccer and Disaster* exposes inexcusable regulatory lethargy, indifference and complacency. The progress of attempts at crowd control is not lineal. In Elizabethan England professional drama advanced in the teeth of resolute opposition from city authorities throughout the kingdom and especially in London, where men strongly objected to this burgeoning entertainment on grounds, among other things, of public order.[4] The civil authorities of late

Victorian England took a casual stance towards the growth of association football with long-term regrettable consequences. Laissez-Faireism provided a dowry of death to later generations. It proved to be a myopic libertarianism.

Its legacy contained a compelling truth: ' ... in every single tragedy, the audience is left with a balance of conflicting emotions as regards... the bid for liberation and its cost. And in that equilibrium lies much of the power of tragedy.'[5] Thus the final impression left by *Soccer and Disaster* is one of tragedies too often preventable.

Without question, ' (Association) football has literally cost many people their lives, usually in circumstances that could, or should have been avoided '.[6]

J.A. Mangan
Boria Majumdar
Series Editors, Sport in the Global Society

NOTES

1. Bertrand Russell, *History of Western Philosophy*, (London: Allen & Unwin, 1955), p.34.
2. Ibid., p.35.
3. Ibid., p.34.
4. Pat Rogers (ed.), *The Oxford Illustrated History of English Literature* (London:OUP,1987), p.112.
5. Ibid., p.150.
6. Paul Darby et al., (eds), *Soccer and Disaster: International Perspectives* (London: Routledge, 2005), p.132.

Introduction
Football Disasters: A Conceptual Frame

PAUL DARBY, MARTIN JOHNES, GAVIN MELLOR

Disaster is an overused word in football. Goals scored against a team, heavy defeats and relegations are all regularly described as 'disasters' by fans, journalists, players and the game's administrators. Within the contemporary context of football, where playing success is paramount and supporters have significant emotional investments in the outcomes of matches, a team being knocked out of a tournament or relegated to a lower league may well be classified in line with the *Oxford English Dictionary's* definition of a disaster as an incident of 'great or sudden misfortune'. Yet, to a detached observer, when compared to episodes associated with football that have led to people losing their lives, events on the pitch must seem entirely trivial. Moreover, even when deaths occur in the context of football, some may question the appropriateness of using the label 'disaster' to describe incidents, such as those outlined in this book, that involve relatively small numbers of fatalities. This is particularly likely when football-related deaths are compared with events such as the terrorist attacks on New York on 11 September 2001, the Bam earthquake in December 2003, or more recently, the Tsunami in the Indian Ocean all of which resulted in catastrophic loss of life.

There are clear difficulties associated with establishing what actually constitutes a 'disaster' within football-related contexts and beyond. In purely quantitative, 'measurable' terms (numbers of dead, physical damage, economic cost, etcetera) the incidents described in this book are manifestly different from the large-scale natural or man-made disasters that periodically blight particular regions of the world. Nonetheless, the same descriptor is routinely applied. This conceptual problem has featured prominently in the development of disaster studies as a field of academic enquiry. By acknowledging that there are significant quantitative differences between events that are popularly depicted as disasters, much of the early work in this field attempted to provide a fixed quantitative measure that could define which incidents qualify as disasters and which do not.[1] This proved to be a difficult task. As Alexander notes, 'these [definitions] proved unworkably simplistic, as too many elements are involved to enable one to define the phenomenon purely on the basis of, for example, numbers of people killed...or monetary losses'.[2] More recent attempts to resolve this conceptual problem have tended to define disasters in qualitative rather than quantitative terms. These definitions have been much more liberal and inclusive and have identified the social, economic, political and emotional *consequences* of particular incidents as key factors in allowing them to be accurately categorised as disasters.[3] By drawing on a classification system that accords more significance to the qualitative rather than the quantitative consequences of disasters, it becomes less problematic to label single incidents involving relatively small numbers of deaths as culturally disastrous events.

The 'beautiful game' of football has often been a deadly one, especially for its fans. Whilst it is extremely difficult to attempt to list all of the disasters that have befallen football's supporters in the game's history (not least because of the difficulty of defining a 'disaster'), it is worth noting that significant numbers of football supporters have died at football matches throughout the world since at least the beginning of the twentieth century. The first major football crowd disaster in Britain occurred at Glasgow Rangers' Ibrox stadium in 1902 when 25 people died and over 500 were injured after terracing collapsed during an international match between Scotland and England. Since that incident, four other significant stadium disasters have occurred in Britain - at Bolton in 1946, at Glasgow in 1971, at Bradford in 1985, and at Sheffield in 1989 - that resulted in a combined total of 251 deaths. British football fans were also involved in the Heysel Stadium disaster in Belgium in 1985, when 39 fans died after crowd disorder led to a wall collapsing in the ageing stadium.

Whilst British football supporters have been subject to relatively frequent stadium disasters, they have not been the victims of the world's most deadly soccer tragedies. The Lima stadium disaster in 1964 cost 320 people their lives, and the Moscow disaster of 1982 is estimated to have resulted in at least 340 deaths. These disasters, whilst exceptional in scale, are by no means the only international football disasters to result in significant loss of life. Argentina (1968), Lebanon (1968), Turkey (1968 and 1974), Egypt (1979), Nigeria (1979), Greece (1981), Columbia (1982), Nepal (1988), Guatemala (1996), South Africa (2001), and Ghana (2001) have all experienced football stadium disasters that have killed at least twenty people.

Images of some crowd disasters, such as Hillsborough (1989) where 96 Liverpool fans died, were broadcast around the globe and have become lodged in the game's public history; yet others that took place outside the western world, like the Lima tragedy in 1964 or the disaster in Buenos Aires four years later, are remembered far less widely beyond those immediately affected.[4] While it is occurrences of mass deaths that have had the most impact on the consciousness of the game, countless more supporters have died in individual incidents, sometimes as a consequence of crushing, sometimes as a result of violence by other fans. The impact of these deaths on the culture and industry of football has taken various forms according to the specific circumstances and contexts of the incidents. Football and political authorities have ignored some deaths, whereas others have been defined squarely as 'disasters' and have given rise to structural changes in the whole governance and economy of the game in the countries where they have occurred.

Stadium-related football disasters have undoubtedly been the most deadly, in terms of loss of life, which have occurred around the game. They are not, however, the only disasters to have blighted football in recent decades. Since the end of the Second World War, a significant number of football players, coaches and administrators have been lost from the game in air crashes. Whilst it is difficult to ascertain the exact number of fatal air crashes that have resulted in the deaths of professional footballers, it is possible to note the most significant air disasters to have affected the game. The first of these occurred in 1949 when a plane carrying the Italian champions Torino home from a friendly in Lisbon crashed killing eighteen players, along with the team's technical staff and trainers, and three journalists. Since this event, a number of other air disasters have affected teams across the world. In 1958, eight members of the 'Busby Babes' Manchester United team died when their plane crashed on take-off in the German city of Munich. In 1961, staff and players from Green Cross of Chile perished when their aircraft hit a mountain. The Andes claimed Bolivia's most popular team, The Strongest, in 1969, whilst fourteen players and three members of staff from the Russian team Pakhtakor Tashkent died in a mid-air collision in 1979. Players and officials from Alianza Lima, of Peru, were lost in the Pacific Ocean in 1987, and fourteen Surinamese members of Dutch clubs were killed when their aircraft attempted to land in fog at Paramaribo in 1989. In the most recent air disaster to occur in world football, and the only one so far to affect a national team, eighteen Zambian national team players died after their military aircraft plunged into the Atlantic off Gabon in 1993.

When defined in purely quantitative terms, many of these air crashes are not particularly significant, especially when compared to incidents such as the Lockerbie air disaster that resulted in the deaths of 259 passengers and 11 people on the ground. If approached from a more cultural perspective, however, the majority of these incidents are hugely significant, not least in terms of their emotional consequences. The links between sport, social identity and community have been a central focus of much sport sociology and history, and these links have often been thrown into sharp focus at the time of air crashes and other incidents that have resulted in the untimely deaths of football players and managers. The deep, emotional connections that football supporters have with 'their' teams ensure that when tragedies befall team players and other club representatives, fans often feel an acute sense of shared loss. In the wake of many of the air crashes that have blighted football, supporters and wider communities have gone into deep mourning, expressing their connection to those that have died. This mourning has frequently coalesced into prolonged remembrance around the deaths. Indeed, as we shall see in this book, some football clubs' supporters now define who they are and what they stand for by constant reference to tragic events that have affected their clubs. In this sense, these fans have defined certain deaths and tragedies as significant 'disasters' because of emotional consequences that they produced for them, and because of the specific cultural milieus in which those disasters occurred.

Football disasters are not unusual in being constructed according to particular cultural contexts and values. As Horlick-Jones points out, disasters 'take place, and are perceived in, specific socio–economic, historical, cultural and chronological contexts'.[5] It is these circumstances that determine what is actually regarded as a disaster. Indeed, a disaster is ultimately any event constructed and viewed as such by the society or community in which it occurs. Thus the death of eighteen Zambian international football players in 1993 might seem trivial when compared with the fact that prevalence rates of HIV/Aids in Zambia are currently running at more than twenty percent of the total population.[6] However, the Zambian people, the Zambian media, and a variety of other institutions defined the deaths of the Zambian football players as a 'disaster', illustrating how the construction of an event as a disaster is always contingent on wider social processes.

Analyses of disasters that consider not only the 'causes' of disastrous incidents, but also the ways in which societies and communities construct and respond to tragedies, can reveal much about the social, economic and political cultures in which we exist. This is why the study of disasters in football, or indeed any other context, is a worthwhile exercise. The disasters that are analysed in this collection are not studied for their own sake. The reader will not find in most chapters long explanations of the technical details of why and how individual tragedies occurred. Rather, the disasters are analysed to reveal the social tensions, economic and organisational deficiencies, political structures, and cultural practices that exist in various societies and football cultures across the world. Thus this collection sets out to explore different football disasters within the social, economic and political contexts in which they occurred. It should not be regarded as a definitive account of every football disaster or even a guide to what the main disasters are in the game's history. Instead, it offers an analysis of particular disasters that have resonance for a wider understanding of the game's social and political economies in different cultural times and places.

The first article in this collection sees Martin Johnes offer an overview of the regulatory and political responses to crowd disasters in twentieth-century Britain. He argues that the responses were too often characterized by an apathy towards safety amongst the football authorities, central government and fans. This apathy was rooted in a desire to exclude sport from legislation, in the terrace culture of the game, in the characterization of fans as hooligans and the exclusion of the safety of soccer fans from the concerns of central government.

The British game has suffered more disasters than anywhere else. This perhaps owes something to the age of its grounds, so many of which were built in the late nineteenth century.[7] The date and design of British football stadiums led many clubs in the 1990s to completely rebuild their homes or even move to new stadia, a process which was an integral part of a wider reinvention of the game in the wake of the Hillsborough disaster and the influx of television money. One ground to be recently demolished was the world's most famous, Wembley Stadium. Yet despite its iconic stature, the stadium was actually the venue of a near-disaster during the first match that it ever hosted. The 1923 FA Cup final which opened Wembley Stadium, is the topic of this collection's second study. In it, Jeff Hill illustrates how what should have been a celebration of English football and its new stadium turned into chaos due to the sheer size of the huge crowd that attended the game. Yet despite the large number of injuries that resulted from the day's event, the fact that the match went ahead peacefully came to symbolize the orderliness of English crowds and the wider working class. The event is thus lodged in the game's public history as a proud moment rather than a narrowly avoided disaster.

Outside Glasgow, Ibrox stadium is perhaps best known as a conduit for the sectarianism associated with the 'old firm' rivalry. Yet, on at least three occasions, there have been multiple deaths in the ground caused by its design rather than the misbehaviour or violence of the fans. The third article here, by Graham Walker, explores the most recent and lethal of those incidents, the 1971 Ibrox disaster where 66 fans were killed in a crush on a stairway while trying to exit an 'old firm' derby. This context was paramount to the impact of the disaster. As Walker argues,

> The unique character and atmosphere of this fixture cannot be detached from the tragic events, and the disaster's impact on the Old Firm rivalry was significant, if not the catalyst towards change that was widely hoped for by civic society in Scotland. Moreover, a perception of the disaster outside Scotland as resulting from quasi-religious passions with no parallel elsewhere in Britain may have prevented a more attentive appreciation of the lessons that might have been learnt from it in relation to crowd safety in England.

The disaster did lead to the first safety regulation of sports grounds in the UK but it took the 1989 disaster at Hillsborough for the country's top stadia to be totally overhauled. The move to all-seater grounds in the English game's top two divisions may have been underpinned as much by the desire to eradicate hooliganism as it was to ensure the safety of fans but it had a radical impact on not only the game's built environment but also the whole culture of fandom. Ticket prices escalated and leading stadia became more sanitised, maybe even quieter.

While many fans were unhappy about such changes, they are insignificant when compared to the injustices endured by the victims of the Hillsborough disaster, which provides the focus of the article by Phil Scraton. Ninety-six fans were crushed to death after the police failed to manage the entry and distribution of supporters to a packed ground. Fences, designed to keep hooligans off the pitch, prevented the caged supporters escaping the fatal crush. Those 'in authority' treated the bereaved and survivors shockingly, from the immediate aftermath, through the identification of the dead to the various inquests and legal proceedings that followed. Salt was added to these wounds by the continued reference to the disaster by sections of the media, the football industry and academia as a tragedy caused by hooliganism rather than the mismanagement of the police authorities in charge of crowd control and safety that day.

Occurrences of stadium-based football disasters have not only been confined to British football. To illustrate this point and compare the causes, consequences and legacies of British football disasters with those that have happened elsewhere in the world, this book includes three articles that examine incidents involving loss of life at football stadiums in other countries. The first to be examined, the Heysel tragedy, actually involved hooliganism by fans of a British club, Liverpool FC. Whereas at Hillsborough they were the victims, four years earlier they had widely been believed to have been the main perpetrators of the deaths of 39 fans at the 1985 European Cup final. Chisari presents a passionate account of the disaster from the perspective of Juventus, the club whose supporters bore the brunt of the tragedy. He investigates how the disaster was received in Italy and firmly assigns responsibility to those Liverpool supporters involved in hooliganism, the football authorities who chose the venue, and the Belgian authorities that policed it. When viewed alongside the 56 deaths in the Bradford fire, 1985 was a dire year for British football. Whatever the current fashionability of the game, Chisari's article reminds us of a more shameful past.

In the second non-UK stadium disaster covered in this collection, Yigit Akin investigates, what he terms, 'one of the most catastrophic events in Turkish sports history': the stadium disaster that occurred in 1967 during a match between teams from the two major Anatolian cities of Kayseri and Sivas. In his analysis of this event, Akin explains a range of post-war socio-economic developments in Turkey, and investigates how these influenced the expansion of professional football into rural areas of the country. In this context, Akin goes on to explain how strained relations between the cities of Kayseri and Sivas contributed to a heightened sense of tension when Kayserispor and Sivasspor played each other for the first time in 1967; a tension which resulted in a stadium crush that killed 42 people and injured more than 300 others. In the remainder of his chapter, Akin investigates the consequences of the disaster for the people of Kayseri and Sivas, and explains how the Turkish government and Turkish football authorities reacted to the event.

In the next chapter on an international stadium disaster, Peter Alegi examines the Ellis Park Stadium disaster of 11 April 2001, when 43 people lost their lives and at least 158 were injured during a crucial match for the South African League Championship between Soweto rivals Kaizer Chiefs and Orlando Pirates. Nine days after the disaster, South Africa's President Thabo Mbeki appointed a Commission of Inquiry, headed by Justice B.M. Ngoepe. The Commission issued its final report in August 2002 and, although it made several recommendations to prevent future stadium tragedies, many questions were left unanswered. A year or so later, a Johannesburg newspaper voiced the feelings of many in the country when it asked: 'Why did 43 people lose their lives? Why?' The focus of Alegi's chapter is to address this very question. In particular, it analyses the causes of the disaster, and then investigates the strengths and weaknesses of the official findings in light of different interpretations of the events. Alegi concludes with a discussion of the ways in which fan culture and crowd management in contemporary South Africa have been influenced by the apartheid past.

The book then addresses four disasters involving the deaths of players and officials whilst travelling to or from football matches in airplanes. In the first of these, Paul Darby addresses the Zambian air disaster of 1993 which resulted in the loss of eighteen members of the Zambian national squad, along with a number of medical and technical staff and administrators. Darby begins by examining some of the conceptual difficulties associated with describing events leading to relatively small losses of life as disasters in a continent where this term is normally reserved for the massive death tolls associated with famine, drought, extreme poverty, civil war and, more recently, the AIDS pandemic. Darby resolves this difficulty by arguing that the deaths of Zambian footballers and 'ordinary' citizens throughout the continent share a common causal continuum consisting of factors such as poverty, corruption, weak administration and political instability. His analysis of the Zambian air disaster focuses on the ways in which these factors impacted upon Zambia and the administration of football in the country and how they ultimately precipitated the tragedy. The second half of the chapter centres on the aftermath of the disaster. Here, Darby examines the response of the Zambian government, football authorities and citizens in the days, weeks and months following the tragedy. This short-term response was characterised by an intense sense of loss, public grieving and a strong desire to commemorate the victims. However, as Darby's analysis of the official inquiry and the payment of compensation to the bereaved families reveals, these sentiments slowly dissipated in the longer-term aftermath of the disaster.

In the next study of a major football air crash, Gavin Mellor explains the various ways in which English football supporters and the English media 'constructed' Manchester United's Munich air crash of 1958 as a 'disaster'. Mellor explores the narratives that emerged to make sense of the disaster in three historical periods. Firstly, he investigates the narratives that helped to 'construct' the air crash as a disaster in 1958, and interpret the actions of opposing sets of football supporters in response to these narratives. Secondly, he considers the disaster's impact on Manchester United in the late 1960s, and analyses how themes of loss and recovery influenced interpretations and 'readings' of the club during that period. Thirdly, he assesses the influence of the air crash on Manchester United since the 1980s. In particular Mellor comments on the continuing 'consumption' of the Munich disaster by the club's fans, and analyses how Manchester United's close association with the disaster during a period of commercial and playing success influenced the construction of 'negative' contemporary narratives around the club. This chapter draws on a theoretical framework that explains how the 'consumption' of death and tragedy by sports fans (and others) can serve to enhance feelings of connectedness and community.

Aldo Panfichi and Víctor Vich's analysis of the plane crash on 8 December 1987 that resulted in the deaths of sixteen members of the Peruvian team, Alianza Lima as well as a number of team officials examines the context and popular responses to the tragedy. The first part of their chapter describes the circumstances of the crash before moving on to locate the disaster in Peru's socio-economic and political climate in the 1980s. The focus of Panfichi and Vich's contribution is to explore a number of alternative accounts or 'fantasies' that emerged from the victims' families, Alianza Lima fans and the popular media in the aftermath of the crash. This 'hidden' history of the disaster served to help the local population make some sense of the tragic loss of the players, elevated the dead to the status of 'martyrs' and laid blame for disaster on corrupt politicians, government official and the Army.

In the final chapter of the book, Paul Dietschy analyses the causes, consequences and legacies of the Superga disaster on May 4 1949 which involved the deaths of eighteen members of the Torino team along with two trainers and a club official when the plane that they were travelling on crashed in the outskirts of Turin. Dietschy begins by detailing the status of this side as the pre-eminent football force in Italy at the time and argues that their successes, particularly from 1945 onwards can be read as a signifier of Italy's post war reconstruction. Consequently, the loss of the team is framed as a 'national' tragedy and one that had resonance throughout Italy and beyond. The chapter then examines reactions to the crash in Turin and more specifically, the ways that it fed into and impacted upon the rivalry between supporters of the city's two clubs, Torino and Juventus. Dietschy also addresses some of the more practical consequences of the disaster and in particular, he examines the impact that the loss of 'assets' associated with the crash had on Torino's financial stability. Finally, Dietschy charts the emergence of a new activist fandom on the part of the most loyal and 'hardcore' Torino fans in the wake of the tragedy. The analyses here concentrate on how the support of the these fans manifested itself and the extent to which they were motivated by a desire to ensure that the club developed in ways that would provide a fitting memorial to those who lost their lives in the disaster.

Bill Shankly, the renowned manager of Liverpool FC once said, 'Some people think football is a matter of life and death. I don't like that attitude. I can assure them it is much more serious that that'.[8] This infamous quote may illustrate how seriously fans and players take football but ultimately the sentiment is misplaced, even if meant humorously. As this book shows, football has literally cost many people their lives, usually in circumstances that could or should have been avoided. No game, no matter how emotive or commercial, is worth that.

NOTES

1. For an excellent synopsis of the development of the study of disasters as a field of academic enquiry see, D. Alexander, 'The Study of Natural Disasters, 1977–1997: Some Reflections on a Changing Field of Knowledge', *Disasters*, 21, 4 (1997), 284–304.
2. Ibid, p.289.
3. Some examples of such definitions include those by B. G. McCaughey, 'U.S. Naval Disaster: The Psychological Symptomatology', *U.S. Naval Research Centre Report*, 84, 2, 1984, p.8 and G. Shah, 'Social Work in Disaster', *Indian Journal of Social Work*, 45 (1985), pp.462–471. In one of the most inclusive definitions Berren et al classified a disaster as 'any event that stresses a society, a portion of that society, or even an individual family beyond the normal limits of daily living'. M. R. Berren, J. M. Santiago, A. Beigel and S. A. Timmons, 'A Classification Scheme for Disasters', in R. Gist and B. Lubin (eds.) *Psychological Aspects of Disaster* (New York: Wiley, 1989).
4. 320 and 71 people lost their lives in these disasters respectively
5. Tom Horlick-Jones, 'Modern Disasters as Outrage and Betrayal', *International Journal of Mass Emergencies and Disasters*, 13, 3 (1995) p. 306.
6. John Vidal, 'The Stakes Could Not be Higher' in *HIV/AIDS in Africa*, published by *The Observer*, 12 October 2003.
7. John Williams, 'English football stadiums after Hillsborough', in John Bales and Olof Moen, *The Stadium and the City* (Keele: Keele University Press, 1995), pp. 219–53.
8. In *Sunday Times*, 4 October 1981. Quoted in Tony Augarde (ed.), *The Oxford Dictionary of Modern Quotations* (Oxford: Oxford University Press, 1992), p. 267.

1

'Heads in the Sand': Football, Politics and Crowd Disasters in Twentieth-Century Britain[1]

MARTIN JOHNES

Over the course of the twentieth century, 276 people lost their lives in disasters at UK football grounds.[2] Yet it is surprising that such tragedies did not occur more frequently. The rapid speed with which the game's popularity developed in the late nineteenth century meant that football grounds were built quickly and crudely. Any profits that clubs made were usually invested in players rather than spectators' facilities. Eager to see their teams succeed on the pitch, fans were usually happy with such prioritizing. Thus, as the century progressed and the game developed on and off the field, improvements in the condition of grounds were limited. Inside these grounds were often large, compact, swaying and some-times inflamed crowds. Quite simply, the assembly of large numbers of excited supporters on decrepit terraces was a recipe for disaster.

Disasters have powerful emotional, psychological and social impacts. They bring home the realities of risk in a way that abstract possibilities cannot. This creates expectations and demands for action to ensure there can be no repeti-tion.[3] Yet the extent to which expectations are fulfilled, and the force with which they are demanded, depends very much on the political circumstances of the tragedy and those affected. This chapter explores the responses to football disasters in the UK. It aims to show how the responses have been characterized by an apathy towards safety amongst the football authorities, central government and fans. This apathy was rooted in a desire to exclude sport from legislation, in the terrace culture of the game, in the characterization of fans as hooligans and in the exclusion of the safety of football fans from the concerns of central government.

'IN THE KNOW': REGULATION AND HAPHAZARD APPROACHES

On 5 April 1902, at Ibrox Park, Glasgow, a section of wooden terracing collapsed during a match between England and Scotland causing spectators to fall 50 feet. Twenty-five people were killed and over 500 injured. The game was not stopped and, according to one witness, not 'even the cries of dying sufferers nor the sight of broken limbs could attract this football maddened crowd from gazing upon their beloved sport'.[4]

Blame for the disaster was attributed to the quality of wood used in the stand.[5] The disaster was thus seen as a technical failure in the building of stadiums rather than a product of the industry's desire to pack in as many spectators as possible with minimal expenditure on their safety and comfort. It spelt the end of wooden terraces but prompted no public inquiry or wider safety review. Nonetheless, for the football industry, the disaster was a signal of the need to protect itself against litigation from fans in the event of future tragedies. Consequently, the one legal legacy of the disaster was that the Football Association (FA) was registered as a limited liability company.[6]

This was not the first accident at a football match. Part of a stand had collapsed at Blackburn in 1896 injuring five people. Shortly afterwards a boy lost his foot after a railing collapsed at a match in Newcastle.[7] Less seriously, bruises and crushes were fairly common occurrences for spectators at the more popular clubs. The popularity of football had grown rapidly since the sport's codification in 1863. By the turn of the century, crowds of over 20,000 were watching top matches in the English first division.[8] Supporters were hosted in grounds that had been constructed quickly to meet demand. The philosophy was to pack in as many spectators as possible: a ground's capacity was simply whatever the previous record was. The actual location of football grounds was dependent on the availability of cheap land near to urban conurbations. The result was that many chosen sites were unsuitable, with little room for expansion or improvement of facilities as crowds grew. In particular, entrances were often along narrow side streets that were prone to overcrowding. Ton Pentre FC's ground in the Rhondda was perched precariously on a hillside. In 1911 iron fencing gave way in the general rush to leave the ground and a number of men fell into the river below sustaining head injuries.[9] In 1914, a wall collapsed at Hillsborough, home of Sheffield Wednesday FC, injuring 80 people.

The safety of crowds at football matches during the Edwardian period was not regulated by government or any external agency. Regulation, in its most general definition, is 'the imposition of economic controls by government agencies on (usually) private businesses'.[10] Governments have regulated businesses for as long as both have existed. Among the areas regulated are price, quantity and quality of goods and safety, particularly in the transport industries. Despite the wider laissez-faire climate, Victorian statutory regulation of transport in the UK had begun with the first railway regulation act of 1840 and was gradually enhanced and broadened into shipping through the rest of the nineteenth century.[11]

Those safety regulations that did exist tended to be responses to specific known problems rather than anticipated dangers. In the entertainment industry all music halls and theatres had been licensed since the 1880s because of moral concerns about the performances they hosted, while the sale of alcohol subjected such premises to an additional licensing system.[12] Yet this system also allowed a consideration of safety issues by the local authorities responsible for the licenses. The enclosure of a large audience inside a building presented a more obvious hazard than open football grounds. Two horrific disasters in the late nineteenth century drew attention to that potential and cemented the need for regulation. In 1883, 190 children were killed in a crush at a show at Victoria Hall in Sunderland. In 1887, 186 people died in a fire in an Exeter theatre. Specific legislation relating to fire precautions in theatres followed.

Football (like all sports) was seen as a wholesome pleasure, an escape from the realities of life and largely free from the moral concerns associated with bawdy music halls. As such it was not the target of intervention from the authorities whose existence revolve around such realities. Instead, football was left to regulate the safety of its customers itself. The minor accidents that did take place were normalized as part of the unfortunate but inevitable outcome of the congregation of a large and excited crowd, while the 1902 Ibrox disaster was blamed on a specific problem of stand design.

The self-regulation of safety may have had some value in industries where companies were experts in their fields, but in football it represented a misplaced trust. Clubs and the sport's authorities were run by a mixture of small business-men and gentlemen whose full-time professions lay elsewhere. They were far from knowledgeable about crowd management themselves, and they did not employ such expert advisors. Instead, the burden of coping with the large attendances that football attracted tended to fall upon the police. A would-be football spectator cannot tell by inspection the difference between a safe ground and a potentially dangerous one. Therefore it would have been legitimate, even in the era of laissez-faire, for the state to impose safety regulations on football clubs in the way it did (to varying extents) on theatres, music halls, railways and shipping.

A WHITE HORSE AND WEMBLEY: THE INTER-WAR YEARS

In 1923 the inaugural Wembley FA Cup final was in danger of descending into disaster. The official attendance was 126,047 but some estimates put the crowd at 250,000. The overcrowding caused thousands to spill on to the pitch delaying the match. Miraculously no one was killed but there were an estimated 1,000 injuries:

> It would, perhaps, be an exaggeration to say that Wembley Park was turned into a battlefield: but as the stretcher-bearers bore the seeming corpses one after another through the crowd and out of the ground, it looked consider-ably more like a battlefield than like a football field.[13]

This is perhaps an exaggeration and most of the injuries were not serious but, in retrospect, some present realized what might have been:

> Had there not been free access to the pitch from the bottom of the terraces, the casualties would have been colossal. I think the crowd safety was due to the behaviour of the crowd and the absence of any barrier preventing people getting on to the pitch because it was as easy to get on to the pitch as it could be today at a county cricket match, and that was the whole saving grace. Otherwise I think hundreds would have been crushed, literally hundreds.[14]

The organisation of the match attracted severe public criticism in Parliament and the press. Consequently, the government set up an inquiry under former Home Secretary Edward Shortt into 'abnormally large attendance on special occasions'.[15]

The Chief Constable of Birmingham told the inquiry that grounds were not always constructed in the best possible manner and were subject to frequent over-crowding. He thus felt that they should be subjected to a licensing system similar to other places of entertainment. The attitude of the FA to such intervention, in what it regarded as an internal matter, was demonstrated by its refusal to give evidence at the inquiry. The inquiry recommended certain technical measures and, should football clubs and authorities fail to cooperate, the licensing of grounds by local authorities. It did envisage, though, that its recommendations would be implemented through pressure from sport's governing bodies which the inquiry had assured that they were anxious that their sports take place 'under conditions which will promote the public safety'.[16] Given the FA's non-appearance at the inquiry, this was an optimistic stance. The committee's recommendations were not implemented or even debated in Parliament. Its technical recommendations appear to have had little impact on the management of football grounds.

As Hill argues elsewhere in this volume, the lack of firm action following the 1923 cup final was assisted by the myths that grew up around the match. The appearance of the King allegedly calmed the crowd and a single policeman on a white horse was said to have been able to clear the pitch, allowing the match to go ahead. Thus instead of being remembered for the endangering of lives and a breakdown in safety control, the game came to symbolize the supposed orderliness and good discipline of British crowds. With such a discourse dominant, the match was hardly likely to spark a major review of crowd safety in the industry. Instead, the organizational legacy of the event was all-ticket FA Cup finals in order to avoid such chaos, and embarrassment, in the future.

The rest of the inter-war period saw no further disasters but the potential danger remained pronounced and there were a handful of isolated deaths in packed crowds at the most popular games. In 1932 the *Liverpool Echo* spoke of 'these days of overcrowding'.[17] Clubs were not aware exactly of what their ground capacities were, and the decision when to close the gates was often a rather haphazard guess. Even when gates were closed it was not uncommon for people to break into a ground. People spilling off a bank and on to the side of the pitch were a common sight at the biggest matches. Ambulance staff were usually kept busy as men, women and children fainted in the crush. A goal or near-miss would produce surges forward thus increasing the crush, while even the swaying of a crowd singing songs could result in hazardous situations. The following letter to a south Wales newspaper illustrates the experience of many in such conditions:

> to me it appeared the world had congregated to see this match. I am not very tall, about 5'2" in height, and in the crowd that was in the ground, I can assure you, the view of hats and heads was simply wonderful. The feeling of having my ribs staved was not so wonderful ... There were about 10,000 too many people in the ground on Saturday, and it is a wonder that there were not a lot more causalities than there were. We are human beings, not sardines and I hope that in future the directors will bear this in mind. VERY MUCH CRUSHED.[18]

To see the big game, or simply avoid the crush, people used their initiatives and sought any available vantage point, no matter how dangerous. Flagpoles, advertising hoardings, roofs of stands and houses were all scaled at times, occasionally with injurious consequences.[19] Yet with conditions and attendances fluctuating over time and place there was no sustained pressure to take action to make football safer.

Police concern did occasionally surface publicly about conditions in grounds but, in the absence of legislation, they were reliant on the willingness of the football world to cooperate. In 1932, the Chief Constable of Cardiff police stated that Ninian Park was not safe for more than 25,000 spectators, yet it had in the past held twice that number.[20] The issue was raised with the Football Association of Wales who simply promised to speak to the club concerned. The death of a man in the crush of a crowd of 72,841 at a 1934 match at Hillsborough, Sheffield prompted a question in Parliament by a local MP.[21] This in turn led the Home Office to ask chief constables about the situation in their areas. This revealed a number of places where clubs were not following police advice on safety. In Liverpool a lack of cooperation had forced the police to demand that the club would accept responsibility in the light of any accident. In Norwich, the police complained to the Home Office who in turn asked the FA to pressurize Norwich FC. The end result was that the club actually built a new ground in line with the police's wishes. Thus such channels could be reasonably effective in securing compliance but they were also lengthy and failed to satisfy the police. Another death, this time in 1936 at a rugby match in Cardiff, was the spark for a Police Federation resolution calling for a licensing scheme.[22] But in the face of opposition from the football authorities and a government unwilling to legislate, there was little the police could do but continue to voice their concerns and hope that such pressures would force individual clubs to put their house in order.

A SMALL ENOUGH RISK: SELF-REGULATION CONTINUED

In the immediate post-war years, football reached new heights of popularity with people desperate for entertainment after the horrors, disruption and austerity of war. Material shortages limited the options, and football attendances reached an all-time high. The implications of this new popularity, on top of the old problems of overcrowding and poor facilities, were exposed at an FA Cup match at Burnden Park in Bolton on 9 March 1946.

Like many grounds, the facilities at Burnden Park were rudimentary: 'The bank was pretty crude, just dirt really, with any old bits of flagstones they could get for steps. When it rained, the gaps filled with water and the mud spilled out but people didn't mind.'[23] It was estimated that there were nearly 80,000 people in the ground that day. A spectator, wishing to escape the crush, had opened a gate. This had enabled more people to pour in. Others forced closed doors or climbed in over walls. The crowd was helplessly pushed down the bank. For those in the middle it was terrifying:

> I felt the incredible power of a crowd, it was surging like waves of the sea. So my uncle said to me we'd better get you down to the front, so I was passed over the heads of the men, it was like a ride, sliding down. Then as I reached the front the disaster happened, the barriers fell down and the people fell and there was this moving forward, a kind of a release of a tidal force and I just ran out, I pushed, I got on the pitch. There was a lot of crying and shouting and suddenly I was looking at the crowd from the pitch and I remember a policeman on a horse, the people at the top of the banking jumping up and down to see what was going on. People suffering from shock and people who didn't know what to do about the people who were injured. The dead people were just left like bags on the ground. I'd seen dead bodies before because of the bombing but you didn't expect it in a football crowd.[24]

Thirty-three people died and over 400 were injured. The official inquiry, chaired by Justice Moelwyn Hughes, noted,

> how simple and how easy it is for a dangerous situation to arise in a crowded enclosure. It happens again and again without fatal or even injurious consequences. But its danger is that it requires so little additional influences ... to translate the danger into terms of death and injuries. The pastime of football watching is on the increase and the chances of danger among the crowds are arising.[25]

Moelwyn Hughes recommended a licensing scheme run by local authorities with penalties for non-compliance.

Although initially supportive, the Labour government proved to be uncertain about the proposed measures, while the football authorities viewed them with distrust. There was even a debate within government as to whether public safety should include spectators at a football match. The Home Office thought that the existing self-regulatory scheme, based upon inspections by the police, was failing because the relationship between clubs and police was already too close to be effective. Yet the football industry feared that any regulatory scheme run by local authorities might 'err on the side of excessive caution', resulting in clubs 'being put to considerable expense and being subject to a great deal of official interference'.[26] Specific post-war conditions further complicated the issue. The shortage of building materials meant that ground improvements were not easy and required special permission. In the aftermath of a world war, the shock of mass deaths had faded and thus the disaster created no public pressure for safety legislation in football.

The licensing plan met opposition in the cabinet where it was argued that the burden would be too great on local authorities, materials were in short supply and that no legislation could prevent accidents caused by illegal entry. It was thought that 'the risk of a serious incident was small enough to be taken'.[27] Thus, instead of the system of licensing by local authorities that the Moelwyn Hughes inquiry recommended, a system of self-regulation was adopted where clubs simply told the Football Association that their ground had been inspected by qualified persons.

Falling attendances and limited investment in grounds meant that the safety of watching football did improve marginally over the next 20 years.[28] Yet concerns remained. In 1952 the Police Federation called for legislation to give the safety of fans the 'same attention as the safety of audiences at theatres and cinemas'. It called the government inaction 'inexcusable' in light of the various reports, the support of the police and (what it perceived as) the support of the FA.[29] One chief constable noted in 1953, 'Where a football club either through lack of funds or clash of personalities (and this does happen) cannot so well carry out such recommendations for public safety as are deemed necessary by the chief officer of police, apparently the system breaks down.'[30] A system of self-regulation in any industry does not work unless its objectives are deeply rooted in the culture of the industry. Football enjoyed no over-riding commitment to ensuring safety.

The emerging problem of hooliganism meant that the issue of crowd management came to be viewed by clubs and authorities through a different lens. Prompted by hooligan concerns, the 1960s saw three important inquiries into football. Norman Chester's 1968 inquiry into the state of the game and how it could be developed for the public good noted that there was a need for better facilities at many grounds from the viewpoint of crowd safety and behaviour. Yet this brief mention was the only attention paid to the question of safety in the whole of the report. An independent 1968 report into the game noted that the recommendations of the Shortt and Moelwyn Hughes inquiries were often ignored, although they did carry some weight with football directors. The report felt that, in the absence of legislation, some clubs did 'not feel obliged to put their grounds into a state considered by the police to be necessary for crowd control'.[31] A 1969 government report on crowd behaviour noted that although the self-regulation system worked 'satisfactorily', there was an advantage in replacing the 1948 certificates with up-to-date regular inspections.[32] Consequently, the football associations of England, Scotland and Wales asked those clubs whose grounds had a capacity of 10,000 or more for an annual certificate that their grounds had been inspected by (undefined) qualified personnel.

THE FIRST LEGISLATION

The failure of this system of self-regulation became clear in 1971 when 66 people were killed in a crush on a stairway while leaving Ibrox Park, Glasgow. It was the fourth incident of crushing on that stairway in the previous ten years. In 1961, two people had been killed and 44 injured, in 1967 11 people were injured and, in 1969, 30 people were seriously injured. The disaster sparked an immediate debate about the need for legislation.[33] The subsequent Wheatley Report recommended a licensing system operated by local authorities.[34]

In the face of Wheatley's assertion that existing controls were inadequate, legislation was inevitable. Cross-party agreement was demonstrated when the 1975 Safety at Sports Grounds Act was introduced by a Conservative government and passed by its Labour successor. The Act established a system of inspection by local authorities and established a series of technical safety requirements in football grounds. However, the cost to small clubs of implementing large-scale safety measures in their stadiums was potentially crippling. Wheatley felt that the risk was not large enough to jeopardize the existence of smaller clubs in the short term. In the course of the inquiry, a private secretary at the Home Office told Edward Heath, the Conservative Prime Minister, 'All but a few clubs are in need of money and there is evident risk that the cost of quite modest improvements would put some of them out of existence – maybe unnecessarily'.[35] Many fans would have agreed that the continued existence of these clubs was more important than any risk they took in their grounds. The only audible voice of dissent appears to have come from the top. Heath wrote, in private, 'We cannot afford another disaster. Crowd safety ought to be covered by the law – unsafe clubs should go out of existence if they cannot become safe.' However, once Wheatley reported, the government did not disagree.[36] Thus the Act initially only applied to clubs in the English first division and Scottish Premier division (plus the three international rugby grounds in Britain). Clubs in the English second division were brought under the Act in 1979. This system created an anomaly where small grounds, such as Shrewsbury Town's (division two, capacity 16,800), were designated under the Act but large stadiums, such as Sheffield United's (division three, capacity 44,000), were not. The ground improvements required by the Act were partly funded through voluntary levies on 'spot the ball' competitions achieved in return for a government promise not to tax the competition. This deal was achieved through the lobbying of the sports minister Denis Howell.[37] Yet Howell's active sympathies were unusual for a leading politician and he was only a minister of state rather than a full cabinet member.[38] By 1975, football hooliganism was seen as a significant problem.[39] Football might be the national sport but it had become a politically unfashionable pastime that had few vocal supporters in government. There was no political pressure to redress the system's anomalies.

The matter was further complicated by the fact that, for many supporters, the culture and atmosphere of the terraces, complete with pushing, swaying and a sense of unpredictability, was actually part of the attraction of the game. Football's appeal was also rooted in its ability to articulate civic/local pride through success on the pitch; hence many fans would rather see their club buy better players than build a safe and comfortable stadium. Thus there was little consumer pressure for comprehensive safety legislation and fans were tacitly complicit in the risks they had to endure. There are of course clear differences between scientific measures of risk and the subjective interpretations of those at risk. Perceptions and responses to risk are located within social and cultural structures.[40] Fatalistic attitudes towards life and death are particularly common within dangerous working-class industries such as mining. In such circumstances, the risks are normalized as an inevitable part of life that cannot ultimately be changed. Many football fans traditionally worked in dangerous conditions and industries and they brought the resulting fatalistic attitudes with them into their leisure. By the 1970s health and safety may have improved in the workplace but danger had its own attraction. Complaining about safety conditions was not part of the culture of the masculine, 'hard' world of football. Since politicians tend to respond primarily to demand, this was a key reason for first, the absence of legislation and then its limitations.

1980S: A DECADE OF DISASTERS

The Shortt report of 1924 noted that the danger of fire in wooden stands meant the size of a crowd was not the only risk in a football ground.[41] At Valley Parade in Bradford fire extinguishers had been removed from a wooden stand, built in 1909, because of fears that hooligans could use them as missiles. Underneath the stand was flammable rubbish that had not been properly cleared since at least 1968. Some exits were locked during games to help control the crowd. On 11 May 1985 the stand burnt down during a match, killing 56 people. Had the 1975 Safety Act applied to the Third Division, the fire hazard that the stand presented would have prevented it from winning a license. In preparation for the club's pending promotion (and thus its inclusion in the legislation) the fire risk had already been identified. In the wake of Bradford, the 1975 Act was immediately applied to all Football League clubs and the Fire Safety and Safety of Places of Sport Act was passed, introducing new fire prevention requirements.[42] With the disaster having shown that football's problems were not just rooted in hooliganism, the Act was also extended to cover rugby league and other major sports grounds.

18

But in the minds of ministers, like much of the public, football fans were inseparable from the issue of hooliganism. Amidst protests in Bradford and Parliament, a single inquiry was established under Mr Justice Popplewell to investigate Bradford, the Heysel tragedy of two weeks later[43] and a hooligan-related death at Birmingham. Gerald Kaufman MP (Labour) called the joint inquiry 'insensitive and in the worst possible taste'. The parliamentary debate on the disaster and inquiry report was dominated by a discussion of violence rather than safety. This was aptly illustrated by the comments of Eldon Griffiths MP (Conservative) who told the Commons that 'a number of police officers plunged into the fire to pull out fans who in other circumstances would have been pelting them with rocks'.[44] Much good sense came out of the Popplewell report but it was responded to and shaped by the question of hooliganism rather than safety. Fans' interests as consumers remained secondary.

Again, a fatalistic attitude was apparent amongst supporters. Litigation for damages established that the club was two-thirds to blame and the local fire authority (which had informed the club of the risk) one-third.[45] However, few fans appeared to actually blame the club. There is a strong emotional link between supporters and their team, and the knowledge that the poor conditions at the Valley Parade ground were far from unique contributed to an acceptance of the fire as a 'dreadful blow' from fate.[46]

Popplewell noted that, had perimeter fences been erected around the pitch at Bradford, as was the case at many other grounds, the death toll would have been much higher. The importance of his recommendation of adequate exits in such fences was not widely noticed amidst continuing hooligan concerns. On 15 April 1989 such fences proved to be fatal for 96 Liverpool fans attending the FA Cup semi-final against Nottingham Forest at Hillsborough, Sheffield. Inadequate policing and signposting meant that fans were not distributed evenly across the three fenced pens that made up the Leppings Lane end. The overcrowding in the central pen became fatal when the police opened an external gate to relieve a crush outside the ground. Hundreds poured into the nearest pen, which was already full beyond capacity. Exit gates below were locked because of fears of trouble and the police were slow to realize that people were dying in the crush against the fence.[47]

The impact of Hillsborough was very different to previous football disasters. Senior police officers spread misinformation that hooligans were to blame and tabloid newspapers followed this lead. The public inquiry under Lord Justice Taylor was to hear such allegations repeated, to the considerable anger of people in Liverpool and the wider community of football fans. Taylor's report dismissed such theories unequivocally and laid the blame for the disaster at the feet of the police.

Such attempts to deflect the blame thrust the subject of safety firmly onto the public agenda. Fans too had to wake up to the potential danger of vast over-crowded terraces and reassess their attachment to its culture. Hillsborough was the latest in a long line of disasters caused by mismanagement that seemed to plague Britain in the mid–late 1980s, and there was already a wider debate on public safety.[48] Hillsborough fed into this and created a determination to ensure that football did not suffer again. This new determination owed much to the fact that the disaster had unfolded live before a horrified television audience. In the following days, newspapers published graphic photographs of the dead and dying. Not perhaps since the 1966 Aberfan tragedy had a disaster so shocked the nation.

Hillsborough brought a radically different approach to safety within football through the introduction of all-seater stadiums to the top two divisions in line with the recommendations of the Taylor inquiry. This was forced upon generally reluctant clubs[49] by a government that saw football as an embarrassment and irritant. Graham Kelly, then chief executive of the FA, recalls he and his colleagues being 'hauled into Downing Street like naughty schoolboys'. He thought that Thatcher 'despised football, had little or no interest in sport and drove those around her who were interested in the national sport underground'. He went on, 'there was no football lobby because she wouldn't give the game room. I did not see Douglas Hurd or Leon Brittain exhibit any feeling for football at a time when we needed understanding and help.'[50] Thatcher's personal position, the Heysel tragedy and the continuing problem of hooliganism meant that the government was no longer content for football to govern its own affairs. The government's insistence on all-seater stadiums was as much due to their potential to reduce hooliganism as to the safety factor. Hooliganism, not safety, had brought football into the arena of high politics.

A new publicly-funded body, the Football Licensing Authority, was set up to oversee the licensing and regulation of grounds. The financial cost of rebuilding was softened by a fall in building costs brought about by the recession and John Major, a sport-loving chancellor, who made money available to the game for ground improvement by earmarking some of the proceeds of the levy on football pools. Money was distributed through the Football Trust. In the period 1990–97 it distributed £150m to clubs in England, Wales and Scotland. The cost in that period of rebuilding stadiums came to over £500m.[51] It was originally envisaged that all league grounds should become all-seater but divisions three and four were excluded in 1992 because of the cost, and a review that showed smaller attendances and strict regulations on the use of terraces could make standing safe. Notably by this time John Major was Prime Minister and the government appeared to be taking a more sympathetic approach towards sport.

The stadium changes forced on the football industry by the government compelled it to reassess its finances, its treatment of its consumers and, indeed, its whole image and future. Hillsborough thus became a catalyst not only for the rebuilding of Britain's stadiums, but also for the reinvention of the game itself. It focused ideas for a breakaway league and contributed to a chain of events that led to the Premier League, a lucrative deal with Sky television and the current fashionableness and wealth that pervades the upper echelons of football.

FOOTBALL, HOOLIGANS AND HIGH POLITICS

The impact and perceived importance of a disaster is not solely dependent upon the size of the death toll. Rather what constitutes disaster is a social construction. As Horlick-Jones points out, disasters 'take place, and are perceived in, specific socio-economic, historical, cultural and chronological contexts'.[52] Such contexts go far towards determining what is regarded as a disaster. In football, nowhere is this clearer than with regards to the 1958 Munich air crash. The aeroplane carrying Manchester United back from their European Cup quarter-final against Red Star Belgrade crashed while trying to take off after a refuelling stop in Munich, with the loss of 23 lives. Eight of the young team were killed, including the supremely talented Duncan Edwards. The manager Matt Busby was also seriously injured. This tragedy continues to occupy a central place in football's folklore and was integral in creating the image of Manchester United as a unique club. Its memory has completely overshadowed the more deadly post-war disasters of Ibrox and Burnden Park. Football is a sport concerned with glory and heroes: players are immortalized but fans forgotten and the lessons of past disasters easily overlooked.

The history of football disasters in post-war Britain illustrates how the safety of consumers has been submerged beneath wider concerns. The failure to introduce more comprehensive regulatory schemes arose from a tradition of excluding sport from legislation. This tradition, which dated back to the idealistic amateurism of the nineteenth century, was based upon a belief that sport's values were divorced from those that the law regulated. Its competitive but communal ethos, with an emphasis on fair play, had no need of intervention from the world of economics and politics.[53] This stance subsided in the post-war period of welfarism, yet there remained limits to the degree of intervention that governments were willing to undertake and sports willing to tolerate. Government was more concerned with the provision of facilities for participation (which was thought of as benefiting public health) than the regulation of spectator sports.

Denis Howell told the Commons in 1975 that commercial enterprises that put the public at risk should bear the cost of any necessary statutory safety measures and that football was no different.[54] Yet by excluding clubs in divisions three and four from safety legislation he was treating football differently. He thus ensured that it seemed that the game had an importance that could transcend the norms of the law and business world. It took the horror of Hillsborough to elicit a strong regulatory stance on safety in football.

Yet, even then, safety regulation in football had to compete against the characterization of fans as hooligans. The government and the industry's authorities were overly concerned with the misbehaviour of a minority and thus measures to prevent violence overruled safety concerns. The lethal fences at Hillsborough, designed to cage hooligans like animals, are the most tragic example of this. In the aftermath of the Hillsborough disaster, the investigations were influenced by media representations of fans as hooligans. The Taylor Report dismissed such allegations but, as Scraton shows elsewhere in this volume, the association between the disaster and hooliganism distorted the inquest verdicts of accidental death. Government concerns about hooliganism rather than safety were further indicated by the passing of the 1989 Football Spectators Act (which was to curb the civil liberties of fans in an effort to fight hooliganism) without waiting for Taylor to complete his inquiry into Hillsborough and crowd safety. Douglas Hurd, the Home Secretary, had his doubts about the wisdom of this but it went ahead thanks to a delay in the Taylor Report's completion and 'Moynihan [the sports minister] pushing from below and the PM pushing from above'.[55] Lord Graham told the House of Lords:

> To seek to progress this Bill in the midst of such awful, horrific and unbearable tragedy for the bereaved, the injured, the emotionally damaged, the clubs, the players, and the cities of Sheffield and Liverpool seems to be an act of unspeakable obscenity. To intrude Parliament and Parliamentarians into such enormous unbearable grief is an exercise of monumental insensitivity. To do so ... demands progress ... at a time when the evidence of what happened on that awful day has still to be gathered, let alone evaluated.[56]

Fifteen Tory MPs voted against the Bill. Thatcher's memoirs make no reference to either the Hillsborough or Bradford disasters.[57] In 1990 the government was forced to abandon the national membership scheme, which the Act had legislated for, when Taylor expressed doubts about its safety implications.

There has been much theoretical debate as to whether or not the peripheries of the UK are neglected by London-based governments. Jim Bulpitt spoke of territory and power in the UK and argued that the business – what he called 'statecraft' – of the centre was to keep those things which governing politicians cared about in the centre, the realm of high politics. The rest was the periphery, the realm of low politics.[58] Although Bulpitt was primarily concerned with territorial concepts, his ideas can also be applied to other aspects of the political and social life of the nation. The interests of fans were peripheral to government and thus rarely in the realm of high politics. Even in the aftermath of a disaster, the safety of consumers is just one interest competing in the debate over what to do. Whether it wins or not depends as much upon the power and influence of other interests as it does on the validity of its own voice. Before Hillsborough, the safety of fans was submerged beneath the interests of the sport's authorities who successfully lobbied against more stringent legislation, fearing financial pressures and undue external interference. Football fans had too few committed supporters at the heart of UK politics to change that balance of power. Hooliganism may have increased external concern in football's affairs but it ensured that the fans were viewed in light of their potential to misbehave rather than to die in decrepit grounds. Fans themselves remained attached to the culture of the potentially dangerous terraces.

Thus lack of external pressure meant that independent government action was extremely unlikely since it would bring little or no political reward.

Football also suffered as a predominantly working-class sport; this marginalized it from the realms of high politics. The working-class issues that do impinge on high politics are the more fundamental ones of health, education, housing and, above all, jobs. These basic needs are more important to both voters and politicians. Given the difficulty in satisfying these demands, other needs were easily overlooked, particularly when there was no pressure for change from the consumers of the football industry and a resistance to change amongst its producers.

Before the 1980s Labour, the party of the British working class, was essentially uninterested in football. As far back as 1898 Keir Hardie could be found perplexed at the 'unknown world' he discovered when attending a match at Villa Park in Birmingham.[59] For many Labour politicians football not only failed to complement socialism, but was perhaps even a rival for the working man's affection. Even the *Daily Worker* took time to realize that dismissing football as a capitalist distraction was costing it sales.[60] When the veteran Labour politician Tony Benn went to a game in 1989 he recorded in his diary, 'I don't think I've ever been to a professional football match in my life before, an extraordinary confession!'[61] Harold Wilson was the first leading Labour politician to publicly embrace the game but there was something opportunistic about his stance. His autobiography wrongly claims that Huddersfield Town won the League and Cup double twice when he was a boy.[62] His lack of attendance at matches was demonstrated when the crowd at Huddersfield were told that he had never seen them lose.[63] There were of course more committed supporters on both sides of the House[64] but, as the Parliamentary debates after Ibrox and Bradford showed, most MPs who did follow the game could not escape viewing the situation through the lens of hooliganism. This demonstrated an acute failure to grasp what were two distinct issues.

REGULATING SAFETY

Over the course of the twentieth century, detailed policy in the UK has rarely been primarily ideologically driven. Instead, it has leant towards a 'needs must' basis after negotiation within the interested groups that make up policy communities. It is in less glamorous issues such as regulation, which escape the glare of public and media attention, where such communities are most influential. Political responses to football disasters are a prime example of this. Before Hillsborough, finance, the interests of producer groups and practical politics minimized the regulatory regimes that were imposed on the game.

There are many examples from beyond football of wider concerns holding back safety legislation. The repeated failure to implement automated stopping systems on trains in the wake of rail disasters is one notable recent example. There are also other examples of how the status of the victims has dictated the response of the authorities. The sinking of the *Titanic* saw widespread horror and sorrow at the loss of so many lives, and not least so many millionaires and other luminaries. This horror provoked a very strong regulatory response through the introduction of lifeboats for all passengers. Yet the root cause of the disaster lay in the reckless sailing of the captain, not a shortage of lifeboats. The protests of the shipping industry were pushed aside and legislation was introduced because of public concerns and pressures.[65] The Aberfan disaster, which killed 144 people including 116 children, saw rapid legislation covering the management of coal tips to ensure it was never repeated. Yet, as a Welsh, working-class mining community in a safe Labour seat, Aberfan was also isolated from the realms of high politics and, in a series of controversies over the disaster fund and the inquiry, the interests of the bereaved and survivors were marginalized.[66]

In other sports there were varying attitudes towards safety. Motor sports presented obvious dangers to spectators and participants alike and this was recognized long before the Le Mans (France) disaster of 1955, where 83 people were killed when an out-of-control car plunged into the crowd. Such sports thus enforced strict safety regulations at their venues without being prompted by external regulation. Nonetheless, safety was not necessarily an overriding concern as was illustrated by the Auto-Cycle Union prioritizing clean sport over safety in its list of regulations.[67] In contrast, the absence (by and large) of hooliganism from spectator sports such as cricket, rugby league and athletics meant that they were excluded from the 1975 safety act. Not until after the Bradford fire were such grounds brought under the legislation.

Taylor noted in his final report:

> It is a depressing and chastening fact that mine is the ninth official report covering crowd safety and control at football grounds … Why were these recommendations and others not followed? I suggest two main reasons. First, insufficient concern and vigilance for the safety and well-being of spectators. This was compounded by a preoccupation with measures to control hooliganism. Secondly, complacency which led all parties to think that since disaster had not occurred on previous occasions it would not happen this time. But there is no point in holding inquiries or publishing guidance unless the recommendations are followed diligently.[68]

The history of football crowd disasters is one of lessons unlearnt and subsumed beneath wider concerns. No other industry appears to have shown quite the same unwillingness to learn from its tragedies. At the root of this is the fact that football is not an ordinary industry. The custom of fans is dependent on traditional loyalties rather than value for money or safety/comfort considerations. Football's customers were simply not in a position to take their business elsewhere even had they been concerned about ground conditions. Indeed, for so many fans, the heaving terraces and the crumbling grounds were part of the very attraction of the game and its culture. It took the horrific scenes at Hillsborough and the subsequent controversies over who was to blame to revolutionize attitudes towards safety. Only then did fans, authorities and government wake up to the need for a radical new approach to prevent another tragedy.

It was this freedom from normal market forces that engendered the complacency that Taylor saw. Irving Scholar, chairman of Tottenham Hotspur FC, noted that, 'If you'd left it to football, football would have hoped that the problem would go away. It would have been "heads in the sand" … I don't think that they wanted to face up to the facts.'[69] Even Sir Bert Millichip, chairman of the FA, noted that, 'What happened at Hillsborough was something which, quite frankly, could have happened years before. It is surprising that it hadn't happened before. It's surprising the complacency that there was even after it happened.'[70]

That complacency may have been allowed by piecemeal, reactive and unimaginative safety legislation but this is typical of UK lawmaking and does not absolve the football industry from its responsibilities. One of the philosophies of the Football Licensing Authority is 'safety cannot be achieved by means of externally-imposed regulations; those responsible must understand and believe in it for themselves'.[71] In any industry there needs to be a commitment to compliance that does not allow safety regulations to be subsumed beneath the pressures of daily operation and profit seeking.[72] There needs to be a culture of safety in which regulation is internalized – those affected, whether managers or employees, have to believe in the rules that they are meant to obey. Before Hillsborough, the football industry did not understand or believe in prioritizing the safety of its customers.

NOTES

1. The early stages of the research were funded by an ESRC grant (R000222677) to look at responses to Aberfan and other disasters.
2. For the purposes of this paper, disasters are defined as events causing multiple deaths.
3. Bridget M. Hutter and Sally Lloyd-Bostock, 'The Power of Accidents: The Social and Psychological Impact of Accidents and the Enforcement of Safety Regulations', *British Journal of Criminology*, 30, 4 (1990), 410.
4. Quoted in Simon Inglis, *The Football Grounds of Great Britain* (London: Collins Willow, 2nd edn, 1987), p.29.
5. However, the contractor responsible was found not guilty of culpable homicide. See Robert S. Shiels, 'The Ibrox Disaster of 1902', *Juridical Review*, 230 (1997), pp. 230–40.
6. Geoffrey Green, *History of the Football Association* (London: Naldrett Press, 1953), p.192.
7. Inglis, pp.28–9.
8. For a general history of football see Dave Russell, *Football and the English: A Social History of Association Football in England, 1863–1995* (Preston: Carnegie, 1997).
9. *South Wales Daily News*, 13 March 1911.
10. T.E. Keeler and S.E. Foreman, 'Regulation and Deregulation', in P. Newman (ed.), *The New Palgrave Dictionary of Economics and the Law* (London, Macmillan: 1998), vol.3, pp.213–22, quoted at p.213.
11. Iain McLean and Martin Johnes, '"Regulation run mad": The Board of Trade and the loss of the *Titanic*', *Public Administration*, 78, 4 (2000), 729–49.
12. See Peter Bailey (ed.), *Music Hall: The Business of Pleasure* (Milton Keynes: Open University Press, 1986).
13. Quoted in Edward Grayson, *Sport and the Law* (London: Butterworth, 2nd edn., 1994), p.110.
14. Sydney Woodhouse (witness) in Andrew Ward and Rogan Taylor (eds), *Kicking and Screaming: An Oral History of Football in England* (London: Robson, 1995), p.23.

15. Rt Hon. Edward Shortt KC (chairman), *Report of the Departmental Committee on Crowds*, Cmd. 2088 (London: HMSO, 1924), hereafter Shortt Report. The evidence heard by the inquiry is held at the National Archives (NA): HO 73/114 and 115.
16. Shortt Report, paras 46–7.
17. *Liverpool Echo*, 7 Jan. 1932.
18. *South Wales Echo*, 28 Feb. 1923, quoted in Martin Johnes, *Soccer and Society: South Wales, 1900–39* (Cardiff: University of Wales Press, 2002), p.121.
19. A pole, which had been climbed at Swansea, collapsed during a match in 1925, injuring nine people. *South Wales Echo*, 31 Jan. 1925.
20. *South Wales Argus*, 15 Feb. 1932.
21. Capt. Crookshank (Gainsborough, Unionist), Parliamentary Under-Secretary, Home Office, 1934–1935.
22. The inter-war evidence gathered by the Home Office on safety at football matches can be found at NA: HO 45/24798, HO 45/11627, HO 45/25128. For a more detailed examination of the safety issues, based upon Home Office and Metropolitan Police files, see John Walton, 'Football, faintings and fatalities, 1923–1946', *History Today* (Jan. 2003), 10–17.
23. Bert Gregory, member of ground staff, in *Guardian*, 9 March 1996.
24. Harold Riley in *Guardian*, 9 March 1996.
25. R. Moelwyn Hughes, *Enquiry into the Disaster at Bolton Wanderers' Football Ground on the 9th March, 1946*, Cmd. 6846 (London: HMSO, 1946), p.12. Original syntax.
26. FA and Football League representatives quoted in Norman Baker, 'Have they forgotten Bolton?', *The Sports Historian*, 18, 1 (May 1998), 143. The analysis presented here of the aftermath of the Bolton disaster is largely derived from this article. The Home Office records of the disaster can be found at NA: HO 45/25125, 45/25126 and 45/25127.
27. Herbert Morrison (Lord President) quoted in Baker, 144.
28. Declining attendance figures probably even owed something to a reluctance to watch football in uncomfortable grounds when there were other more 'attractive' entertainments now on offer. Russell, pp.184–6.
29. *Police Review*, 4 July 1952. In the early 1950s, following the introduction of floodlit football, there was brief police concern centred on the safety of spectators should the power fail and a ground have to be evacuated in the dark. See NA: HO 42/24798.
30. Chief Constable of Burnley to E. Anstey (Home Office), 11 March 1953. NA: HO 42/24798.
31. G. Dickens (ed.), *Soccer Hooliganism: A Preliminary Report* (Bristol: Wright, 1968), p.9.
32. John Lang (chairman), *Report of the Working Party on Crowd Behaviour at Football Matches* (London: HMSO, 1969), para. 12.
33. *The Times*, 4 Jan. 1971.
34. Rt Hon. Lord Wheatley, *Report of the Inquiry into Crowd Safety at Sports Grounds*, Cmnd. 4952 (London: HMSO, 1972).
35. Memo to Edward Heath, 19 Aug. 1971, NA: PREM 15/796.
36. Note by Heath, 23 Aug. 1971. NA: PREM 15/796.
37. Inglis, p.35. Denis Howell, *Made in Birmingham: The Memoirs of Denis Howell* (London: Queen Anne Press, 1990), pp.260–1.
38. Yet, even then, he was of higher rank than the third-tier ministers who looked after sport under Mrs Thatcher.
39. See Eric Dunning, Patrick Murphy and John Williams, *The Roots of Football Hooliganism: An Historical and Sociological Study* (London: Routledge, 1988).
40. Mary Douglas, *Risk and Blame: Essays in Cultural Theory* (London: Routledge, 1992).
41. Shortt Report, para. 40.
42. In response to the hooligan concerns of the inquiry, the government also passed the Sporting Events (Control of Alcohol etc.) Act 1986 and the Public Order Act 1986.
43. Thirty-nine Juventus fans were killed when a wall collapsed following a charge by Liverpool fans at the European Cup final held in Heysel, Belgium.
44. Hansard, 3 June 1985, vol.79, cols.23, 36.
45. Fletcher & Fletcher v Bradford City AFC, HSE and West Yorkshire Metropolitan Council. *The Times*, 24 Feb. 1987. The exclusion of the ground from the direct provisions of the 1975 Safety Act did not of course free the club from a legal responsibility to ensure the safety of its customers, most notably under the Health and Safety at Work Etc. Act 1974 which created an obligation for companies to protect the safety of non-employees on their premises.

46. Personal communication with editor of *The City Gent* (Bradford City FC fanzine), 3, 26 Aug. 1999.
47. Phil Scraton, *Hillsborough: The Truth* (Edinburgh: Mainstream, 1999) is a comprehensive and powerful history of the disaster and its aftermath.
48. See Iain McLean and Martin Johnes, *Aberfan: Government and Disasters* (Cardiff: Welsh Academic Press, 2000). Between 1966 and 1979 there had been just five disasters in the UK with a death toll greater than 30. Between 1985 and 1989 there were ten.
49. Dominic Elliott and Denis Smith, 'Waiting for the Next One: Management Attitudes to Safety in the UK Football Industry', unpublished paper. Cf. Dominic Elliott, *Organisational Learning from Crisis: An Examination of the Football Industry, 1946–97* (Ph.D. thesis, University of Durham, 1998) and Anthony King, *The End of the Terraces: The Transformation of English Football in the 1990s* (Leicester: Leicester University Press, 1998), p.102.
50. Graham Kelly, *Sweet FA* (London: Collins Willow, 1999), pp.170, 179.
51. Football Trust, *Annual Report*, 1997, p.1.
52. Tom Horlick-Jones, 'Modern Disasters as Outrage and Betrayal', *International Journal of Mass Emergencies and Disasters*, 13, 3 (1995), 306.
53. Ken Foster, 'Developments in Sporting Law', in Lincoln Allison (ed.), *The Changing Politics of Sport* (Manchester: Manchester University Press, 1993).
54. *Hansard*, 19 June 1975, vol.893, col.1751.
55. Hurd diary, 19 April 1989, quoted in Mark Stuart, *Douglas Hurd: The Public Servant, An Authorised Biography* (Edinburgh: Mainstream, 1998), p.218.
56. *Hansard* (Lords), 16 June 1989, vol.508, col.1647.
57. Margaret Thatcher, *The Downing Street Years* (London: HarperCollins, 1993).
58. James Bulpitt, *Territory and Power in the United Kingdom: An Interpretation* (Manchester: Manchester University Press, 1983) and idem, 'The Discipline of the New Democracy: Mrs Thatcher's Domestic Statecraft', *Political Studies*, 34 (1986), 19–39.
59. Quoted in Mark Hayhurst, 'Why Labour Loves Muddied Oafs', *New Statesman*, 21 Feb. 2000.
60. This is not to suggest that the Labour Party at its grassroots was not interested in the game, but even there it was far down its list of priorities. See Stephen G. Jones, *Sport, Politics and the Working Class: Organised Labour and Sport in Inter-War Britain* (Manchester: Manchester University Press, 1988). For a wider view of the left's marginal interest in leisure see Chris Waters, *British Socialists and the Politics of Popular Culture, 1884–1914* (Manchester: Manchester University Press, 1990).
61. Tony Benn, *The End of an Era, Diaries 1980–90* (London: Arrow, 1994), p.561.
62. Harold Wilson, *Memoirs, 1916–64: The Making of a Prime Minister* (London: Weidenfeld and Nicolson, 1986), p.9.
63. Hayhurst, 'Why Labour Loves Muddied Oafs'.
64. David Bull and Alistair Campbell (eds), *Football and the Commons People* (Sheffield: Juma, 1994).
65. McLean and Johnes, 'Regulation run mad'.
66. For the response to Aberfan and disasters since see McLean and Johnes, *Aberfan*.
67. Jack Williams, '"A Wild Orgy of Speed": Responses to Speedway in Britain before the Second World War', *The Sports Historian*, 19, 1 (May, 1999), 11.
68. Peter Taylor, *The Hillsborough Stadium Disaster, 15 April 1989: Inquiry by the Rt Hon. Lord Justice Taylor: Final Report*, Cmnd. 962 (London: HMSO, 1990), paras 19, 23, p.4.
69. Ward and Taylor, p.359.
70. Ibid., p.358.
71. FLA website, www.flaweb.org.uk/fla.intro.html.
72. For an example of how safety regulations can be buried beneath daily concerns see T. Hynes and P. Prasad, 'Patterns of "Mock Bureaucracy" in Mining Disasters: An Analysis of the Westray Coal Mine Explosion', *Journal of Management Studies*, 34, 4 (1997), 601–23.

27

2

'The Day was an Ugly One': Wembley, 28th April 1923

JEFFREY HILL

Since the events of 11th September 2001 the term 'twin towers' has taken on a new and terrible meaning. Before that it signified, to British people at least, something quite different and certainly less awful. The two squat towers that framed the main entrance were the distinctive feature of Simpson and Ayrton's new sports stadium at Wembley Park in north London, hurriedly built to accommodate the Football Association Cup final of 1923. It was also to form a central part of the campus for the British Empire Exhibition, scheduled to open at Wembley in the summer of 1924 and designed both to celebrate the sinews of empire, and to promote trade within it. In the days when building programmes ran to timetable and costs did not escalate too frighteningly over budget, the stadium was completed on schedule. It staged its first event – the Cup final between West Ham United and Bolton Wanderers – on the afternoon of Saturday 28th April 1923. It aroused enormous public interest. An estimated half a million people descended on Wembley, and chaos prevailed across north London that day, which *The Times* newspaper described as an 'ugly one'.[1] By any physical measurement, set either by contemporary experience (of wars, colliery accidents and maritime calamities) or by subsequent sporting tragedies, the circumstances of the 1923 Cup final fell far short of what might be considered 'disaster'. Yet the events of the day nonetheless had far-reaching consequences. They influenced the subsequent management of sports spectacles in twentieth-century Britain, and were responsible for a symbolic representation of Englishness that prevailed well beyond the particular time and space of Wembley in the spring of 1923.

I

The new sports stadium had been completed on what had previously been a golf course and amusement attraction in Wembley Park. The site had a history of commercial initiatives, mostly failed ones.[2] The impetus for the creation there of a new football ground came from two sources. One was the Football Association (FA), which had long been searching for a fitting stadium for its immensely popular cup competition; the other was the company formed in 1920 to launch the British Empire Exhibition (BEE).[3] Without the second development it is unlikely that the first would have succeeded, although the FA's desire for a new London venue was keen. Most of the clubs that had won through to the final after the initial decade of the competition came from the Midlands and North, yet a metropolitan location was thought to be essential. 'There is no denial', wrote the first historians of football in 1905, 'that London is the place for a great sporting event.'[4] Since its inception in 1871 the final tie of the competition had always been held in London except for three occasions in the 1890s, and from 1895 until 1914 it had been permanently based at the Crystal Palace grounds in south London.[5] During this time a day out in London for the final had grown into a popular holiday for supporters of provincial clubs, who descended in their thousands from special trains at the main railway terminals. The attendant rituals of sightseeing and merry-making also quickly established themselves as an informal part of national culture in which provinces and metropolis were brought together in a friendly rivalry that symbolized the harmonious nation.[6]

Large attendances appear to have been achieved at the Crystal Palace without undue strain on local communications and services. How many of those who gained admittance actually saw the match in a stadium that was poorly terraced and in need of renovation is open to question,[7] but this appears not to have deterred people. Attendances increased as the final itself grew in popularity, and by the beginning of the twentieth century crowds of over 100,000 were being accommodated in the football arena. They became a byword for jollity and good humour. Their orderliness drew admiring comments from contemporary observers, sometimes in verse:

> The Sydenham slopes are unsurpassed
> In their essential fitness
> For letting monstrous crowds and vast
> The sports arena witness.
> But, oh, the wobbling, whelming surge
> That ever swayed those masses;
> And on your minds this fact I urge –
> John Bull's behaviour passes.
> All praise for that good-humoured blithe
> Which – in the crush terrific –
> Made each crammed Sydenham slope, and writhe
> And roar, a slope Pacific.[8]

The FA, though, was concerned about the state of the ground, and about the reluctance of the Crystal Palace authorities to embark on improvements. Before the First World War a search was begun for a new venue.[9] The FA would not accede to a request from the Crystal Palace company that the FA should itself make a contribution to ground improvements, though it did offer that if the company were to make alterations so that 125,000 could see the match, it would undertake to stage the final there for 'a series of years'.[10] Although correspondence between the FA and the company on the possible use of the ground for the Cup final continued into the early 1920s, the first final to be attended by the monarch – that of 1914 – was also the last to be staged on the Crystal Palace site.[11] The first three finals after the War were played at Stamford Bridge in London, which accommodated crowds of between 55,000 and 73,000 and lacked the 'junketing' associated with the Crystal Palace, whose 'palmy days' became part of a sweet memory of the pre-War age.[12] In May 1921 the FA reached an agreement with the BEE to play the final in the new stadium to be constructed at Wembley Park.[13]

The Empire Stadium was finished only a few days before the 1923 final and designed to hold 126,000 spectators.[14] The *Morning Post,* in an analysis immediately after the match, commented on what in later years would have been termed the 'hype' surrounding the new stadium. Press coverage, it claimed, was responsible for 'magnifying great events and impressing enormous numbers of people with the importance and glamour of some particular happening'. This, according to the paper, produced the phenomenon of the 'monster crowd', also seen at Wimbledon, Lords and Twickenham in previous years.[15] In spite of this, however, the situation that developed in the vicinity of Wembley from around midday on 28th April took everyone involved in the management of the final by surprise. The coming together of a number of developments was not anticipated. The most obvious of these was the attraction of a brand new stadium – 'a monument to sport so vast as to be unrivalled' as the *Bolton Evening News* described it[16] – which was always likely to encourage speculative attendance from those not normally interested in football. Further, the clubs involved in the final – one of them local and enjoying success which had led to promotion to the First Division that very season – were well supported. Bolton had prepared for what was an already well-established 'northern invasion' of London on Cup final day with 14 special trains. It was estimated that altogether 120 special football trains had converged on London for the match.[17] Indeed, the effectiveness of railway organization was a major reason for the vast crowds, and had been a prime factor in the choice of Wembley as the site of the stadium. Not only did Wembley have four suburban stations within easy distance, but also the major railway companies ran a number of trains direct to Wembley, and the London Midland and Scottish Railway had a ten-minute direct service from Euston for passengers from the North. Finally, and important for Londoners able to make last-minute preparations, the weather was fine. It was this 'irony of fate', as *The Times* put it,[18] which meant that Wembley on that afternoon became out of control – the largest sporting crowd yet seen around a single stadium.

With the benefit of hindsight it is tempting to say that the problems might have been foreseen and operations managed differently. To begin with, little prior control was exercised either over the sale of tickets or the flow of traffic to the stadium. Spectators could reserve in advance only 35,000 seating and standing places. Tickets for other parts of the ground, as was the custom at Cup finals, were on sale at the turnstiles only on the day of the match. This encouraged speculative attendance and added to the crowds. The first signs of disorder came with the traffic congestion experienced on the main roads from central London, some travellers complaining that their journey had taken two hours. The congestion was added to nearer the official time of the kick-off as many people had decided that entry to the match was impossible and had turned back, in some cases prompted by the rumour that the match had been called off. Many abandoned public transport and preferred to walk to the stadium.[19] Fearful of arriving late they took the most direct, though unorthodox, routes, and arrived at the stadium from all points of the compass. 'With scores of others', recounted the football correspondent of the *Bolton Evening News*,

> I made my way across a grass field, crossed a railway, scaled a high wall, and then found my way into the enclosure obstructed by corrugated iron hoardings with three rows of barbed wire above them. Some of the more daring spirits surmounted this formidable obstacle, whilst others less venturesome burrowed under the hoardings only to find more difficulties ahead. Nobody seemed to know how to get inside the enclosure, and there were thousands of people shut out. It was my good fortune to reach the Press seats at the top of the North stand at 3.40, and then greatly to my relief I learned that the match had not started.[20]

This individual's graphic account is typical of the way that Wembley 1923 has been recorded in popular memory: chaos resulting eventually in some kind of order. But it fails to capture the essence of the overall situation. It seems clear from two other accounts – one compiled by Superintendent Landon, the police officer responsible for the strategic oversight of operations, the other by Major Belcher, the assistant general manager of the BEE company which had responsibility for crowd control within the ground – that serious problems began to occur as a result of a late congestion of spectators both outside and inside the stadium. Until around 1.30 p.m. there had seemed little reason to believe that events would be any different from those at previous finals. The stadium gates had opened as planned slightly before 11.30 a.m. and no difficulties had been experienced with the admission of spectators. At 1.30 p.m., however, the crowd outside the turnstiles 'got very large', in the words of Superintendent Landon.[21] At this point in time, according to the report by Major Belcher, some 115,000 people had been admitted to the ground. To prevent overcrowding inside the decision was therefore taken to shut down all turnstiles, allowance being made for a continued entry of spectators during the time the order was given and its being executed. When the stadium was closed it was estimated that there were between 126,000 and 135,000 people inside. But immense crowds outside the ground, pressing forward to gain admittance, now began to climb in. This, to be sure, was partly an attempt by frustrated

31

and determined spectators, some of whom had reserved seats, to see the match at all costs. However, it was also the result of a rational decision by those at the front of the crowd to avoid injury and possible death by crushing from the pressure of those behind. A *Daily Mail* reporter claimed that people climbed in, *helped by police*, as the only way of escape: 'I had to choose between climbing the gates or being crushed to death.'[22] Belcher's report estimated that in the three-quarters of an hour following the closure of the turnstiles between 50,000 and 100,000 people gained entry without paying. Because of this the inner circulating corridors between the turnstiles and the arena became so jammed that the internal gateways to the stands and terraces, which had already been closed, were re-opened purely in order to alleviate the crushing in the corridors. Thus thousands of additional people were admitted to terraces which, already full and (at the maximum occupancy of 18 square inches for each person) afforded no extra space. The playing area was therefore the only vacant space into which an escape from the crush could be made, and understandably it was quickly occupied.[23]

The main details of Belcher's account were largely corroborated in Landon's report. Landon, however, introduced additional observations that render the overall situation yet more complex. It should be noted that Landon, as a senior officer at 'X' Division, Harrow Road, had been involved in a series of discussions with the BEE management before the match to reach agreement on the numbers of policemen needed for crowd control inside the stadium. These were far in excess of those deployed at any previous Cup final, and there is no indication that the BEE, which was paying for the police presence, sought to reduce numbers in order to save costs. During the course of the afternoon, moreover, the numbers were greatly added to on Landon's initiative by the drafting in of officers from other duties in neighbouring areas. Yet the police presence inside the stadium appears not to have been sufficient to prevent a rush of some 200–300 people who climbed over a three-foot iron fence separating the unreserved standing accommodation in the south-west section of the ground and occupied the reserved ring seats around the playing area. This occurred 'shortly after 1.30 p.m.' and was followed by a similar rush over the corresponding fence on the eastern side of the stadium. These events happened, therefore, *before* the crush outside the stadium had worked its effects upon the situation inside. According to Landon 'there was ample room inside the standing terraces at the time and the action of these people in both instances was not attributable to pressure from behind'. Various explanations might be suggested for this behaviour. It could have been that the capacity of the unreserved standing accommodation had been overestimated, and that although as Landon stated 'there was ample room' it did not seem so to those at the front of the terraces at the time. Landon himself had noted what he felt to be a fault in the design of the stadium, in that the positioning of the entrances to the terraces caused spectators naturally to turn *downwards* as they emerged from the stairs leading up from the circulating corridors, and that as a result the lower portions of the terraces might have become disproportionately crowded compared with the upper sections. But all reports are unclear on this point, and Landon finally opted for a dubious explanation that is inconsistent with the otherwise sober tone of his account. He placed blame squarely on the shoulders of the spectators themselves.

> The crowd was not composed of the best class of Association Football supporters, the London team hailing from the East End and the Provincial team from a manufacturing centre. They were difficult to control, and their action in climbing over the railings into the arena before the place was filled was deliberate and inexcusable.[24]

Landon was not alone in attributing some responsibility for the chaos to what was regarded as anarchical behaviour on the part of working-class or provincial supporters. The *Manchester Guardian* also believed that the presence of thousands of Lancashire supporters who had travelled overnight and were determined to see the match added to the problems. Unlike Londoners who, the paper claimed, were 'less resistant to authority', the Lancashire men would not turn back when shut out of the ground.[25] Landon, however, commenting upon this phase of the events, cast doubt on this view, acknowledging the legitimacy of the actions of the crowd outside the ground: 'there was every excuse ... if some of them had not escaped the pressure loss of life and severe injuries would have resulted'.[26] Indeed, it was Landon who first noted the fact that the stadium's very recent completion – in fact being in some respects 'not ready' – was, as events turned out, fortunate. There were still many builders' ladders and planks lying around and these were used to climb over turnstiles and fences.[27]

The commotion in the stadium was partly captured in a letter to *The Times* by the novelist Frank Swettenham, who described how he arrived with a ticket to find the stadium organization completely wanting. Signs were misleading, seats were difficult to locate, many who eventually got to their appointed seats found other people sitting in them, and there were few stewards.[28] Landon, in fact, had described the stewarding system as 'useless', and it seems that in the face of the chaos many stewards panicked and fled: 'some of them became so nervous that they removed their distinguishing badges'.[29] Inevitably there were casualties. The *Daily News*, in a feature entitled 'The Battle of Footerloo',[30] reported a grim scene of 'seeming corpses' being carried away on stretchers from the stadium, 'which looked considerably more like a battlefield than like a football field'. But more balanced accounts suggested a less dramatic outcome. The *Daily Telegraph's* estimate of 1,000 cases, mostly minor, dealt with by the first aid organizations, accords with most other verdicts. Those seriously enough injured to warrant being removed to Willesden General Hospital were reckoned by the *Telegraph* to number 50, their injuries being mostly limb and rib fractures, and crushing to the chest and abdomen.[31] A Home Office memo described the allegation by Jack Jones, Labour MP for Silvertown (the constituency in which West Ham United was located) of 1,000 casualties 'more or less seriously injured' as 'ludicrous', pointing out that only six or seven cases were serious and that these were progressing favourably.[32] Answering questions in parliament on the Monday after the match the Home Secretary, W.C. Bridgeman, reported that only 22 people had been removed to hospital for treatment, ten of whom were allowed home the same day. Three cases were described as 'serious'.[33] What press reports had noted, however, was that the officers of first aid organizations had experienced great difficulty in stretchering the injured to casualty stations because the safety corridors had become impassable as a result of the rush of spectators onto the pitch.[34] It was, perhaps, more as a result of luck than good management that no deaths were recorded. In spite of everything, the match started some 45 minutes later than the designated kick-off time.

This was possible because of the clearing of the pitch by mounted policemen who employed the method of pushing back a front line of spectators with linked arms in ever increasing circles. This procedure has become the main image in the folk memory of Wembley 1923, symbolized in the figure of the policeman on the white horse. At the time, however, the white horse was linked in the public mind with another image, that of the King, George V. It was claimed that the presence of the King had a calming influence over the crowd. Superintendent Landon, for example, observed that when the King made his appearance in the arena at 2.59 p.m., the stadium was 'completely thronged with people'. But when the Guards' band struck up the national anthem everyone broke into song, a response that underlines Belcher's claim in his report that the crowd was in 'good temper and good humour'.[35] Writing some ten years after the events the Secretary of the FA, Sir Frederick Wall, claimed that George V had not been pleased with the scene that met him on his arrival, especially a suggestion that the match might have to be abandoned. Such thoughts were dispelled, according to Wall, largely by the fact that the King himself became an attraction in his own right. His presence in the Royal Box (which appears not to have been occupied by interlopers) started a counter-surge by spectators anxious to cast eyes on their monarch. 'Tens of thousands', in Wall's words, filed past him thence to be directed through a tunnel out of the arena.[36] In this way space was cleared in the ground. The match, which then proceeded, was won 2-0 by Bolton Wanderers. It was, claimed West Ham's local paper the *Stratford Express*, a 'fiasco'.[37]

Apart from a parochial reaction from the *Bolton Evening News*, which regretted that the crowd scenes had overshadowed the decisiveness of the Wanderers' victory,[38] most sections of opinion opted for the fiasco interpretation. The general view might be summed up as, 'it must not happen again'.[39] As early as the afternoon of Monday 30th April questions were being asked in Parliament. They continued over the next few weeks. MPs were concerned not only about the safety of future football crowds in this stadium but, understandably, about the effectiveness of the safety arrangements for the far greater crowds expected for the Empire Exhibition to be held the following year. For the most part MPs asked about the

provision of adequate entrances and exits, the traffic arrangements, measures both
to prevent and deal with injuries, the deployment of police, and the question of
where responsibility should rest for overall control of such large-scale crowds.
Nobody objected when the Clydeside MP George Buchanan – in an attempt to
correct the Anglo-centric hysteria that had enveloped the subject of Wembley
over previous weeks – suggested that the Cup final should in future be held in
Glasgow, 'in order that it may be properly conducted'.[40] Questions took a more
serious line, however, when the prospect of delinquency was raised. Sir Alfred
Butt referred to the delays that had been experienced on crowded trains from
central London with no lighting facilities and which had in many cases had been
stopped for lengthy periods in tunnels, with consequent dangers of mass panic and
robbery.[41] The point was taken. But many MPs took exception to the elaboration
of this theme by Oswald Mosley, the Independent Conservative MP for Harrow,
some of whose constituents lived near Wembley. Mosley alleged that 'hooliganism' had been imported into the district by the football supporters,[42] a charge hotly
rejected by Jack Jones, many of whose own constituents were West Ham fans.[43]
The crowd, claimed Jones (echoing the point made by several others), had been
'good humoured'. Mosley's attempts to continue in this vein were met with cries
of 'Order' and 'Sit Down' by other Members. Moreover, in spite of further criticisms from Mosley in subsequent questions about policing arrangements, it was
the police who emerged as the heroes of the afternoon. Or rather *a* hero. It was in
these very Commons debates that the image of the policeman on the white horse
began to assume prominence. There were a dozen mounted policemen on brown
horses on the pitch, but it was the white one that captured the imagination. And
this horse, Billy, was not even white: 'really a dirty grey colour' according to
another policeman, but it showed up white in press photographs.[44]
   What is interesting about the whole episode is the way in which the threat of
the crowd – as imagined by Mosley – was transformed into a reassuring image of
the virtues of the nation. In this respect the 1923 Cup final represents one of those
moments in the creation of the mythology of a nation. In the constructing of
stories that tell of the people and their habits, what is remembered is not always
exactly what happened. A day which, if not 'ugly', was at the very least extremely
disorganized, came to be embedded in popular memory as a source of pride in a
nation where people knew how to behave and remained calm in difficult situations. Constable Scorey – the policeman on the white horse – later admitted that
on arriving at Wembley from his base in Rochester Road he thought the situation
hopeless and did not know what to do; but, he said, 'the crowd was good-natured
and seemed to respect the horse'.[45] *The Times* moderated its judgement of the
'ugly' situation in two respects – the spirit of people and police working together,
and the absolute loyalty of the 'mixed congregation' to the King.[46] For years afterwards millions of English football followers were inducted into the game's culture
through a literature of books, magazines and pictures in which the image of the
white horse took a prominent place. And since English football culture was always

informed by a sense of the nation's place in the wider world, a notion of 'the other' was latent in it. Thus the *Daily News,* in spite of its sensational headlines, commented on the essentially moderate nature of both crowd and police, with the latter conspicuously preferring to spend time in patient crowd control rather than attempting a quick dispersal by violent methods, 'as the police in more excitable lands might do'.[47] In stark contrast to the portrayal of the riotous and violent behaviour of crowds at foreign football grounds, with their moats, fences and armed police, the Wembley final of 1923 worked as an icon representing English fans to themselves as self-disciplined, peaceable, essentially cooperative, needing only the firm coaxing of a single policeman and his horse to bring them to order. Moreover, this image to a large extent influenced later assumptions about crowd control measures at big sporting events. It generated a belief that crowds could manage themselves, and thus delayed for many years the use of statutory regulations to ensure safety.

II

Nonetheless, the pressure of parliamentary debate and press discussion produced a committee of enquiry. The Home Secretary in Bonar Law's cabinet, W.C. Bridgeman, appointed a departmental committee chaired by his predecessor Edward Shortt.[48] It reported in March 1924 to Bridgeman's successor, Arthur Henderson. The Committee was made up of Shortt as chairman, H. Hughes-Onslow, who had experience in the administration of amateur sport, H.P.P Lane, the Chief Constable of Lancashire, Frank Pick, Assistant Managing Director of the Metropolitan District Railway, C.D. Carew Robinson of the Home Office, and F.C. Toone the Secretary of Yorkshire County Cricket Club (and later in 1924 manager of the MCC cricket tour to Australia). A.S. Hutchinson of the Home Office served as the committee's secretary.

Their terms of reference were difficult ones. Though occasioned by the events at Wembley the committee was charged with making recommendations applicable to 'abnormally large attendances on special occasions', especially at athletic grounds, and to consider whether, in view of improved transport services, further steps needed to be taken to ensure the safety of the public. This being the case, the committee's report made few direct references to Wembley, though the Wembley events clearly influenced the committee's deliberations. The Shortt report made clear, however, that it had not been part of the committee's brief to apportion blame for the events of 28th April. Its proceedings had dilated upon a number of safety issues, some of which were pertinent to what had happened at Wembley, others of which were not. Shortt's committee met on 13 occasions to interview senior police officers, representatives of transport organizations, officials of sports clubs, and the architect and engineer of the new stadium. It made visits to various sporting venues, including major football grounds in England and Scotland, Doncaster racecourse, and the RAF Pageant at Hendon. Amidst all the thoroughness, however, there was one conspicuous absentee in the entire proceedings and this was the Football Association, the prime mover of the Cup final, which had refused to comply with a request to give evidence. The committee produced a comprehensive analysis of the many problems attending the staging of big sporting events, ranging from the transporting of spectators to and from the stadium, to the managing of crowds inside grounds, and their eventual exit from them. Its report distinguished between safety features required at grounds of different sizes, pointing out that its recommendations were not designed to apply to small venues (with a capacity of less than 3,000).[49]

To begin with, the committee spent some considerable time on the traffic arrangements for bringing spectators to grounds. This had been a major problem in north London at the 1923 Cup final, where the provision of plentiful rail and road transport had been the major reason for the congestion: trains and buses debouched people more rapidly than the stadium's immediate environment could absorb them. The committee's discussions were conducted in the light of this. Absence of coordination between transport services, police and ground management had been partly responsible for the chaos at Wembley and, in proposing a greater degree of cooperation between these key elements, the Shortt committee found a willing response from each. Where an event might involve the passage of spectators through several distinct boroughs, each with its own powers of controlling traffic, it was proposed that the police should be the natural authority to exercise an overall coordinating control, their aim to be to keep traffic moving, however slowly. In relation to the approach of crowds to the ground once they had been set down by road or rail transport, there was a general view that a sufficient distance should be available (at least two hundred yards was suggested where new grounds were being constructed) between the disembarkation point and the ground entrance, and that an open area free of vehicular traffic would permit crowds to be dispersed into smaller gatherings for marshalling by the police into queues. Reducing pressure on turnstiles, which had been a major problem at Wembley, was considered to be a necessity. There should always be an unscaleable perimeter wall to prevent unauthorized entry into the stadium. In view of another problem experienced at Wembley, that of spectators continuing to arrive at an already full ground, it was felt that when grounds became full notices should be displayed at the traffic embarkation points away from the ground to prevent the further transporting of spectators. Bridges and subways were recommended, where possible, as a means of avoiding the need for spectators having to cross busy roads, which would add to the congestion of both people and traffic. In the light of the experience at Wembley, mounted police were recommended as being of particular value in controlling crowds. In general terms a principle expressed in evidence to the committee by Sir Edward Stockton, Treasurer of Lancashire County Cricket Club, was endorsed by the committee as one of its most significant recommendations. This was the need to start the control of crowds at a point well back from the stadium itself. It was particularly pertinent to the Wembley case, and one that had an obvious relevance to all similarly large sporting gatherings.

A number of points were made about crowd control once the spectators had arrived inside the ground. Considering that the police presence within sports grounds was paid for by the ground authorities, the committee was at pains to point out that this did not make them employees of the ground authorities. It was felt, for example, that police officers, whilst often very experienced in 'packing' large crowds into confined spaces, were not stewards; they might assist stewards but should remain first and foremost policemen, doing the job of policemen, under the direction of their own officers. Stewarding, which had been palpably inadequate at Wembley, needed to be improved, and the committee proposed the creation of disciplined and trained stewards, whose distinguishing badges should not be removable. Alongside stewards there should be trained ambulance staff at all grounds with a capacity over 10,000. The committee recommended that the overall management of the event should be in the hands of a central coordinator in telephonic communication with all parts of the ground. There should be an 'adequate' number of turnstiles (one for every 1,250 'units of capacity') and where possible turnstiles should be built into walls and operated by one man; groups of turnstiles should be overseen by a controller who could assess the overall situation, keeping a check on numbers passing through, and close turnstiles when necessary.

On the design and construction of the interior of grounds the committee made a number of important recommendations:

- Crowds should preferably be segregated into small units ('pens'), both to minimize disturbances and to achieve more effective control.
- Space outside the ground was preferable to interior circulating corridors as a means of crowds sorting themselves out and finding their sections of the ground; though if exterior space was limited circulating corridors serving as an 'expansion chamber' were useful in avoiding congestion.
- Entrances to the terracing should be at the top of the terrace, and where the terracing exceeded 50 feet a second tier of entrances should be provided at the top of the terrace section they served; the fundamental principle here was that a crowd 'will find its way downwards but not upwards'.
- The pitch of the terracing may be 1:2 but should not exceed 1:3. (A pitch of 1:1, found in some American stadiums, was considered to be too steep.)
- There should be both vertical and horizontal gangways in stands and terraces to facilitate packing of crowds and to avoid congestion.
- At least 15 feet, and preferably 25 feet, should be allowed between the front row of spectators and the playing area.
- The lower tiers of standing should be sunk approximately three feet below the playing surface to prevent an 'onrush' of spectators on to the field.

- 'Ring' seats, as were provided at Wembley within the boundary fence, should be done away with except for use by disabled people (or spectators sitting on the grass at cricket matches).
- Adequate toilets and direction signs should be provided.
- All construction should be such that it would pass the safety standards laid down by local authority surveyors.

The Committee also spent time considering a feature of crowds that was familiar to all those who attended football matches in Britain before the arrival of the 'all-seater' stadium in the late-twentieth century. This was the frightening and potentially very serious problem of 'surging' or 'swaying' on open terraces. There were two possible remedies. As we have seen, the committee's favoured option was the 'pen' system, though this existed to any great extent only on relatively few grounds. The alternative was the far more common method of placing crush barriers at strategic points along the terracing. Such barriers were themselves of two main types – a 'continuous wire rope along the length of the terrace', as used at Hampden Park in Glasgow – or the more usual individual rigid barrier. In reflecting upon the relative merits of barriers the committee noted the need to ensure, whichever method was employed, that there existed 'no long stretches' of open gangway up and down a terrace, and that the corners of the terracing were barred to prevent horizontal surging. All barriers should be spaced so as to permit no more than 15 rows of spectators between them.

The committee also took up the important question, which had been a central one to the problems of the 1923 Cup final, of the purchase of tickets in advance. This simple expedient, which in future was to be the one single measure preventing a recurrence of the problem that had afflicted Wembley, occasioned a good deal of controversy in the months following the 1923 final. It was a novel idea, especially at football matches. There had been no such arrangement at the Crystal Palace where people simply arrived and paid for entrance to the grounds. At football grounds only grandstand seating (usually amounting to a small proportion of the total ground capacity) could be reserved. At Wembley there was additionally some reserved standing in front of the two grandstands. The Committee's view on the question of requiring tickets for *all* spectators was an equivocal one:

> While we consider that any such arrangement would be in itself impracticable and open to objection on the ground that it would provide undue opportunities for profiteering in tickets, we are certainly in favour of an extension of the principle of advance booking as far as possible, but we do not believe that it would go more than a short way towards solving the difficulties of the control of crowds. (p.17)

It was felt that, because there was no tradition in football of such a system, spectators would not bother to book in advance, and would simply turn up on the day as they had always done.[50] The Football Association, concerned about forgery and profiteering, but which had taken no responsibility for crowd management at Wembley in 1923, was completely opposed to the idea of booking in advance. Moreover, as a report in the *Evening Standard* showed,[51] there was a worry that spectators with tickets and therefore guaranteed places might be inclined to arrive at grounds at the last minute, thereby intensifying rather than reducing the problems of 'late rush'. But in contrast the Home Office, the Wembley Stadium authorities, and the police were in no doubt that the 'all-ticket' system was the obvious answer to controlling large crowds. The BEE, which spent £50,000 to £60,000 in the months following the 1923 Cup final to make improvements at Wembley for staging the event in future, sought to enlist the support of the Home Office to bring pressure to bear on the FA.[52] The Metropolitan Police also gave its strong backing.[53] Sir John Anderson, at the Home Office, pointed out that his department had 'no power to direct that all seats must be sold beforehand' though was clearly in favour of such a scheme, at least as applied to the Cup final. He would have pressed it upon the FA had the latter not finally acquiesced 'of their own motion' (*sic*) in February 1924.[54] Thus the new system was introduced for the 1924 Cup final between Aston Villa and Newcastle United, though it was not without problems in the early years. After four years of operation the *Athletic News* reported that the all-ticket system 'ensures peace, orderliness and comfort in the stadium', but noted also the vast excess of demand over supply: two thirds of applications for tickets were turned down.[55] There were also complaints from clubs about the difficulties of obtaining allocations for their supporters.[56] In 1930 the system of allowing the general public to apply directly to the stadium was stopped; three-quarters of the tickets were kept by the FA for distribution to its affiliated bodies,[57] and this was to remain the procedure for years to come.

The Shortt Committee report concluded with a consideration of the means of ensuring that its recommendations were observed. This hinged on the dual problem of regulations and licences. Most of those who gave evidence to the committee favoured some degree of regulation over the design and maintenance of sports grounds to ensure the safety of spectators. Indeed the report mentioned only one witness, Mr Chapman, the Secretary of Manchester United FC, as being opposed to regulation on the grounds that 'most clubs already know what to do' (p.26). Since the previous century the conventional approach to the problem of regulating public spaces of entertainment such as theatres and music halls had been provided through a system of licensing operated by local authorities. Shortt's committee, however, recognized differences between sport and other commercial leisure businesses, and in particular sought to preserve the influence exercised in sport by the various governing bodies. In view of what was considered to be the relative absence of crowd problems in the past, and assuming that in the future crowds would continue to behave sensibly, the committee was anxious to avoid removing the power of governing bodies and placing it in the hands of national and local government. Wishing to maintain the principle of self-government, therefore, the committee recommended that the governing bodies themselves should administer the system of regulations: 'we feel that at this stage it is safe to leave the matter to them' (p.26.) However, it was noted that should these voluntary arrangements break down at any point in the future, resulting in negligent administration that in turn might cause serious crowd disturbances, 'then the time would have arrived for the establishment of a full system of licensing with proper legal sanction' (p.26).

The problem for the future was in deciding when that time had arrived. The cardinal principle espoused by Shortt and his members had been that of consensus: to permit the various parties involved in sports events to come together and through cooperation arrive at a reasonable solution. In relation to the question of how many police should be deployed at large football matches, for example, the Committee noted that traditionally it had been resolved by discussions between police and ground authorities:

> [we] feel that the present system should be allowed to continue, by which the spirit of co-operation between the parties concerned is encouraged. To this we attach considerable importance. (p.13)

In general, therefore, rather than prescribe predetermined strategies, faith was placed in the sound sense that would emerge if the managers of the main organizations sat down together to work out how best to deal with a particular event. It placed a good deal of responsibility in the hands of senior police officers, with their experience of traffic and crowd control, to advise event organizers on matters such as ground capacity. It also displayed a degree of expectation and trust in the way crowds behaved. Press reports of the events at Wembley played their part in fostering such an assumption, as did the evidence of the police. An example of this was found in the reports of both Landon and Belcher, when they commented pointedly on the fact that, in spite of the chaos at Wembley, the cash boxes with the turnstile takings had been transported safely from the turnstiles to the main office. Disorder, of which there was plenty, did not imply lawlessness. Crowds acted better for minimum policing, as phrases such as 'sorting themselves out' and 'knowing a ground' suggested. Indeed, the situation at Wembley was partly accounted for by the stadium's not being a 'home' ground for any club, and therefore having no 'home' spectators who were habituated to its layout and peculiarities (p.6). For all these reasons, therefore, Shortt and his committee held back from making recommendations that depended on legislation to ensure the safety of crowds at large sporting events. The committee's dilemma over the proper balance between the legal and the voluntary approach was nicely captured in a letter from Frank Pick to Arthur Henderson shortly after the report's publication in March 1924:

The subject ... turned out [Pick wrote] to be a much more difficult one than I imagined. There seemed to be no easy way of dealing with it: either very little had to be done, or a great deal had to be done ... I hope ... we have produced a report which will be generally acceptable, and which will effect some improvement without at the same time establishing any elaborate system of control of sports' [*sic*] grounds.[58]

As time was to prove, and as other studies in this collection show, this faith in the principle of self-regulation was misplaced. Many of the Shortt committee's recommendations on safety were either casually administered or ignored altogether.

III

The chief legacy of Wembley 1923, therefore, is to be found in its impact on the minds, rather than the bodies, of English people. In this respect Wembley was to take its place alongside another event that became emblematic of British character in the twentieth century: Dunkirk. It is not by any kind of fictional accident that Ian McEwan made Dunkirk the centrepiece of his novel *Atonement*.[59] It is a cardinal metaphor for a novelist interested in exploring British manners and social relationships. The industrial port in northern France has possessed a particular resonance for British people since the events there in the summer of 1940 when a serious military defeat was prevented from being an outright disaster by the mass evacuation of troops. But instead of being a warning of the consequences of outmoded thinking and poor leadership – things in themselves to be atoned for – Dunkirk was remembered in the public mind as a symbol of the courage, discipline and self-sacrifice of soldiers and civilians. Until well into the late twentieth century, the name 'Dunkirk' instantly evoked thoughts and images of the British people and their character, in many cases working its meaning on people who knew little of the historical circumstances of 1940. It was perhaps the central British myth of the second half of the twentieth century, speaking of a spirit to be invoked when times were hard to pull the nation out of its troubles. Prior to Dunkirk, and then in company with it, the events at Wembley in 1923 provided a similar mythic vision. On that spring afternoon was seen a nation in microcosm, caught up in disorder but sorting itself out with good sense and minimal guidance. As with Dunkirk the myth took precedence over the lessons to be learnt, preventing a serious consideration of those lessons. The reasons are many why it took so long before statutory regulation of sports crowds was introduced in England, but the myth of the British crowd is one of them.

NOTES

1. *The Times*, 30 April 1923.
2. See Adam Spencer, *Wembley and Kingsbury* (Gloucester: Alan Sutton, 1995); Geoffrey Hewlett (ed.), *A History of Wembley* (London: Brent Library Service, 1979).

3. See Simon Inglis, *The Football Grounds of Europe* (London: Willow Books, 1990); British Empire Exhibition, *Official Guide* (London: Fleetway Press, 1924); Sir E. Owen Williams, 'The Construction of the British Empire Exhibition', *Concrete and Constructional Engineering*, XIX (1924), 420–32; Gavin Stamp (ed.), *Sir Owen Williams, 1890–1969* (London: Architectural Association, 1986).
4. Alfred Gibson and William Pickford, *Association Football and the Men Who Made It* (London: Caxton Publishing, n.d.), vol.4, p.41.
5. William Pickford, *A Few Recollections of Sport* (Bournemouth: Bournemouth Guardian Ltd., n.d.).
6. See Jeff Hill, 'Rite of Spring: Cup Finals and Community in the North of England', in Jeff Hill and Jack Williams (eds), *Sport and Identity in the North of England* (Keele: Keele University Press, 1996), pp.85–111.
7. Sir Frederick Wall, *Fifty Years of Football* (London: Cassell, 1935), pp.159–60; Geoffrey Green, *The Official History of the FA Cup* (London: Naldrett Press/Football Association, 1949), p.96.
8. Quoted in Tony Pawson, *100 Years of the FA Cup: The Official Centenary History* (London: William Heinemann Ltd, 1972), pp.112–13. 110,000 attended this match; there were 120,000 at the final of 1913.
9. Football Association (FA) Minutes, Finance Committee (FC), 5 July 1913.
10. FA Minutes, FC, 4 Nov. 1913; 2 Feb., 21 Dec. 1914.
11. FA Minutes, FC, 4 Nov. 1913.
12. *The Times*, 28 April 1922; FA Minutes, FC, 30 May, 2 July, 21 Aug. 1921.
13. FA Minutes, FC, 30 May 1921.
14. See Oscar Faber, 'The Concrete Buildings', *Architectural Review*, I (1924); 'The Architects, Engineers and Contractors of the British Empire Exhibition', *Wembley Historical Society Journal*, 2 (1963).
15. *Morning Post*, 30 April 1923.
16. *Bolton Evening News*, 30 April 1923.
17. Ibid., 27 April 1923.
18. *The Times*, 30 April 1923.
19. See accounts in *The Times, Morning Post, Daily News, Daily Mail*, 30 April 1923.
20. *Bolton Evening News*, 30 April 1923.
21. National Archives (NA), HO 45/11627/ 445340/12, Commissioner of Police, 2 May 1923 (hereafter 'Landon Report').
22. *Daily Mail*, 30 April 1923.
23. See Landon Report; and NA, HO 45/11627/445340/13, report by Major Belcher, Assistant General Manager British Empire Exhibition, to Colonel Cole, Department of Overseas Trade, April 1923 (hereafter 'Belcher Report').
24. Landon Report.
25. *Manchester Guardian*, 30 April 1923.
26. Landon Report.
27. Landon Report; see also NA, HO 45/11627/ 445340/1, notes used by Home Secretary (W.C. Bridgeman) in answering questions in House of Commons.
28. *The Times*, 30 April 1923. Other accounts also note the poor signage, which meant that many spectators were milling around the corridors unsure of where to go.
29. Landon Report.
30. *Daily News*, 30 April 1923.
31. *Daily Telegraph*, 30 April 1923.
32. NA, HO 45/11627/445340/1A, Home Office memo, 30 April 1923.
33. Parliamentary Debates, 163 HC Deb. 5s, pp.1381–2.
34. *The Times*, 30 April 1923.
35. Landon and Belcher Reports.
36. Wall, p.164.
37. Quoted in Charles P. Korr, 'A Different Kind of Success: West Ham United and the Creation of Tradition and Community', in R. Holt (ed), *Sport and the Working Class in Modern Britain* (Manchester: Manchester University Press, 1990), p.145.
38. *Bolton Evening News*, 30 April 1923.
39. The *Daily News*, under a headline 'The Wembley Fiasco', commented 'the marvel is that the breakdown of the much-vaunted arrangements for dealing with the crowd ... did not culminate in a tremendous tragedy' (30 April 1923).
40. Parliamentary Debates, 163 HC Deb 5s, p.971.

43

41. Ibid., p.1650.
42. Ibid., pp.971–2, 2259–60.
43. Ibid., p.971.
44. Alan Brown, 'Didn't We Have a Lovely Time the Day We Went to Wembley', *Guardian*, 1 April 1995, p.22.
45. Idem.
46. *The Times*, 30 April 1923.
47. *Daily News*, 30 April 1923.
48. See HO 45/24798/446941. The committee was appointed in June 1923.
49. Crowds Committee, *Report of the Departmental Committee on Crowds* (London: HMSO, 1924), Cmd. 2088.The absence of the FA is explained by its considering that responsibility for crowd matters at Wembley rested with the BEE. This was a complacent attitude, of course, especially since the FA Ground Committee had met in May 1923 to make a series of recommendations to improve safety and crowd control at Wembley, though the BEE's proposal to reduce the capacity of the stadium for the 1924 final was rejected by the FA. (See FA, Ground Committee Minutes, 3, 17 May, 22 Oct. 1923.) There is a brief summary of the Crowds Committee report in Simon Inglis, *The Football Grounds of Great Britain* (London: CollinsWillow, 1978 edn), pp.28–30, which misses some points, and incorrectly states that the report was commissioned by the first Labour government. It was commissioned by W.C. Bridgeman, Home Secretary in the Bonar Law (subsequently Baldwin) Conservative government, which left office following the general election of December 1923 to be replaced by MacDonald's first Labour administration.
50. NA, HO 45/11627/ 446941, ADH to Buckland, 29 Jan. 1924.
51. *Evening Standard*, 5 Feb. 1924.
52. NA, HO 45/11627/445340/30, Travers Clarke to Sir John Anderson, 28 Jan. 1924.
53. Ibid., Horwood to Anderson, 1 Feb. 1924.
54. NA, HO 45/11627/445340/30, Anderson to Travers Clark, Feb. 1924; see also FA Minutes, 4 Feb. 1924.
55. See *Athletic News*, 25 April 1927.
56. FA Minutes, FC, 23 April 1926.
57. FA Minutes, Report of Final Tie Committee, 24 Nov. 1930.
58. NA, HO 45/24798/446941, Pick to Henderson, 19 March 1924.
59. Ian McEwan, *Atonement* (London: Jonathan Cape, 2001).

3

'The Ibrox Stadium Disaster of 1971'

GRAHAM WALKER

I

On 2 January 1971 66 football fans were crushed to death and 145 injured while attempting to leave Ibrox Stadium in Glasgow after the traditional New Year fixture between Rangers and Celtic, Scotland's 'Old Firm' rivals of many years standing. Up to this date it was the worst football disaster the British Isles had known. It eclipsed, in terms of the death toll, the previous major cases of Bolton in 1946, and Ibrox again back in 1902. The latter tragedy resulted from the collapse of a section of the terracing and resembled the 1971 case in respect of the crucial factor of crowd pressure. It might be added that the essential nature of spectating at large football matches in Britain had also changed little since the beginning of the century: the risk of crushing was considered normal and fans tolerated the possibility of losing control of their movements both while watching the match and exiting the ground afterwards.

The Wheatley Report, which was compiled in the wake of the 1971 Ibrox disaster, addressed issues of crowd safety hitherto largely neglected in official circles, and in 1975 the Safety of Sports Grounds Act was passed. During the years following the disaster Rangers Football Club embarked on the radical reconstruction of Ibrox into a predominantly seated stadium by 1981, and an all-seater by the mid-1990s. In so doing the club anticipated the directives of the Taylor Report in the aftermath of the Hillsborough disaster of 1989, which surpassed 1971 in loss of life and proved to be the decisive turning point in the development of British football crowd culture.[1]

II

The Rangers-Celtic match of 2 January 1971 was a typically keenly contested and tense affair watched by, for these games, a customary huge attendance, in this case over 80,000. The match was level 0-0 until the closing stages when Celtic took the lead with a goal from their diminutive winger Jimmy Johnstone. One minute later, with the last significant kick of the game, Rangers equalized through their centre forward Colin Stein. In the days following, a theory was floated as to the disaster's cause which quickly took root and which persists both in popular and academic writing about football to the present.[2] This theory explained the deaths by suggesting that many disappointed Rangers fans made their way out of 'the Rangers End' of the strictly segregated stadium when Celtic scored and, on hearing the roar which greeted the Rangers equalizer, attempted to return by climbing back up the steps of the exit, in this case the stairway at the north-east of the stadium which took its name from the terracing passageway it led directly on to: 'Stairway 13'. In so doing, the theory ran, they collided with fans leaving when the match ended, and were caught up in a deadly crush. The widespread currency enjoyed by this explanation led the scorer of the equalizing goal, Colin Stein, to admit 20 years later to the anguish he felt about possibly, if unwittingly, being responsible for the accident. The theory has endured in spite of the dearth of evidence for it in the findings of the Fatal Accident Inquiry (FAI), and in spite of the efforts of fans, many of whom were at the match and either were involved in, or witnessed, what happened, to explode it.[3]

The evidence of the proceedings of the FAI and a subsequent court case taken by the relatives of one of the victims against Rangers Football Club, reveals the much more probable cause to have been that of someone stumbling and falling almost halfway down the staircase, precipitating a surge forward by a densely-packed crowd.[4] Bodies, the police evidence stated,[5] were piled on bodies to a height of some six feet, and the victims, some of whom died standing, had the life literally sucked out of them. The cause of death for the vast majority was traumatic asphyxiation. It also was made clear that the fatal accident occurred some minutes – the best estimate is four to five – after the end of the match. In the minds of all witnesses bar one who testified to seeing one individual try to go back up the stairway, there was no question of fans coming down colliding with fans going up. Several witnesses claim to have seen, or been aware of, someone falling in front of them as they descended the staircase, and there were those witnesses, both on the stairway and watching from the tenement flats opposite the exit, who laid great stress on the possibility that someone on top of a friend's shoulders in a posture of celebration lost his balance, toppled and created a snowball effect. The conclusion of the FAI was that the precise cause remained obscure but that the effective cause was the overwhelming crowd pressure on the stairway.

The perils of large crowds using exits at football stadia were well recognized, but Ibrox had an especially ominous recent history. In 1961, again following an Old Firm game in which Rangers scored a late equalizer, two fans were killed in an accident on the same stairway. At this time, the steep exit was divided only by a wooden handrail down the middle, which gave way in the crush. Fans were able to escape to the grass banking alongside the stairway by breaking down the wooden side fence. With the hindsight of the knowledge of the 1971 disaster this was a vital factor, since the fans on the latter occasion were not able to break down the fence. The fence had been put back in place after the 1961 accident, and, it is claimed by some, was strengthened after another accident, in which over 30 were injured, following the Old Firm encounter of 2 January 1969, exactly two years before the disaster. In September 1967, indeed, there had been yet another incident after yet another Old Firm match leading to minor injuries and the twisting of steel hand-rails installed by Rangers in their extensive re-fashioning of the stairway following the 1961 tragedy. In 1961–62 the club concreted the stairs as well as dividing the exit into seven passageways by means of the rails. Rangers were widely praised for such improvements but, in retrospect, it can be seen that too little attention was paid to the design, as opposed to the condition, of the staircase. The exit was what was termed a 'waterfall staircase', and during the inquest into the 1971 disaster several experts voiced the opinion that the dangers inherent in such a structure might have been minimized by altering the design to create a 'fanning out' effect near the bottom, or that the stairway ought to have been reconstructed into a 'zigzag' style with regular turning points.[6]

Certainly, the serious incidents in 1961, 1967 and 1969 ought to have concen-trated the minds of the club's board of directors on the question of the safety of the staircase, more than appeared to be the case from the evidence presented to the Inquiry in 1971. The minutes of the meetings of the board of directors that were produced suggest that the issue was neglected, and confirm that the club took no action in 1969 beyond repairing the handrails and fencing which had been damaged. This was in spite of receiving letters of complaint from fans whom, the board minutes indicate, it was decided to 'appease' with complimentary tickets, an offer promptly withdrawn when the club was informed by its insurers that it was not liable for the injuries incurred in the 1969 incident.[7]

As was also made clear at the inquest, Rangers and the police were well aware that 'Stairway 13' was the most popular exit of all those in the stadium. This was on account of its proximity to public transport facilities and to the location of supporters' coaches. It was estimated that over 20,000 would have used the exit in crowds the size of which attended the Old Firm game of 2 January 1971. Rangers had in fact requested a special meeting with the police about matches at Ibrox back in February 1970, but this had been concerned with the subject of hooligan behav-iour, not safety.[8] During the Inquiry in 1971, senior police officers stressed that their interpretation of their role on match days was to curb disorder, and that no effective control could be exercised over departing crowds at exits. The Chief Superintendent of the Govan division of the Glasgow police stated: 'There is always crushing leaving football matches, normal rushing, they seem to enjoy it and can take it. If we see any person in danger or anyone liable to fall, or anyone being injured through this crushing we would have a duty to act. Until we see this danger we don't act.'[9]

Superintendent Angus MacDonald was forced to acknowledge that the police had a responsibility to prevent dangerous crowd pressure developing and to try to arrange for the crowd to be spread as evenly as possible.[10] It was, however, admit-ted by his superior that there were no policemen detailed to go to the exit stairways at the end of the game.[11] The police's priority, as is clear from the Inquiry evidence, was the prevention of hooligan behaviour and many officers were instead instructed at the end of the match to take up positions outside the stadium in case of fighting between rival sets of fans. When it became clear that an accident had occurred on the stairway some officers who remained inside the stadium were directed to the top of the terracing to prevent overcrowding at the head of the stairs. By this time it was too late. As was pointed out by the advocate for the relatives of the deceased at the FAI, the police were admitting responsibility where there was danger to life on the one hand, and on the other saying that they were powerless to control departing crowds.[12] It might be suggested that police could at least have been positioned at the top of the terracing to attempt to spread the departing spectators as evenly as they could down the different lanes of the stairway. The Inquiry found that the crowd pressure was far greater in the first three lanes of the stairway looking north, while the ones furthest away from this point were relatively free of crowd pressure. In this respect there was a parallel of a sort with Hillsborough and the overcrowding in the central pen of the Leppings Lane terrace.[13]

What became apparent at the FAI was the profound lack of clarity pertaining to the responsibilities held by the police and the club regarding safety,[14] and the ambiguities surrounding the issue of crowd disorder and where it could be said to have overlapped with crowd safety. As with the Hillsborough disaster, there was much confusion of the issues of crowd behaviour and crowd safety.[15] The Inquiry into the tragedy in 1961, moreover, had concluded that crowd pressure at the top of the stairs had been the crucial factor in the accident, and a police sergeant who gave evidence agreed that police should in future be stationed at the top of terracing to control the exit of people.[16] The events of 1971 demonstrated that neither Rangers Football Club nor the police had absorbed the lessons of the 1961 tragedy, even after the further warnings of 1967 and 1969. The two parties evidently did not purposefully combine to address this specific problem, although relations between them were mutually acknowledged to be excellent, and meetings took place, as noted, about hooliganism.

It should be stressed that the police did call a meeting after the 1969 accident when concern over safety was raised. This meeting was indeed the focus of much attention at the FAI in 1971 and the subsequent court case taken against Rangers. While the police evidence concerning the meeting was presented in a clear and informative fashion, the Rangers officials who were questioned about it were vague in their recollections, and failed to demonstrate that the club took the safety issue seriously enough in the aftermath of the third serious incident on the same stairway. It was this failure, combined with the evidence of the board minutes, which led the Sheriff presiding over the later court case to lambast the club for the manner in which they conducted their business and kept records.[17] The Rangers directors, all of them elderly men out of their depth, cut a pitiful collective figure in the aftermath of the disaster in 1971, and the club's dignity was only salvaged by the organizing ability and strength of character shown by the team manager of the time, the legendary Willie Waddell. It would be Waddell's vision of a new Ibrox that would be pursued and eventually realised.[18]

The 1969 meeting about the staircase involved the police, a Rangers director (probably David Hope), and the Glasgow Corporation Master of Works and his deputy. Ideas were floated about the redesign of the stairway, the replacement of the side fence with handrails was discussed, and the vital issue of crowd pressure at the top of the terracing was addressed in relation to schemes for a tunnel to provide an alternative exit, and the division of the terracing to enforce a more even use of all exits. However, the impression that emerges out of the Inquiry evidence is of insufficient agreement being reached as to any one idea, sharp discrepancies between testimonies as to what was suggested, and no significant pressure being exerted on Rangers by the police and/or the Master of Works to adopt a specific scheme to improve safety.[19] There was no follow-up meeting after the 1969 accident before the disaster two years later.

Both the police and the club, as expressed by respective representatives at the Inquiry and the court case, were keen to stress the factor of crowd behaviour as something which could not always be predicted, or to allow for which measures could not be taken with certainty of success. The consumption of copious amounts of alcohol at the 2 January 1971 match was reflected in the amount of cans and bottles littering the terracing afterwards, yet this was not in itself unusual, and certainly not if the factor of a Scottish New Year was borne in mind. Moreover, the relative absence of alcohol among the victims was clearly recorded at the Inquest.[20] Some fans may well have been drunk and this may have influenced their behaviour while departing, but it is doubtful that it was more than a peripheral cause.

Perhaps more pertinent was the intensive mood of jubilation among the Rangers supporters arising out of the dramatic closing moments of the match. The Chief Superintendent described it as follows: 'The excitement was tremendous, jubilation, they were singing, shouting, they were jumping up and down, waving their arms, hugging their friends, the terracing was in an uproar. I would say it was football mania at its highest.'[21] The Rangers Chairman, John Lawrence, was also convinced that the fans' euphoric state had much to do with what happened.[22] An eyewitness who lived opposite the exit in question claimed that the Rangers goal instilled such energy and exuberance among the fans that due care was not taken on the stairway.[23]

It is certainly necessary to be aware of the feverish emotions generated by an Old Firm match with all its traditional ethnic and sectarian trappings. By 1971 it was well established as Britain's premier sporting rivalry, and meetings of 'Protestant Rangers' and 'Catholic Celtic' had frequently been accompanied by violence between the two sets of fans and much general disorder.[24] The scale of the police operation on the day of 2 January 1971 was well in excess of the suggested measures for the management of such a crowd contained in the report of the Lang

Inquiry into football crowd behaviour, which was published in 1969.[25] Ironically, the crowd on the day was exceptionally well-behaved, with police making only three arrests. Before disaster struck it was being considered as one of the quietest Old Firm contests in the history of the fixture. The outbreak of unconfined joy at the Rangers end was spiced by the satisfaction derived from depriving Celtic of a victory and keeping Aberdeen top of the Scottish League. Rangers by this time only had a remote chance of winning the championship. The mood of the fans may well have lent increased volatility to the perennially hazardous business of exiting the stadium.

Yet it must be reiterated that there had been precedents. The circumstances of the 1961 fatal accident bore an uncanny resemblance to that of 1971. On the former occasion the departing Rangers fans were in a similarly rapturous mood after a late goal for their team. In 1967 and 1969 the fans were in celebratory spirits following victory over their greatest rivals. Once more it is difficult not to draw the conclusion that Rangers and the police should have addressed more seriously the potential problems that the large exiting crowd posed, especially if happenings on the field had created a mood conducive to recklessness. Again, it is pertinent to ask why the problem of crowd pressure at the top of the stairway, identified in the FAI of 1961, was not thoroughly investigated.

The complacency arguably shown by Rangers and the police was, however, symptomatic of a wider culture of neglect and ignorance of football crowds at the level of state policy formation and decision-taking. Callum Brown has demonstrated in detail how the Scottish Office displayed a lack of knowledge about football, and how pejorative notions concerning football fans and their behaviour inhibited proper evaluation of problems of crowd safety and the question of licensing football grounds.[26] In the post-war era, notwithstanding the warning delivered by the Bolton disaster, there was a lack of urgency around the matter: the buck, in effect, was passed from the Scottish Office to the Scottish Football Association and thereon to the clubs themselves. No legislation was passed to enforce clubs to take safety measures, and this in turn reflected the absence of a consensus of opinion in Britain generally regarding standards of ground safety.[27] In Scotland, moreover, Brown shows how the Scottish Office habitually confused the issues of crowd behaviour and safety and was mesmerized by the law and order ramifications of the Old Firm rivalry.[28] Just six months before the disaster of 1971 a licensing system for Scotland's football grounds was ruled out on the advice of senior civil servants. They maintained that the time was not right for legislation and indicated that such a system would not do anything substantial to prevent the consequences of 'loss of control' and 'panic'. It was doubted that a licensing system would make any significant contribution towards controlling hooliganism and improving crowd behaviour.[29]

The findings of the FAI into the Ibrox disaster of 1971 spared Rangers, and other parties, from blame, and it has been remarked since that there was no real 'blame culture' at the time.[30] It is in more recent years that some Rangers fans have identified the then custodians of their club as guilty men.[31] However, in 1974 the club was condemned as negligent by the Sheriff presiding over a test case brought by the wife of a victim of the 1971 tragedy, and she was awarded over £26,000 in damages. By this time only the club's declared intention to modernize Ibrox saved its image from further ruin, and it was also increasingly under pressure regarding its apparent refusal to sign players of the Catholic faith. Scottish football and society were now facing momentous social and cultural challenges.

III

The profound sense of shock induced by the disaster led many to hope that the historic sectarian antagonisms which marked west-central Scotland and found most vivid expression through football would cease, or at least diminish. There were indeed signs of a softening of the Old Firm rivalry in the immediate aftermath of the tragedy when the joint efforts of the two clubs encouraged some supporters to make conciliatory gestures. Players and officials of both clubs attended memorial church services for the victims at St Andrews Roman Catholic Cathedral and at Glasgow Cathedral. Both clubs gave generously to the Lord Provost of Glasgow's Disaster Fund, and later in January took part as a Rangers and Celtic 'select' team in a special match in aid of the fund held at Hampden Park, Scotland's national stadium.[32]

However, it was not long before old hatreds resurfaced. Rangers' league championship challenge faded quickly after the New Year of 1971 but they won through to the Scottish Cup Final in May where their opponents were Celtic. The typically enormous cup final Hampden crowd of over 120,000 produced an 'Orange versus Green' occasion as charged and acerbic as ever. Sectarian anthems and battle hymns rang out from the packed terracing with undiminished fervour. This was a rivalry the depth of which bore no comparison with the high-profile derbies of English football. The short-lived nature of Old Firm fans' conciliatory attitudes in 1971, for example, presented something of a contrast to that exhibited by Liverpool and Everton fans in the wake of Hillsborough.

Nevertheless, it can still be argued that the Rangers management had an opportunity, in the aftermath of the disaster, to address the question of sectarianism and declare their intention to sign Catholic players as well as Protestants. The club had come under pressure to do this since the events of Newcastle in May 1969 when Rangers fans rioted during and after their team's defeat in a Fair Cities Cup semi-final. The consequent glare of national (British) publicity resulted in the club's all-Protestant character being widely and critically scrutinized.[33] This marked a turning point: until then Rangers had not been held to account in a significantly public fashion. The club was now seen by opinion-formers and commentators to be decidedly out of step with the changing times and changing social values, although the continuing strength of religious identity and sectarian attitudes and assumptions in Scotland should not be underestimated.[34]

Certainly, the Rangers board seemed to fear that ending the 'tradition' would lose them considerable support; the club's vice-chairman, Matt Taylor, said precisely this in 1967.[35] As a body, Waddell included, the men who ran Rangers in 1971 possessed neither the courage nor the inclination to attempt it, even in circumstances which for a short time at least lessened the likelihood of an outraged reaction from their own supporters. Had he been as forward-thinking on this matter as on the reconstruction of the stadium, Willie Waddell could have used the latitude his powerful personality afforded him to bring the club truly into a new era. However, as is evident in his response to a question about Rangers' signing policy at a meeting of Glasgow magistrates in August 1972, Waddell simply preferred to deny that sectarianism was practised by the club or was in any way part of its ethos.[36]

Waddell instead focused his efforts on the club's continuing problem with hooliganism among its fans, calling for sectarian songs and chants to cease. He issued public statements to the effect that the club did not want this type of support, and even made an appeal from the Ibrox pitch at the start of season 1972–73 – this followed the tarnishing by the fans (albeit in a battle with Franco's ruthless police force) of the club's greatest achievement in winning the European Cup Winners' Cup in Barcelona. However, while encouraging the Chief Constable of Glasgow that the club was doing all in its power to dissociate itself from sectarianism, this did not extend to altering a *de facto* policy of signing players on a religious basis.[37] By this time, moreover, the issue of hooliganism was overshadowing that of safety as the motivation for the installation of more seating in the stadium.[38] The issue of crowd pressure at the top of the terracing had been tackled by means of the construction of a wall to break the flow of spectators, and the wooden side fences of Stairway 13 (since renumbered) had been replaced by handrails.[39]

To the discomfort of the Rangers management the issue of hooliganism continued to be resolutely connected to the club's all-Protestant image by the media, and later outbreaks of trouble at Manchester in 1974 and, most significantly, Birmingham in 1976 forced the club to state that they intended to sign players of all faiths. No such signing was made until that of the promising schoolboy John Spencer in the early 1980s, and the practice was not widely acknowledged as having changed until the sensational acquisition of Maurice Johnston by the then manager Graeme Souness in 1989. By this time Rangers had much to live down in the eyes of those outside the traditionally-minded of their support, although the catalogue of refusals on the part of Catholics pursued by Souness from 1986 indicated how entrenched were the outlooks of many across the divide. Moreover, the perpetuation of sectarian tensions in Scotland has been viewed by many as the outcome of several other factors besides the symbolism of Rangers.[40] Certainly, the implication of Waddell's defensive form of argument in the 1970s – that signing Catholic players would not of itself resolve sectarian problems in Scotland – has proved true enough.[41]

Further evidence of the absence of any reforming intentions over the signing of players at Ibrox can be found in the events which conspired to deny the Chairmanship of the club to director David Hope in 1973.[42] Hope had masterminded the successful development of the Rangers pools operation since the 1960s, and it was in fact the income generated from this venture which allowed the extensive rebuilding of Ibrox to take place in the late 1970s and early 1980s. Nonetheless, it seems to have been the case that Hope's marriage to a Roman Catholic, and possibly his own suspected conversion to Catholicism, stymied his elevation to the Chair when John Lawrence signalled his intention to step down. However, it should be kept in mind that Hope had not acquitted himself well at the FAI after the disaster and was perceived to have let down the club.[43]

The Ibrox disaster of 1971 had a global significance too: it affected expatriate Scots across the world, particularly in places like Canada and Australia where Rangers and Celtic supporters clubs formed a link with home. The Scottish actor John Cairney, a Celtic supporter, has provided a moving recollection of the profound impact of the disaster on his fellow Scots entertainers who were touring Canada at the time, including the legendary singer and 'bluenose' (Rangers fan) Andy Stewart, and on the exiles.[44]

However, Scotland and the Scottish diaspora apart, the disaster reverberated most strongly in nearby Northern Ireland. Here the sectarianism of the Old Firm rivalry was but a strand in a densely woven tapestry of conflict, and the troubles which had erupted in the Province two years earlier were now reaching new peaks of political violence and sectarian carnage.

The *Belfast Newsletter* estimated that 2,000 fans from Ulster attended the match,[45] and the same paper reported in mid-January that a Catholic mob in the Upper Springfield Road area of the city taunted Protestants with cries of 'Rangers 66 Celtic 0', a grim reference to the fact that it was Rangers fans who had died.[46] A week later riots on the Shankill Road between mobs and troops resulted in a Rangers supporters club, among other buildings, being destroyed by fire.[47] The impact of the Northern Ireland troubles on Old Firm supporters had already been evident in the additions to respective Orange and Irish Republican repertoires of songs about Ian Paisley and Bernadette Devlin. A popular Rangers anthem of the time, later to be taken up and rendered more bloodthirsty by Ulster Loyalists, was 'I was born under a Union Jack', an adaptation of Lee Marvin's hit 'I was born under a wanderin' star'. The song contained the lines: 'Do you know where hell is, hell is in the Falls; heaven is the Shankill Road, we'll guard old Derry's Walls.'[48] The upsurge in communal violence in Northern Ireland in 1971, pitching the Province very close to all-out civil war, might be said to have been a factor in maintaining sectarian tensions around football at a high level when the tragedy of Ibrox could in other circumstances have diluted them.

As in Ulster it was the working class, particularly of the west of Scotland, which held most tenaciously to the tribal-like identities celebrated through football. Aside from the 13 schoolboys in their early teens, and an eight-year-old boy, the victims of the disaster were overwhelmingly adult male manual workers. There was one young woman victim who was a machinist, and there was a soldier, a prison officer, a railway clerk and a factory foreman. There were six labourers and two unemployed. The occupations of the rest comprised welders, platers, panel beaters, machine operators, sheet metal workers, bakers, tailors, plumbers, electricians, painters, drivers, printers, joiners, engineers, glaziers, boilermakers, fitters, steel workers; there were several young apprentices of various trades.[49] Of the many witnesses who gave evidence at the FAI, most of whom attended the match and were close to the tragic events, the social profile was identical: over-whelmingly male manual workers, predominantly skilled or semi-skilled.[50]

Just as the spread of addresses of the deceased, albeit with a concentration in Glasgow, reflected the long-standing appeal of Rangers throughout Scotland, this occupational profile attests to the traditional nature of the club's bedrock support since its emergence as a major force in Scottish football in the late nineteenth century.[51] Additionally, it was an indication of the extent to which football remained overwhelmingly the workingman's pastime in the 1970s, and Glasgow and west-central Scotland's heavy industrial character. As the research of John Williams has shown, the predominance of the manual category in general, and skilled manual in particular, among Rangers supporters shrank significantly by the early 1980s, and to a level (30 per cent) at which it was barely stronger than the category of 'skilled non-manual' in 1990. Williams also found that as the club modernized and improved its facilities, and society's work and leisure structures altered, Rangers drew more fans from a wider geographical radius, more females and more white-collar workers.[52] Indeed, Rangers could be said to have reflected at an early stage the trends that would come to define the spectator experience in England post-Taylor.

IV

The Ibrox disaster moved the Scottish folk singer, Matt McGinn, whose back-ground was Catholic of Irish descent, to write a song in honour of the victims which became locally well-known, and was appreciated greatly by Rangers supporters.

New Year bells had been ringing
All Scotland was singing
The old year had died, and the new had been born
As the news of disaster, from Ibrox came spreading
The news that would cause a whole nation to mourn.[53]

Thus the opening verse of the song which went on to proclaim 'the Old Firm united' and 'no Billy, no Dan', noble sentiments which proved all too fleeting in reality. It was not long until Celtic supporters would coin chants that mocked the victims, a practice taken up from the late 1980s by Aberdeen supporters as a token of the bitterness that has come to define relations between many of the fans of this club and Rangers.[54] This was ironic given the manner in which Rangers fans had sung in support of Aberdeen on the fateful day of 2 January 1971, including spirited renderings of 'The northern lights of old Aberdeen'.[55] The Ibrox disaster, like that of the Manchester United Munich air crash of 1958 and other tragedies, has been commemorated in the context of changing football crowd rivalries and cultures in a deeply offensive fashion.

Commemoration of a well-meaning and respectful kind also became a notable issue in the decades following the disaster. For many years afterwards it seemed that the tragedy was destined to be quietly forgotten, at least in terms of public recognition and visible reminders. At the time, as a Rangers fan has recently observed, 'the public reaction was of quiet shock, nothing like the more recent disasters at Bradford, Heysel and Hillsborough'.[56] This reflected the very different 'mourning culture' of the era, in Britain generally but perhaps especially in Scotland where ostentatious shows of emotion were considered culturally at odds with the prevailing values and self-image. Much was to change in this respect in the 1980s and 1990s, and the reaction to the Hillsborough disaster of 1989 was particularly cathartic and transformative. As Ian Taylor has pointed out, the overnight decoration of the Leppings Lane entrance at Hillsborough with football memorabilia was 'a mass popular rite largely without parallel in Britain this century'.[57] It seemed to provide the example which football supporters felt appropriate to follow in mourning the subsequent deaths of victims of other tragic occurrences or of players and managers who had attracted adulation at specific clubs. Thus, in the case of Rangers, there were huge displays of supporters' tokens of respect and affection following the deaths of former winger Davie Cooper and former manager Jock Wallace in the 1990s. This kind of ritual had never before been observed following the deaths of ex-players and managers who had attained similar legendary status.

This changing pattern of behaviour also came to focus on the Ibrox disaster. By the time of the twentieth anniversary there was considerable pressure put on the club by the fans to honour the memory of the victims.[58] The line taken by the club for many years – that the new Ibrox stadium was in itself a memorial to those who lost their lives – was regarded increasingly by fans as inadequate, however important and creditable such rebuilding had been. On 2 January 1991, when Rangers again faced Celtic at Ibrox, the fans paid their own tributes by laying scarves and other club mementoes at the disaster site. A commemorative plaque, organized by the management of the club in response to popular demand, was also unveiled at this corner of the stadium, although the man who arguably ought to have performed the ceremony, Willie Waddell, was absent. A minute's silence was then held before the match started, but some Celtic supporters interrupted it with jeers, catcalls and chants. The further acrimony caused by this to relations between the two sets of fans was predictable.[59]

The continuing pressure exerted by supporters for a more prominent and visible memorial finally resulted in the commission of a statue that was unveiled at a special commemorative service at Ibrox to mark the thirtieth anniversary in 2001.[60] The statue was of the club captain of the period, John Greig, and it was intended as a tribute not only to the victims of the 1971 disaster, but also to those of 1902 and 1961. 'The players, managers and directors come and go', wrote the editor of one of the Rangers supporters fanzines at the time of the statue's unveiling, 'but the faceless and nameless crowd is the raw material out of which the club is made. Sadly those who died in the Disasters did not remain faceless and nameless. Remember them all and the reasons why they died.'[61]

V

The Ibrox disaster of 1971 reflected the fact that British football stadia of the period were in general dangerous places. Ibrox was a typical example of a stadium which had taken shape at the beginning of the twentieth century and which housed huge numbers of fans with the provision of minimal standards of spectator safety and comfort. If anything, Ibrox was one of the better-appointed grounds, and Rangers could not be said to have neglected in any way the essential maintenance and condition of the stadium. Nevertheless, too little thought was given to the question of safety, particularly in relation to exiting the ground, when warning had been served in the form of previous accidents on the same stairway.

The disaster also assumes a more singular character when it is borne in mind that it happened after an Old Firm game, as indeed had the previous accidents. The unique character and atmosphere of this fixture cannot be detached from the tragic events, and the disaster's impact on the Old Firm rivalry was significant, if not the catalyst towards change that was widely hoped for by civic society in Scotland. Moreover, a perception of the disaster outside Scotland as resulting from quasi-religious passions with no parallel elsewhere in Britain may have prevented a more attentive appreciation of the lessons that might have been learnt from it in relation to crowd safety in England.

A study of the disaster also helps shed light on the social composition of the football crowds of the time, and indicates that the early 1970s was perhaps the last point at which a particular social strata – that of skilled manual workers – so dominated the culture of football crowds, at least in the case of Rangers.

The Ibrox disaster has been much more the subject of popular inquiry and personal remembrance since the late 1980s than before. Partly this reflects the popularity of new technology and the extent to which the internet has allowed more supporters to participate in discussion and reminiscence;[62] yet the main factor seems to have been the general trend towards more explicit displays of commemoration in Scotland and in Britain as a whole, which was clearly visible in fans' reaction to the Hillsborough disaster.

NOTES

1. For a discussion of football grounds and the nature of spectating see R. Giulianotti, *Football: A Sociology of the Global Game* (Cambridge: Polity Press, 1999), ch.4; for Ibrox see S. Inglis, *Football Grounds of Britain* (London: Collins Willow, 1996), pp.466–71; for legislation on football grounds and spectator safety, Ken Foster, 'Developments in Sporting Law', in L. Allison (ed.), *The Changing Politics of Sport* (Manchester: Manchester University Press, 1993); *Report of the Working Party on Crowd Behaviour at Football Matches* (The Lang Report), (London: HMSO, 1969); Report on Crowd Safety at Sports Grounds (The Wheatley Report), (Cmnd. 4962, 1972); for the Bolton disaster in 1946 and earlier incidents, J. Walton, 'Football, Fainting and Fatalities', *History Today*, 53, 1 (Jan. 2003), 10–17; for Hillsborough see P. Scraton, *Hillsborough: The Truth* (Edinburgh: Mainstream, 1999); and I. Taylor, 'English Football in the 1990s: Taking Hillsborough Seriously?', in J. Williams and S. Wagg (eds), *British Football and Social Change* (Leicester: Leicester University Press, 1991).
2. R. Forsyth, *The Only Game* (Edinburgh: Mainstream, 1990), pp.109–10, and A. MacPherson, *Blue and Green* (London: BBC Books, 1989), pp.76–86 are examples of popular accounts; Giulianotti, *Football*, p.74 is an example of an academic treatment.
3. See letters to *The Herald* (Glasgow), 2 Jan. 1996, 3 Jan. 1996 and (to Sports Editor), 15 Jan. 1996.
4. The Report of proceedings of Fatal Accident Inquiry (FAI) into the Ibrox disaster of 2 January 1971 and material relating to the compensation case brought against Rangers Football Club are contained in a special Ibrox Disaster Archive (hereafter referred to as 'Ibrox Archive') located in the Mitchell Library, Glasgow. This is the main source on which this study is based.
5. Strathclyde Regional Archives, SR 22/51/1.
6. See, for example, evidence of William Gow and Professor Alexander Coull at FAI, Ibrox Archive, A5–A7, and the summing up of the advocate for the relative of the deceased at the court case in 1974, Ibrox Archive, B16–B17.
7. Ibrox Archive B36, minutes of board of directors, 28 Jan. 1969; 24 Feb. 1969.
8. Ibrox Archive, A4, FAI evidence of Superintendent Angus MacDonald.
9. Ibrox Archive, A4, evidence of Chief Superintendent Robert Purdon.
10. Ibrox Archive, A4, evidence of MacDonald.
11. Ibrox Archive, A4, evidence of Purdon.
12. Ibrox Archive, A4, examination of MacDonald by advocate.
13. See Scraton, chs.1–3.
14. There was, for example, some confusion over the precise role of stewards inside the ground.
15. Scraton, passim.
16. Ibrox Archive, A10, Report of proceedings of Fatal Accident Inquiry, 16 Nov. 1961, evidence of John Paterson.
17. Ibrox Archive, B85, Sheriff's final judgment. The Sheriff also took the view that Rangers had been guilty of the deception of the Scottish Football Association in 1969 over the latter's request that the club furnish it with details of when the ground was last inspected for safety.
18. See A. MacPherson, *Action Replays* (London: Chapmans, 1991), ch.6; S. Halliday, *Rangers: The Waddell Years* (London; Chameleon Books, 1999); D. Mason, *Rangers: The Managers* (Edinburgh: Mainstream, 2000), pp.95–116.
19. Ibrox Archive, A4, see evidence of Hope, White, Gow, Shepherd and Nicholson especially.
20. Ibrox Archive, A2, evidence of Celtic Football Club doctor.
21. Ibrox Archive, A4, evidence of Robert Purdon.
22. Ibrox Archive, A6, evidence of John Lawrence.
23. Ibrox Archive, A1, evidence of Robert John Duncan.
24. For an excellent guide to the Old Firm phenomenon and its place in Scottish society see Bill Murray, *The Old Firm: Sectarianism, Sport and Society in Scotland* (Edinburgh; John Donald, 2nd edn, 2000).
25. See Lang Report (note 1). Lang visited Ibrox and according to the minutes of the Rangers board of directors of 17 June 1969, was impressed by the condition of the stadium. The Lang Report, however, made the point about 'funnelling' at entries and exits. A member of the Lang team, former England manager Walter Winterbottom, gave evidence at the court case taken against Rangers. He was inclined not to lay the blame on the club. See Ibrox Archive, B80.
26. Callum G. Brown, 'Sport and the Scottish Office in the Twentieth Century: the Control of a Social Problem', in J.A. Mangan (ed.), *Sport in Europe: Politics, Class, Gender* (London: Frank Cass, 1999).
27. See Inglis, pp.466–71.

28. Brown, 'Sport and the Scottish Office'.
29. *The Herald*, 1 Jan. 2002.
30. 'Ibrox', BBC Scotland documentary programme broadcast January 2001.
31. *Follow, Follow* (Rangers Fanzine), No.115.
32. See press cuttings collected in Ibrox Archive, C1. See also Murray, pp.183–4. Hampden was the biggest sports stadium in Britain at this time, and several witnesses at the FAI concerning Ibrox made the point that Hampden's steep exits resembled those of Ibrox.
33. See Murray, pp.182–4; also Graham Walker, "There's Not a Team Like the Glasgow Rangers": Football and Religious Identity in Scotland', in G. Walker and T. Gallagher (eds), *Sermons and Battle Hymns: Protestant Popular Culture in Modern Scotland* (Edinburgh: Edinburgh University Press, 1990).
34. See discussion in Callum G. Brown, *Religion and Society in Scotland since 1707* (Edinburgh: Edinburgh University Press, 1997).
35. Quoted in Murray, p.181.
36. Ibrox Archive, B36, board of directors minutes, 21 Aug. 1972. See also Murray, p.185.
37. Ibrox Archive, B36, board of directors minutes, 8 Aug. 1972.
38. Ibid.
39. Ibrox Archive, B36, board of directors minutes, 6 April 1971.
40. See T.M. Devine (ed.), *Scotland's Shame? Bigotry and Sectarianism in Modern Scotland* (Edinburgh: Mainstream, 2000) for a recent audit of the debate surrounding sectarianism.
41. Since the signing of Johnston Rangers have fielded many Catholic players including the Italian Lorenzo Amoruso who was for a time club captain.
42. See G.P.T. Finn, 'Faith, Hope and Bigotry: Case Studies of Anti-Catholic Prejudice in Scottish Soccer and Society', in G. Jarvie and G. Walker (eds), *Scottish Sport in the Making of the Nation* (Leicester: Leicester University Press, 1994).
43. See comment by editor in the Ibrox disaster feature contained in *The Rangers Historian*, 3, 3 (1991).
44. J. Cairney, *The Man Who Played Robert Burns* (Edinburgh: Mainstream, 1987), pp.113–19.
45. *Belfast Newsletter*, 4 Jan. 1971.
46. *Belfast Newsletter*, 18 Jan. 1971.
47. *Belfast Newsletter*, 25 Jan. 1971.
48. See S. Walsh (ed.), *Voices of the Old Firm* (Edinburgh: Mainstream, 1995), pp.129–31; G. Bell, *The Protestants of Ulster* (London: Pluto Press, 1976), p.52.
49. Strathclyde Regional Archives, SR 22/51/1.
50. Strathclyde Regional Archives, SR 22/51/2.
51. See Walker, '"There's Not a Team Like the Glasgow Rangers"'; also R. Holt, *Sport and the British* (Oxford: Oxford University Press, 1989), pp.159–60 for commentary on the social profile of victims of the 1902 Ibrox disaster.
52. John Williams, *Seven Years On: Glasgow Rangers and Rangers Supporters, 1983–90* (Leicester: Sir Normal Chester Centre for Football Research, 1990).
53. Matt McGinn, *McGinn of the Calton* (Glasgow: Glasgow District Libraries, 1987), p.132.
54. See R. Giulianotti and M. Gerrard, 'Cruel Britannia? Glasgow Rangers, Scotland and "Hot" Football Rivalries', in G. Armstrong and R. Giulianotti (eds), *Fear and Loathing in World Football* (Oxford: Berg, 2001).
55. Ibrox Archive, A1-A7, recollections of various witnesses.
56. Recollections of Kenny Bell on Ibrox disaster, BBC website, 2 Jan. 2001.
57. Taylor, p.4.
58. 'Twenty Years Ago', *Follow, Follow*, No.17.
59. See various articles and letters in *Follow, Follow*, No.17.
60. See feature on sculptor Andy Scott in *The Herald Magazine*, 26 April 2003.
61. *Follow, Follow*, No.115.
62. For example see http://uk.geocities.com/ibrox_disaster/disaster.html.

4

Death on the Terraces: The Contexts and Injustices of the 1989 Hillsborough Disaster

PHIL SCRATON

The crush came … it wasn't a surge. It was like a vice getting tighter and tighter and tighter. I turned Adam 'round to me. He was obviously in distress. There was a police officer, about five or six feet away and I started begging him to open the gate. I was screaming. Adam had fainted and my words were 'My lovely son is dying' and begging him to help me and he didn't do anything. I grabbed hold of Adam's lapels and tried to lift him over the fence. It was ten feet or thereabouts with spikes coming in. I couldn't lift him. So I started punching the fence in the hope I could punch it down. Right at the beginning when I was begging the officer to open the gate, if he'd opened it I know I could've got Adam out. I know that because I was there.[1]

This is Eddie Spearritt's testimony to the last moments of his son's life. Adam, eventually evacuated from the Hillsborough terraces, was pronounced dead at the Northern General Hospital, Sheffield at approximately 4.45 p.m. on 15 April 1989. He was one of 96 men, women and children who died as a result of injuries sustained on the terraces or, as became increasingly clear, because the police response to the impending disaster and the medical response that followed were inadequate. Of the 96 who died only 14 were taken to hospital. The rest were pronounced dead at the ground and, in body bags, were laid out on the floor of the Hillsborough gymnasium. Pat Nicol, whose ten-year-old son, Lee, was killed, spoke for many when she said, 'You don't expect to go to a football match and die'.[2]

Eddie Spearritt came close to death. Having struggled in vain to save Adam he lost consciousness and collapsed under foot in the crush of pen 4. This was some time around 3 p.m., six minutes before the FA Cup Semi-Final between Liverpool and Nottingham Forest was stopped, and 20 minutes before the dead and dying in central pens 3 and 4 were dragged through two narrow gates across the perimeter track and onto the pitch. Two hours are missing from Eddie's life. The first medical record of him at the hospital is his admission to intensive care at

5 p.m. Following the chaos of the pens' evacuation, and given the paucity of immediate necessary medical treatment and facilities, it is clear that an unknowable number of those who died could have been saved. Eddie has no knowledge of his whereabouts between 3 p.m. and 5 p.m. It appears he had been presumed dead, as were others who also recovered. He agonizes over Adam's death and whether he too might have been saved.

As the disaster was happening, in full view of the police control box high above the Leppings Lane terrace, a further tragedy was set in motion. The South Yorkshire Police match commander, Chief Superintendent David Duckenfield, informed Graham Kelly, then Chief Executive of the Football Association, that Liverpool supporters had forced entry through an exit gate causing an 'inrush' onto the already packed terraces. Within minutes this version of events was broadcast worldwide. Jacques Georges, then President of UEFA, railed against 'people's frenzy to enter the stadium come what may, whatever the risk to the lives of others'. They 'were beasts waiting to charge into the arena'.[3] Thus, Liverpool fans were responsible for the deaths of 'their own'. The lens of hooliganism was firmly in place.

This was also the version relayed by the police to the South Yorkshire Coroner, Dr Stefan Popper en route to the stadium. He instructed the taking and recording of blood alcohol levels of all who died, including children. This was unprecedented. As the pathologists' reports would establish the medical cause of death it was clear that the Coroner considered alcohol to be a significant factor in the disaster. Within hours, bereaved families queued outside the gymnasium to identify their loved ones. The presentation of bodies in body bags, and the casual treatment of the bereaved, combined insensitivity with callousness. Grief-stricken relatives were 'interrogated' regarding the drinking habits and 'criminal' records of their loved ones. The next day the Prime Minister Margaret Thatcher visited Sheffield accompanied by the Home Secretary, Douglas Hurd. She was briefed that there 'would have been *no* Hillsborough if a mob, who were clearly tanked up, had not tried to force their way into the ground'.[4]

Two days later the *Sheffield Star* (18 April 1989) published the first serious police allegations as facts concerning Liverpool supporters not only causing the disaster, but also attacking rescue workers and stealing from the dead. Its headline was: 'Drunken Attacks on Police: Ticketless Thugs Staged Crush to Gain Entry'. This included an allegation that 'yobs' had 'urinated on policemen as they gave the kiss of life to stricken victims'. Local politicians and Police Federation representatives, without any substantiating evidence, reiterated the allegations, and on 19 April the *Sun* cleared its front page. It pronounced: 'The Truth: Some Fans Picked Pockets of Victims; Some Fans Urinated on the Brave Cops; Some Fans Beat Up PC Giving Kiss of Life'. A further eight newspapers carried the allegations including 'sex jibes over a girl's corpse' (*Sheffield Star* 19 April 1989). It later transpired that the *Sun* editor, Kelvin Mackenzie, had considered running the headline 'You Scum'.[5] As the Home Office Inquiry under Lord Justice Taylor commenced, Duckenfield's instant reaction to blame the fans, thereby exonerating the police, had established a broad and seemingly legitimate constituency. Not only did it determine the course of events in the immediate aftermath, but it set a wider media and political agenda.

THE HILLSBOROUGH STADIUM

One of the greatest problems we have is access to the ground, particularly at the Leppings Lane end. The redesigned turn stiles [*sic*] do not give anything like the access to the ground, either on the Leppings Lane terraces or in the West Stand, needed by away fans. On occasions last season when large numbers attended, we had away supporters who were justifyably [*sic*] irate because of the inefficiency of the system, which was turned on the police and could have resulted in public disorder.[6]

The Hillsborough Football Stadium opened in 1899 and, like so many other football stadia, had been modified to meet the requirements of the 1975 Safety of Sports Grounds Act, and, subsequently, revisions to the 1976 Home Office Guide to Safety at Sports Grounds, brought about by the Popplewell inquiry into the deaths at Bradford, Birmingham and Heysel.[7]

Hillsborough was considered by the football authorities to be one of England's best grounds. While parts of the stadium had been upgraded, the essential fabric of the Leppings Lane terrace was unchanged. Previous lessons regarding crowd safety had been ignored and the modifications to the terrace prioritized crowd control and segregation. Following serious crushing in 1981, resulting in injuries to 38 fans, the Leppings Lane terrace was divided by lateral fences into three separate enclosures or pens, thus preventing movement along the terrace. Tragedy had been narrowly avoided by opening the gates in the trackside perimeter fencing. In 1985 the police requested further lateral fences and the terrace was divided into five pens. Both central pens, directly behind the goal, were fed by a 1 in 6 gradient tunnel beneath the West Stand, built in 1965 in preparation for the 1966 World Cup. Emerging from the tunnel, fans walked to the right or left of a fence into pens 3 or 4 respectively. A high, overhanging fence mounted on a wall separated the terraces from the perimeter track. There was restricted access into each pen through a narrow, locked gate. The crush barriers were reviewed in 1979 leaving a mixture of relatively new and old. Modifications made in 1985 and 1986 resulted in different barrier distribution in each pen. In pen 3, for example, a diagonal gap stretched from the front barrier to the back of the terrace. A crush down this channel would clearly place the front barrier under considerable pressure.

The West Stand seated 4,500 spectators. The uncovered Leppings Lane terrace held 10,100. Entry into the North Stand was also from the Leppings Lane turnstiles. Thus 24,256 fans converged on 23 turnstiles located in a small, divided outer concourse. The 10,100 fans with tickets for the Leppings Lane terrace walked through outer gates onto the concourse to queue at seven turnstiles. The remaining 14,156 ticket-holders for North and West Stands accessed 16 turnstiles through the adjoining concourse. In the hour before kick-off this tightly confined area, a shop wall to the left and a fence above the River Don to the right, had to cope with 25,000 people unfamiliar with the layout of the stadium. The outmoded turnstiles regularly malfunctioned. Although an electronic counting system recorded the numbers accessing the terrace there was no way of knowing the distribution between the pens. The two central pens, with capacities of 1,000 and 1,100, were always the first to fill. The doors at the head of the tunnel feeding the central pens could be closed once it was estimated that the pens' capacities had been reached. It was a calculation based on observation rather than actual numbers entering.

It flew in the face of the Moelwyn Hughes' Inquiry's recommendations after the Burnden Park disaster of 1946 that all terrace enclosures should be accurately monitored. Moelwyn Hughes 'feared that the disaster at Bolton might easily be repeated at 20 to 30 grounds'. He concluded: 'How simple and how easy it is for a dangerous situation to arise in a crowded enclosure. It happens again and again without fatal or even injurious consequences.' All that was necessary was the occurrence of one or two additional factors and that inherent 'danger' would be transformed into 'death and injuries'.

15 APRIL 1989

It was a beautiful spring morning as Liverpool fans embarked on their trip across the Pennines to Sheffield. The last thing on anyone's mind was danger. For the second time in successive years their team had drawn Nottingham Forest in the semi-finals of the FA Cup. Hillsborough was hired by the Football Association as a neutral venue and policing and crowd control arrangements were virtually identical. Liverpool fans were allocated the West Stand, the Leppings Lane terrace and the North Stand. It was an all-ticket match and the only instruction on the tickets was that spectators were expected to be inside the stadium 15 minutes before kick-off. Fans travelled by train, coaches, transits and cars. Coaches and transits were stopped en route and searched by police. Arriving in Sheffield, all were directed to designated car parks, searched and briefed by South Yorkshire Police officers. Those arriving by train were escorted to the stadium. Delays on the journey meant that thousands of Liverpool fans arrived in Sheffield in the hour before the 3 p.m. kick-off.

At 2.30 p.m. a police officer noticed coaches 'arriving one after another'. Ten minutes later fans were disembarking coaches 'about a quarter of a mile away' and a 'large number of Liverpool supporters were trying to park'. With train escorts arriving just before 2.30 p.m., coaches backed up along main roads and cars attempting to park, it was clear that the steady stream of supporters arriving at the

62

Leppings Lane turnstiles prior to 2.15 p.m. would become a torrent. And so it happened. Lack of stewarding and the absence of filtering along Leppings Lane contributed significantly to the sudden and intense build-up in the narrow outer concourse area. Any semblance of queuing evaporated as the bottleneck, the concern raised by the 1986 internal police memorandum, began to take its toll. The simple equation was that more people were arriving at the rear of the enclosed concourse than were passing through the turnstiles at the front. A serious crush ensued. Even mounted police became trapped in the crowd and fans struggled to breathe. The senior officer outside decided that the 'only practical way to prevent deaths outside would be to open the [exit] gates' thereby allowing people into the stadium and relieving the crush. He 'radioed ground control [the police control box inside] and asked for the gates to be opened. There was no acknowledgement'. Thinking his radio was defective he used another and 'repeated my request'. Again, 'there was no acknowledgement'.[8]

Chief Superintendent David Duckenfield assumed responsibility for policing Hillsborough Stadium just 21 days before the semi-final. He and his assistant, Superintendent Bernard Murray, watched the congestion build at the turnstiles on CCTV monitors. It was tense in the control box as the request to open the exit gates came through. Duckenfield, a match commander with virtually no experi-ence of policing football in a stadium with which he was unfamiliar, faced a massive dilemma. He thought: 'A man who I have known for many years, a man who I respect and admire, was demanding of me something I would not normally give … [he] was telling me that unless I opened the gates there would be serious injury and possibly death.' He was 'all consumed'. Murray broke the long silence: 'Mr Duckenfield, are you going to open the gate?' After further hesitation, and as if thinking aloud, Duckenfield responded: 'If there's likely to be death or serious injury outside I have no option than to open the gates.' He instructed Murray to open the gates.[9]

Despite being located in a control box directly above the Leppings Lane terrace, they did not consider that the crowd distribution in the pens might be a problem. Yet photographs taken moments before show both central pens were packed while the side pens were sparsely populated. The clear and obvious danger was that in relieving the life-threatening crush at the turnstiles a worse situation would develop on the terraces. Murray's mind-set is evident from an earlier inter-change with a chief inspector who had inquired whether the terrace should be filled one pen at a time. Murray's reply was that all pens should be open from the outset and fans could be left to 'find their own level'.[10]

When gate 'C' opened there was instant relief around the outer concourse. Fans, including Eddie and Adam Spearritt, who had stood back from the crush walked through unstewarded and without police direction. Directly opposite was the 1 in 6 gradient tunnel beneath the West Stand, signposted 'STANDING'. It led into the packed central pens. Neither police nor stewards thought to close the tunnel and redirect incoming fans to the side pens. Over 2,000 fans walked down and compression was immediate. Faces were jammed against the perimeter fence, people fell and in pen 3 a barrier, near the bottom of the diagonal channel, collapsed bringing down a tangled mass of bodies. As the match kicked-off the thunderous roar of the crowd drowned out the screams of the dying. The police failed to respond and forced those trying to escape the crush back into the pens. Officers on the perimeter track were under explicit orders not to open the narrow perimeter gates without authorization of a senior officer.

The failure to close off the tunnel before opening Gate C was compounded by the failure to respond immediately and effectively to the disaster unfolding on the terraces. Once the two narrow perimeter track gates were opened the full horror began to dawn. Over 500 people were dead, dying or injured. Restricted access prevented effective and speedy evacuation of the pens. The match was abandoned at 3.06pm and fans and some police officers tried to resuscitate those who had lost consciousness. As these distressing scenes were taking place, Duckenfield told the Assistant Chief Constable that it was a 'pitch invasion'. He radioed for reinforcements including dog handlers. Minutes later he lied to the FA officials, not mentioning that he had directed his officers to open the exit gates. In giving evidence to the Taylor Inquiry, Duckenfield stated: 'The blunt truth [was] that we had been asked to open a gate. I was not being deceitful ... I just thought at that stage that I should not communicate fully the situation ... I may have misled Mr Kelly.'[11] He did. And, unwittingly, Kelly reiterated the lie to the awaiting media. As the disaster happened the fans were blamed.

FROM OFFICIAL INQUIRY TO JUDICIAL SCRUTINY

In the immediate aftermath the Home Secretary, Douglas Hurd, appointed Lord Justice Taylor to conduct an Inquiry 'into the events at Sheffield Wednesday Football Ground on 15 April 1989 and to make recommendations about the needs of crowd control and safety at sports events'.[12] Hurd appointed the West Midlands police to assist in the Inquiry. The Force also conducted the criminal investigation and serviced the inquests as 'coroner's officers'. Apart from oral evidence to the public hearings, the Inquiry team processed 2,666 telephone calls, 3,776 statements and 1,550 letters. Taylor produced an Interim Report within four months concluding that the 'main cause' of the disaster was 'overcrowding' and the 'main reason' was a 'failure of police control'. He also criticized Sheffield Wednesday Football Club, their safety engineers and the local authority which had failed to issue an up-to-date licence for the stadium. But he directed his most damning conclusions towards South Yorkshire police.

Taylor condemned senior officers as 'defensive and evasive', considering 'neither their handling of problems on the day nor their account of it in evidence showed the qualities of leadership to be expected of their rank'. It was 'a matter of regret that at the hearing, and in their submissions, South Yorkshire Police were not prepared to concede that they were in any respect at fault for what had occurred'.[13] Duckenfield's 'capacity to take decisions and give orders seemed to collapse'. He had failed to give 'necessary consequential orders' after he had sanctioned the opening of the gates and he failed 'to exert any control' once the disaster was in train. Worse still, he lied; his 'lack of candour' triggering around the world 'a widely reported allegation' against fans.[14] The severity of Taylor's criticisms, alongside his exoneration of the fans' behaviour, took many commentators by surprise. In December 1989 the South Yorkshire police accepted civil liability in negligence and paid damages to the bereaved. Subsequently, in a House of Lords judgment, Lord Keith concluded that the Chief Constable had 'admitted liability in negligence in respect of the deaths and physical injuries'.[15] In a later Divisional Court judgment Lord Justice McCowan stated that the force 'had admitted fault and paid compensation'.[16] These words were reiterated in the House of Commons by the AttorneyGeneral.[17]

In March 1990, following consultation with the Director of Public Prosecutions (DPP), the Coroner resumed the adjourned inquests on a 'limited basis' ahead of the decisions regarding criminal prosecution or disciplinary action. He held unprecedented 'preliminary hearings' for each of the deceased dealing only with the medical evidence, blood alcohol levels, the location of bodies prior to death and the identification. There was no discussion of 'how' the person died. The often sparse and inconsistent evidence in each case was summarized and presented to the hearing by a designated West Midlands police officer. Witness statements on which summaries were based were not disclosed and no cross-examination was allowed. What the jury heard was a mixture of interpretation, selection and conjecture presented, unchallenged, as fact. Unable to access primary statements and cross-examine the evidence, bereaved families were left with numerous unanswered questions, disqualified as being outside the agreed parameters of the preliminary hearings.

Four months later the DPP decided there was 'no evidence to justify any criminal proceedings' against any organization involved and 'insufficient evidence to justify proceedings against any officer of the South Yorkshire Police or any other person for any offence'.[18] The Coroner resumed the inquests in generic form. They ran from 19 November 1990 to 28 March 1991. Two hundred and thirty witnesses were called and 12 interested parties (six of whom were police interests) were represented. One barrister represented 43 families. Despite the cost and length of the inquests and the number of witnesses called, disclosure of evidence was limited. Once again, police witnesses emphasized the very issues discounted by Taylor: fans' drunkenness, hooliganism, violence and conspiracy to enter the ground without tickets. In summing up, the Coroner steered the jury away from returning a verdict of unlawful killing. He told them that an accidental death verdict could 'straddle the whole spectrum of events' including 'a situation where you are … satisfied there has been carelessness, negligence … and that someone would have to make compensation payments in civil litigation'.[19] Accidental death would not mean absolution 'from all and every measure of blame'. There could have been mistakes made and 'very serious errors' but being 'incompetent is not the same as saying that a person is being reckless'.[20] After two days of deliberation the jury returned a majority verdict of accidental death.

Despite the Police Complaints Authority's determination to bring disciplinary proceedings against the match commander and his assistant for 'neglect of duty', Duckenfield left the police on ill-health grounds and the case against Murray was withdrawn. Six families took test cases to the Divisional Court aiming to quash the inquests' verdicts on the grounds of irregularity of proceedings, insufficiency of inquiry and the emergence of new evidence. The Court ruled in favour of the Coroner, finding that the inquests had been properly conducted, evidence had not been suppressed and his direction of the jury had been 'impeccable'. In June 1997, following publication of *No Last Rights*[21] and the screening of Jimmy McGovern's award-winning drama documentary *Hillsborough* (ITV, December 1996), Jack Straw, the recently-elected Labour Government's Home Secretary, announced an independent judicial scrutiny 'to get to the bottom of this once and for all'.[22] The Scrutiny, without precedent and conducted by former MI6 Commissioner Lord Justice Stuart-Smith, would review evidence not available to previous inquiries or investigations. 'New' evidence had to be of such significance that it would have resulted in prosecutions or changed the outcomes of the Taylor Inquiry or the inquests. Stuart-Smith visited the South Yorkshire police and took evidence from 18 bereaved families, submissions from the Hillsborough Family Support Group and other concerned parties. In February 1998 he presented his report to the Home Secretary who greeted it as 'thorough', 'comprehensive', 'dispassionate', 'objective' and 'impartial'. Stuart-Smith's conclusion was that neither the Taylor Inquiry nor the inquest had been flawed and the so-called 'new' evidence did not add 'anything significant' to what was already known.[23]

The Home Secretary ignored serious allegations made to Stuart-Smith by the author and a former South Yorkshire police officer. They revealed that in the immediate aftermath police officers were instructed not to record events in their pocket books but to submit hand-written 'recollections' of events. Unusually, they were encouraged to include emotions, comment and opinion as they were solely for the information of legal advisors, were 'privileged' and, therefore, not subject to disclosure. The 'recollections' were gathered by senior officers, submitted to the force solicitors and returned to the Head of the South Yorkshire Police Management Services as part of a systematic process of 'review and alteration'.[24] A review team of senior officers, appointed by the Chief Constable, then transformed the 'recollections' into formal statements and had them signed by individual officers. It amounted to an institutionalized process clearly intended to remove all criticism of senior officers and operational policy while emphasizing misbehaviour by fans.

Over 400 'recollections' were processed. In a confidential transcript of a meeting between Stuart-Smith and the former Head of Management Services, the latter stated that 'the police had their backs to the wall' and it was 'absolutely natural for them to concern themselves with defending themselves'.[25] A former police officer, interviewed by the author, gave oral evidence to Stuart-Smith. He stated that 'a certain chief superintendent' took him and his colleagues for a drink. They were told, 'unless we all get our heads together and straighten it out there are heads going to roll'.[26] None of this impressed Stuart-Smith. He concluded that in a few cases 'it would have been better' not to have made alterations. At worst it constituted an 'error of judgement' but not 'unprofessional conduct'.[27] There would have been serious implications in finding otherwise. It transpired the West Midlands police investigators, the Treasury solicitor, the Coroner and Lord Justice Taylor were aware that the statements were written initially as personal recollections, under the guarantee of non-disclosure, and then transformed into criminal justice act statements through a carefully managed process of review and alteration.

Despite Taylor's unequivocal condemnation of senior police officers, he condoned their privileged access to the investigations and inquiries and the reconstitution and registration of the 'truth' to best advantage the interests of the force. His silence on the process of review and alteration compromised his Inquiry.[28] Yet lack of disclosure of evidence, alongside ignorance of the process through which police statements were taken, severely hindered and disadvantaged bereaved families and their lawyers. The DPP's decision not to prosecute on the grounds of insufficiency of evidence gave no indication of the quality of evidence in his possession. At the inquests the use and selective presentation of evidence by West Midlands police officers prevented disclosure of the original statements and their cross-examination. The South Yorkshire police held all the evidence and used it to establish and sustain their defence.

A CASE TO ANSWER

In August 1998 the Hillsborough Family Support Group initiated a private prosecution against David Duckenfield and Bernard Murray. It was the culmination of a decade's campaigning to establish criminal liability and to access key documents, witness statements and personal 'body files' on each of the deceased compiled by the police investigators. On 16 February 2000 Mr Justice Hooper committed the officers for trial. They were charged with manslaughter and misconduct in a public office. Duckenfield was also charged with misconduct 'arising from an admitted lie told by him to the effect that the [exit] gates had been forced open by Liverpool fans'. The judge summarized the cases for the prosecution and defence as follows:

> It is the prosecution's case that the two defendants are guilty of manslaughter because they failed to prevent a crush in pens 3 and 4 of the West Terraces [Leppings Lane] 'by failing between 2.40 and 3.06 p.m. to procure the diversion of spectators entering the ground from the entrance to the pen'

... that police officers should have been stationed in front of the tunnel lead-ing to the pen to prevent access. It appears, at this stage, to be the defence case that neither of the officers, in the situation in which they found them-selves, thought about closing off the tunnel or foresaw the risk of serious injury in the pen if they did not do so. The prosecution submit that they ought to have done. This is likely to be the most important issue in the case.[29]

The judge noted the bereaved had been left with 'an enduring grief' and 'a deep seated and obviously genuine grievance that those thought responsible' had not been prosecuted nor 'even disciplined'. Yet both defendants, 'must be suffer-ing a considerable amount of strain'. The 'greatest worry' for a police officer was 'the thought of going to prison' where they would run the risk of 'serious injury if not death'. While committing them for trial he took a 'highly unusual course' to 'reduce to a significant extent the anguish being suffered'.[30] He assured them that if found guilty of manslaughter they would not face a prison sentence. It was an extraordinary decision. Again, it appeared that police officers were receiving special treatment. The bereaved families and their lawyers were stunned but noth-ing could be voiced, published or disclosed until after the trial.

The trial opened on 6 June 2000 at Leeds Crown Court and ran for seven weeks. A sombre mood prevailed. The prosecution's case was 'described simply'. People died because they could not breathe and the crush was due to overcrowding 'caused by the criminal negligence of the two defendants ... They had been grossly negligent, wilfully neglecting to ensure the safety of supporters'. Their negligence was not the sole cause of the disaster. The ground was 'old, shabby, badly arranged, with confusing and unhelpful sign-posting ... there were not enough turnstiles'. There existed a 'police culture ... which influenced the way in which matches were policed'. Yet, the 'primary and immediate cause of death' lay with the defendants' failures. Each defendant 'owed the deceased a duty of care ... his negligent actions or omissions were a substantial cause of death' and the 'negli-gence was of such gravity as to amount to a crime'. For the first time the essence of the case had been articulated in full, in public and without interruption. A bereaved mother commented: 'Whatever happens now I have the satisfaction of seeing those men brought to court because it has been decided that there is a case to answer.'[31]

Duckenfield did not give evidence but considerable time was devoted to detail-ing his evidence to the Taylor Inquiry. The judge called Duckenfield's predeces-sor, former Chief Superintendent Mole, as he had drafted the police operational order. The judge introduced him as a crowd safety 'expert'. Murray also gave evidence, stating he had been 'haunted by the memory' of Hillsborough. Closing off the tunnel was 'something that did not occur to me at the time and I only wish it had'. While not recognizing how packed the central pens had become, he denied he had been 'indifferent to the scenes ... I did not see anything occurring on the terrace which gave me any anxiety'.[32]

68

The judge presented the jury with four questions. First, 'Are you sure, that by having regard to all the circumstances, it was foreseeable by a reasonable match commander that allowing a large number of spectators to enter the stadium through exit gate C without closing the tunnel would create an obvious and serious risk of death to the spectators in pens 3 and 4?' If 'yes' they were to move to question 2, if 'no' the verdicts should be 'not guilty'. Second, could a 'reasonable match commander' have taken 'effective steps … to close off the tunnel' thus preventing the deaths? If 'yes', they were to move to question 3, if 'no' the verdicts should be 'not guilty'. Third, was the jury 'sure that the failure to take such steps was neglect?' If 'yes', it was on to question 4, if 'no' the verdicts should be not guilty. Finally, was the 'failure to take those steps … so bad in all the circumstances as to amount to a very serious criminal offence?' If 'yes', the verdicts should be 'guilty'; if 'no' they should be 'not guilty'.[33]

Each question had to be contextualized 'in all the circumstances' in which the defendants had acted. Centrally, did the circumstances of chaos and confusion impede or mitigate the senior officers' decisions? On opening Gate C, was an obvious and serious risk of death in the central pens 'foreseeable' by a 'reasonable match commander?' Not someone of exceptional experience and vision, but an 'ordinary' or 'average' match commander. Even if *gross* negligence could be established, question four demanded that it had to be so bad in the *circumstances* that it constituted a serious criminal offence. For, while gross negligence might result in death, it does not necessarily amount to a serious criminal act.

The prosecution argued that the police 'mind-set' of 'hooliganism' at the expense of crowd safety amounted to 'a failure' best illustrated 'in the word neglect'. It was not a failure caused by the urgency of a 'split-second decision' but 'a case of slow-motion negligence'. The prosecution had presented witness evidence that drew a 'clear, cogent, overwhelming picture from all four corners of the ground': the pens were already dangerously overfull when Duckenfield ordered the opening of the exit gate. If all the witnesses could recognize this fact then Duckenfield and Murray, in the control box, could not miss it. Not only could Duckenfield and Murray see the 'dangerously full pens' but they had adequate 'thinking time' to seal the tunnel and redirect the fans. Their failure amounted to negligence. Not postponing the kick-off 'intensified the responsibilities of those who had taken the decision to get it right'. It was a serious criminal offence because 'thousands of people' had been affected by the breach of trust in the officers.[34]

Duckenfield's counsel replied that the events were 'unprecedented, unforeseeable and unique'. Rather than offering hooliganism as the cause of the crush he maintained that a 'unique, unforeseeable, physical phenomenon', without precedent in the stadium's history, occurred in the tunnel. It projected people forward with such ferocity that it killed people on the terraces. His explanation was that a small minority of over-eager and enthusiastic fans who had caused crushing at the turnstiles *perhaps* was responsible for the explosion of unprecedented force in the tunnel. It was a far-fetched explanation aimed at producing a hidden cause that could not have been anticipated and could not be verified.[35]

Murray's counsel argued that what happened was not 'slow-motion negligence', as described by the prosecution, but 'a disaster that struck out of the blue'. The deaths could not have been foreseen and no reasonably competent senior officer could have anticipated the sequence of events. While the overall police operation might have 'had many deficiencies' Duckenfield and Murray should not be singled out to 'carry the can'. The terraces had been authorized as safe, the fans 'finding their own level' was taken for granted. It was 'Mole's policy, Mole's custom and practice'. A conviction would make Murray a 'scapegoat'.[36]

In his summary the judge emphasized that the case had to be assessed 'by the standards of 1989' when 'caged pens were accepted' and 'had the full approval of all the authorities as a response to hooliganism'. The defendants had to be regarded as 'reasonable professionals', meaning 'an ordinary competent person', not a 'Paragon or a prophet'. When the exit gates were opened, 'death was not in the reckoning of those officers'. They were responding to a 'life and death situation' at the turnstiles and the jury had to 'take into account that this was a crisis'. The jury should 'be slow to find fault with those who act in an emergency', a situation of 'severe crisis' in which 'decisions had to be made quickly'. He noted the 'huge difference between an error of judgement and negligence', that 'many errors of judgement we make in our lives are not negligent' and 'the *mere* fact that there has been a disaster does not make these two defendants negligent'. A guilty verdict would mean that the negligence was, 'so bad to amount to a very serious offence in a crisis situation'. The judge presented two crucial questions to the jury: 'Would a criminal conviction send out a wrong message to those who have to react to an emergency and take decisions? Would it be right to punish someone for taking a decision and not considering the consequences in a crisis situation?'

After 16 hours of deliberation the jury was told that a majority verdict would be accepted. Over five hours later Murray was acquitted. Eventually the jury was discharged without reaching a verdict on Duckenfield. The judge refused the application for a retrial; the case was over. A bereaved father reflected the families' shared feelings: 'I never expected a conviction, especially after I heard the judge's direction. But people on that jury held out. The case went all the way.'[37] The judge's direction covered the debates over circumstances, hindsight, foreseeability, negligence, obvious and serious risk, and what constituted a 'serious criminal act'. Yet it was his comments on the impact of a guilty verdict on the future actions and responses of emergency services' professionals that caused the most surprise and concern. This conflated and confused a policy matter with legal direction. Further, his casual remark that the '*mere* fact' that 96 people had died did not necessarily mean that a serious criminal act had been committed deeply offended and distressed the families.

The private prosecution of David Duckenfield and Bernard Murray was possibly the most significant in recent times. It was not malicious or vengeful; neither was it about attributing *all* blame and *all* responsibility to two men. Given the DPP's decision not to prosecute and the lack of disclosure of evidence, the families had little choice. It remains instructive that the inquest jury and the private prosecution jury each requested further direction on negligence. In both courts the relationship between negligence and unlawful killing or manslaughter was central to their mammoth deliberations. The fact that there was a case to answer and, in the end, the jury remained deadlocked over Duckenfield's culpability, demonstrates that the families' pursuit of limited justice was not ill-conceived.

'JUSTICE FOR THE 96'

Before this Inquiry began, there were stories reported in the press, and said to have emerged from police officers present at the match, of 'mass drunkenness'. It was said that drunken fans urinated on the police while they were pulling the dead and injured out, that others had even urinated on the bodies of the dead and stolen their belongings. Not a single witness was called before the Inquiry to support any of those allegations ... Those who made them and those who disseminated them, would have done better to hold their peace.[38]

Such was their strength and widespread dissemination, the 'grave and emotive calumnies', explicitly stated and unequivocally condemned by Lord Justice Taylor, not only persisted but intensified. The South Yorkshire Chief Constable, who had initiated the process of review and alteration of police recollections and had been contrite at the Taylor Inquiry, publicly welcomed the inquests as an opportunity to challenge Taylor's rejection of hooliganism and drunkenness as primary causes. The Inquiry had left his force with a 'very strong feeling of resentment and injustice'.[39] In the build-up to both the preliminary hearings and the generic inquests, the media reiterated the police allegations. As individual cases were presented, recorded blood alcohol levels were announced. The inference was clear: presence of alcohol suggested culpability for the death of the person and for the deaths of others. Calculated or not, it was a process that attached blame to the deceased and brought shame on the bereaved.

Duckenfield's initial lie became part of a much wider and deeper deceit. The recording of blood alcohol levels by the Coroner, the orchestration of fabricated allegations by police officers and the reaffirmation by senior officers of charges of 'hooliganism' left a durable impression, reinforced and seemingly legitimated by journalists, politicians and academics. Writing in the *Sunday Telegraph* (4 February 1990) Simon Heffer argued that 'the problems of Hillsborough, though Taylor was reluctant to say it, was one [*sic*] of hooliganism'. 'However much it might enrage Liverpool' he continued, 'Liverpool fans were killed by the thuggishness and ignorance of other Liverpool fans.' On his chat show

Terry Wogan commented that unlike soccer's other disasters, Hillsborough was 'self-inflicted'. Following a serious confrontation between English fans and the Rotterdam police, David Evans MP remarked that the Hillsborough disaster, as 'everyone in football knows although they won't say it, was caused by thousands of fans turning up without tickets, late and drunk' (Today, *BBC Radio 4*, 14 October 1993).

Brian Clough, Nottingham Forest's manager at Hillsborough, wrote that he would 'always remain convinced that those Liverpool fans who died were killed by Liverpool people' and 'had all the Liverpool supporters turned up at the stadium in good time, in orderly manner and each with a ticket, there would have been no Hillsborough disaster'.[40] His widely reported comments reignited the public debate over Hillsborough and hooliganism. Faced with a mass of criticism from a range of sources he remained unrepentant. He repeated his allegation that 'Liverpool people killed Liverpool people' on national television.[41] Reflecting on Liverpool City Council's call for a boycott on his autobiography he retorted, 'half of them can't read and the other half are pinching hub caps'.[42] There was astonishment, hurt and anger among the bereaved and survivors and many wrote directly to Clough.[43]

Academic researchers seemed to confirm the relationship between the disaster and violence. For example, in the preface to a book on soccer hooliganism, Kerr recalls watching on television the 'chaotic horror at Hillsborough' caused by a 'late inrush of spectators' who 'had run into an already full enclosure of Liverpool fans, causing a desperate crush'.[44] For Young, Hillsborough was one of 13 international 'noteworthy incidents of sports-related collective violence' between 1955 and 1989; '94 fans' had been 'crushed to death as fans arriving late attempted to force their way into the game'.[45] In a text on disasters and their aftermath Cohen wrongly attributes allegations about Hillsborough to Heysel: 'some fans … urinated on the dead, on police and on ambulance men'.[46] Lewis and Scarisbrick-Hauser propose the application of McPhail's 'behavioural categories' 'as a guide for analysing crowd behaviours'. In their overview of contemporary football crowd safety reports they add four 'new' categories: 'climbing, falling, kicking and public urinating'. Without any attempt to evidence, locate or contextualize behaviour that might warrant inclusion in these categories, they attribute 'surging', 'jogging', 'climbing', 'falling' and 'public urinating' to fans' behaviour at Hillsborough.[47] Cohen situates this behaviour in Liverpool city's 'darker side: a massive drugs problem, endemic unemployment and a resultant capacity for mass disorder'. Liverpool fans had developed a 'ferocious reputation' bearing 'the hallmarks … of Neanderthal man'.[48]

In an insightful analysis of the political-economic context of the disaster, Ian Taylor discusses the Thatcherite obsession with 'secure containment', resulting in the penning of fans, the acceptance of stadium neglect and the compromising of crowd safety. In a subsequent version of this article, however, while challenging 'a series of unpleasant stories … circulat[ing] about the behaviour of Liverpool fans',

Taylor notes 'persistent reports of some [fans] snatching wallets from the dead or dying and also of some obstructive action by drunken and aggressive fans'.[49]

These few examples are taken from a mass of media, political and academic commentary on Hillsborough. They are typical and they were not without consequences. When Lord Justice Stuart-Smith arrived in Liverpool to take evidence from bereaved families, some of the Hillsborough Family Support Group were delayed by a few minutes. On the steps of the Maritime Museum he asked the Group's Secretary, 'Have you got a few of your people or are they like the Liverpool fans, turn up at the last minute?'[50] At the opening of the private prosecution at Leeds Crown Court the judge warned families that 'any display of campaigning, written or verbal, would constitute intimidation and be considered contempt of court'. Further, 'any demonstration would jeopardise the trial'. Seven weeks later as the trial ended and the bereaved families left the court, 'a West Yorkshire police video-surveillance team ... filmed their dignified, calm yet unbowed departure'.[51] Over time such comments and actions were regarded by the bereaved and survivors as intimidatory, constituting slurs on their reputation and that of their loved ones. 'We felt like criminals', was the common response.[52]

Following the publication of the Stuart-Smith report, a South Yorkshire Assistant Chief Constable wrote, 'perhaps the greatest tribute to those who tragically lost their lives, and the firmest indicator that the deaths were not in vain, lies in the transformation of football stadia'.[53] He demonstrated an unwitting yet crass insensitivity towards the long-term suffering of the bereaved. As stated elsewhere, there was 'not the slightest acknowledgement that it took a disaster, for men, women and children to be killed, to shake the reckless complacency that had infected football; its ownership, its organisation and its policing'.[54] Conn states that Taylor's 'most fundamental recommendations', including a full 'reassessment of policy for the game', were 'ignored'. Yet 'directors wheeled and dealed to make fortunes for themselves'.[55] As the Premier League was launched its clubs were obliged to provide all-seater stadia. Supported, and dependent on, unprecedented investment from Rupert Murdoch's media empire, Premiership clubs enjoyed unforeseeable, if not over-inflated, wealth and prosperity.[56]

However safer the reconstructed or new stadia were, and however welcome the facilities provided, the inexorable rise in football's popularity – and notoriety – represents a triumph in rebranding, publicity and marketing. Personal reputations, David Beckham for example, were lost and rebuilt in the media-fuelled hype of celebrity and fame. Beckham's club throughout this period, Manchester United, became the most wealthy sports club in the world and overseas players, many of great talent and all with agents, gravitated towards the new prosperity of the English Premiership. Meanwhile, back in Liverpool, the Hillsborough Family Support Group and the *Justice* campaigns provide a poignant reminder that, despite Taylor's attribution of responsibility for the disaster, there followed no state prosecutions, no disciplinary proceedings and no full and appropriate disclosure of the documentary evidence. What remain are the inquest verdicts of accidental death and a hung jury, unable to decide on Duckenfield's guilt. Stuart-Smith's judicial scrutiny was exposed as little more than a politically motivated attempt to quell the outrage of the bereaved and survivors. On finally receiving 'body files' detailing the last hours of their loved one's lives, families were soon aware that much of the 'factual' information provided was partial, inaccurate and/or contradictory.

The significance of the Hillsborough disaster is not limited to its broader context and immediate circumstances. A sequence of injustices followed: the appalling treatment of the bereaved and survivors by the police and other authorities in the immediate aftermath; the inhumane police and coronial procedures adopted for body identification of loved ones; the conduct and outcome of the inquests; the systematic review and alteration of police recollections, their transformation into criminal justice statements and Taylor's acceptance of the process; the judge's direction of the jury in the private prosecution of Duckenfield and Murray; the taking of body tissue from the deceased without the knowledge or permission of the bereaved. And Eddie Spearritt has received no information regarding his whereabouts between 3 p.m. and 5 p.m. when he was admitted to intensive care. The aftermath of the Hillsborough disaster reveals the shortcomings, failings and manipulation of the state's systems of inquiry and investigation. Over time, it shows how disproved and discredited accounts can be reconstituted and legitimated, how 'truth' can be degraded through propaganda to protect powerful interests and how public servants, supposedly legally and politically accountable, can evade the reach of the law.[57]

ACKNOWLEDGEMENTS

Many thanks to my former colleagues at the Centre for Studies in Crime and Social Justice at Edge Hill, to the ESRC-funded Disaster Research Seminar Group and to Deena Haydon for her critical comments and personal support. Most of all, continuing respect to the bereaved and survivors of Hillsborough and the campaign groups who have retained immense dignity in the face of continuing injustice.

NOTES

1. P. Scraton, *Hillsborough: The Truth* (Edinburgh: Mainstream, 2000), pp.60–1.
2. Personal interview, *The Hillsborough Project* 1989. Held in the Disasters Research Archive, Centre for Studies in Crime and Social Justice, Edge Hill.
3. *Liverpool Echo*, 17 April 1989.
4. Sir Bernard Ingham, Press Secretary to the Prime Minister, personal correspondence, 13 July 1994. Correspondence held by author.
5. D. Chippindale and C. Horrie, *Stick It Up Your Punter! The Rise and Fall of the Sun* (London: Mandarin, 1992), p.283.
6. South Yorkshire Police Memorandum from Inspector Calvert to The Chief Superintendent, 'F' Div, dated 11 June 1986. Document held by author.

7. For an overview of the evolution of safety regulation at UK football grounds see Martin Johnes, '"Heads in the Sand": Football, Politics and Crowd Disasters in Twentieth-Century Britain', chapter one in this volume.

8. References taken from officers' statements. Held by author.

9. See Scraton, *Hillsborough: The Truth*, pp.52–4.

10. Rt Hon. Lord Justice Taylor, *The Hillsborough Stadium Disaster: 15 April 1989, Interim Report*, Cmnd. 765, (London: HMSO, 1989) paras 171–4, pp.30–1.

11. Taylor Inquiry Transcripts, May–June 1989, Day 8: 112–13.

12. Rt Hon. Lord Justice Taylor, *The Hillsborough Stadium Disaster: 15 April 1989, Interim Report*, Cmnd. 765, (London: HMSO, 1989), p.1.

13. Ibid., p.50.

14. Ibid.

15. Lord Keith of Kinkel, *Copoc (AP) and Others v. Wright; Alcock (AP) and Others v. Wright*, House of Lords Judgment, 28 Nov. 1991.

16. *R.v.H.M.Coroner for South Yorkshire ex parte Stringer and Others*, Divisional Court Judgment, 5 Nov. 1993.

17. *Hansard*, 26 Oct. 1994: col. 981.

18. Letter from the Head of the Police Complaints Division to the Chief Constable, 30 Aug. 1990. Held by author.

19. *Inquest transcripts*, Day 75, 21 March 1991: 63. Disaster Research Archive, Centre for Studies in Crime and Social Justice, Edge Hill, Ormskirk.

20. *Inquest transcripts*, Day 78, 26 March 1991: 31. Disaster Research Archive, Centre for Studies in Crime and Social Justice, Edge Hill, Ormskirk.

21. P. Scraton, A. Jemphrey and S. Coleman, *No Last Rights: The Denial of Justice and the Promotion of Myth in the Aftermath of the Hillsborough Disaster* (Liverpool: LCC/Alden Press, 1995).

22. *Guardian*, 1 July 1997.

23. *Hansard*, 18 Feb. 1998: cols 1085–97.

24. Correspondence between Peter Metcalf, partner in Hammond Suddards Solicitors and the Head of Management Services, South Yorkshire Police, 15 May 1989. Held by author.

25. *Scrutiny Transcript*, 1 Dec. 1997. Held by author.

26. *Scrutiny Transcript*, 24 Oct. 1997. Held by author.

27. Rt Hon. Lord Justice Stuart-Smith, *Scrutiny of Evidence Relating to the Hillsborough Football Stadium Disaster*, Cmnd. 3878 (London: HMSO, 1998), p.80.

28. See P. Scraton, 'From Deceit to Disclosure: The Politics of Official Inquiries in the United Kingdom', in G. Gilligan and J. Pratt (eds), *Crime, Truth and Justice: Official Inquiry, Discourse, Knowledge* (Cullompton: Willan Publishing, 2004), pp.46–70.

29. Mr Justice Hooper, *Regina v David Duckenfield and Bernard Murray* Case No: T19991569, Leeds Crown Court, 16 Feb. 2000.

30. Ibid.

31. See Scraton, *Hillsborough: The Truth*, pp.216–19; full text of opening speech by Alun Jones, Q.C. available at www.hfsg.org/opening 11 June 2000.

32. Bernard Murray, in evidence, 10 July 2000 (research notes, held by author).

33. Mr Justice Hooper, questions put to the jury, 12 July 2000 (research notes, held by author).

34. Alun Jones, Q.C., closing speech, 12 July 2000. Available at www.hfsg.org/closing.

35. William Clegg, Q.C., address to the jury, 13 July 2000 (research notes).

36. Michael Harrison, Q.C., address to the jury, 13 July 2000 (research notes).

37. Mr Justice Hooper, summing up, 12–18 July 2000.

38. Taylor, *Hillsborough Stadium Disaster Interim Report*, p.44.

39. Peter Wright, Chief Constable of South Yorkshire, quoted in the *Sheffield Star*, 6 Feb. 1990.

40. B. Clough, *Clough: The Autobiography* (London: Corgi, 1995), p.258.

41. *Sunday Mirror*, 6 Nov. 1994.

42. *Daily Mirror*, 8 Nov. 1994.

43. See Scraton, Jemphrey and Coleman, *No Last Rights*.

44. J.H. Kerr, *Understanding Soccer Hooliganism* (Milton Keynes: Open University Press), p.18.

45. K. Young, 'Sport and Collective Violence', *Exercise and Sports Sciences Reviews*, 19 (1991), 540.

46. D. Cohen, *Aftershock: The Psychological and Political Consequences of Disasters* (London: Paladin, 1991), p.143.

47. J.M. Lewis and A.-M. Scarisbrick-Hauser, 'An Analysis of Football Crowd Safety Reports using the McPhail Categories', in R. Giulianotti, N. Bonney and M. Hepworth (eds), *Football, Violence and Social Identity* (London: Routledge, 1994), p.170.
48. Cohen, *Aftershock*, p.146.
49. I. Taylor, 'Hillsborough, 15 April 1989: Some Personal Contemplations', *New Left Review*, 177, Sept.–Oct. (1989), 89–111; I. Taylor, 'English Football in the 1990s: Taking Hillsborough Seriously?', in J. Williams and S. Wagg (eds), *British Football and Social Change: Getting into Europe* (Leicester: Leicester University Press, 1991), p.9.
50. Scraton, *Hillsborough: The Truth*, p.169.
51. Ibid., p.235.
52. Ibid.
53. I. Daines, 'Hillsborough Legacy', *Police Review*, 13 March 1998, 20.
54. Scraton, *Hillsborough: The Truth*, p.241.
55. D. Conn, *The Football Business: Fair Game in the '90s?* (Edinburgh: Mainstream, 1997), p.126.
56. Scraton, *Hillsborough: The Truth*, p.241.
57. See P. Scraton, 'Policing with Contempt: The Degrading of Truth and Denial of Justice in the Aftermath of the Hillsborough Disaster', *Journal of Law and Society*, 26, 3 (Sept. 1999), 273–97; P. Scraton, 'Lost Lives, Hidden Voices: "Truth" and Controversial Deaths', *Race and Class*, 44, 1 (2002), 107–18.

5

'The Cursed Cup': Italian Responses to the 1985 Heysel Disaster

FABIO CHISARI

INTRODUCTION

Eleven-year-old Andrea Casula loved football above anything else. He played in the youth team of Cagliari, his hometown club. And he loved Juventus. His father had promised after Juventus's defeat in the 1983 European Cup final that if Juve made the final again he would take him to the match. When his father kept the promise and secured tickets for the 1985 final Andrea went to school triumphantly, happy that he was to watch Platini and Boniek and his other idols in the flesh. When Andrea's lifeless body was found following the collapse of a wall in the stadium, it was wrapped in the corpse of his father who had attempted to shield his son from the carnage and chaos that erupted prior to the final.

Although far from the most fatal, the Heysel Stadium disaster of 29 May 1985 is one of the highest profile soccer tragedies. The 39 deaths – 32 Italians, 4 Belgians, 2 French and 1 Briton – took place at the European Cup final between Liverpool FC and Juventus FC, a match between two of the world's most famous clubs. A huge television audience tuned in to watch what should have been the annual highlight of European club football, but instead witnessed scenes of indelible horror and despair. The tragedy was quickly considered to be the nadir of a history of football hooliganism that had preoccupied a generation of sports administrators, journalists, sociologists and politicians.

Yet despite the game's infamy and the large popular and academic literature on hooliganism, that Wednesday night in May 1985 has only been written about in journalistic reports, press articles each anniversary, short citations within broader works on hooliganism in general, and inaccurately on some websites. Even in Italy, where the disaster's impact was most profoundly felt, there has been no scholarly analysis of the tragedy. This study thus aims to present the facts of that night as they actually happened and examine how they were perceived in Italy. Using a detailed review of the press and television coverage, this study examines the tragedy from an Italian perspective. More specifically, the paper presents a view of the disaster through the lens of Juventus supporters who were actually present in the stadium,[1] and analyses the television coverage that broadcast the horrifying pictures of the disaster into the homes of 20 million Italians. The study concludes by considering where responsibility for the disaster lies in the eyes of the Italian football fans, administrators and the Italian media.

This Italian perspective does not chime with how the disaster was often seen in England, during its aftermath and since. There, many placed part of the responsibility for the disaster on the Italian supporters. A public poll published by *The Times* suggested that two out of three respondents thought that Italian fans were as guilty as English supporters.[2] Even today it is possible to read, especially on the Internet, reports suggesting that English and Italian supporters were jointly responsible. This thesis was expounded by the Liverpool FC secretary, Mr Robinson, who, the day after the disaster, did not feel like accusing only his supporters. On the Liverpool FC official website it can be read what former player and manager Kenny Dalglish said about the troubles: 'I can't condone the action of some Liverpool fans, but it is difficult not to react when the opposing supporters are throwing missiles at you.'[3] This chapter seeks to offer an alternative explanation.

'REDS ANIMALS'

Liverpool FC was regarded as the strongest side in Europe in the 1980s. By 1985, the club had won seven out of the last nine English league championships and the European Cup itself in 1977, 1978, 1981 and 1984. Juventus FC in contrast had never managed to extend its historic dominance of Serie A into European club football. Eleven assaults on the European Cup had resulted in nothing more than two runners-up places. Juventus had won the Cup Winners' Cup in 1984 but that was little consolation compared to the game's greatest prize. Nonetheless, the club remained one of the biggest names in European football and Liverpool's Ian Rush told the press on the eve of the 1985 final that it was 'A logical final, it will be a clash between two of the best European clubs'.[4] Unfortunately, there was to be nothing logical about the massacre that was to unfold.

The afternoon of the final was not a quiet one. A group of Juventus fans had stabbed a Liverpool supporter; around 20 English supporters had robbed a jewellery shop; and there had been fights, with the throwing of bottles and stones, between the two opposing sets of supporters in Brussels city centre. However, such trouble was almost routine during the 1980s and there was no omen of what was about to happen inside the *Heizelstadion*.

The stadium's gates were due to be opened at 5 p.m., but it was an hour later before the first supporters were allowed to enter. By this time there was such a crowd outside that entering through the very narrow turnstiles was difficult. A large number of Liverpool fans without tickets managed to get into the stadium by forcing some breaches on the enclosure wall near the section of the ground designated to English supporters. Nonetheless, the 400 policemen on duty seemed to be in control of the situation. At 7 p.m., 75 minutes before the scheduled kick-off, the two main stands were still half empty, while the two sections containing supporters from England and Italy were already packed. The terraces to the right were divided into three sectors: M, N and O. Blocks N and O were designated for supporters coming from Italy. The M block, which was the closest to the central stand, was originally intended as a buffer section occupied by neutral spectators. In fact it was also packed with Juventus fans, mainly Italian emigrants, of whom there were a large number in Belgium. The terraces on the left side of the grandstand should have had the same kind of distribution, at least according to the organized plans, with sectors X and Y for English supporters, and sector Z occupied by locals. The organizers had overlooked the possibility that tickets for sector Z might end up in Italian hands. This is what actually happened and replicated the situation in Sector M.

Skirmishes broke out on the terraces on the left at 7 p.m., with Liverpool fans throwing bottles and other missiles at the occupiers of Z block. By 7.15 p.m. the trouble had escalated considerably. The local authorities had not banned the sale of alcohol, while poor security at the turnstiles had allowed English fans to enter the stadium with entire packs of bottles and cans of beer. Alcohol was not the only cause of the exaggerated excitement amongst the Liverpool fans. The unexpected proximity of opposing supporters raised tensions and offered an opportunity to antagonise the Juventus fans by throwing missiles of all kinds including bottles, cans, petards and even stones pulled up from the upper parts of the terraces where the pavement was made of porphyry cubes. These latter missiles were described in *Corriere della Sera*, as the 'powder magazine of the beasts from Liverpool'.[5] One Juventus supporter recalled, 'I had never seen men behaving so furiously, I had never witnessed such unmotivated violence'.[6] Some Italian fans retaliated by throwing stones, which further excited the hooligan element amongst the Liverpool fans that was now advancing towards Z block, easily scaling the five-feet-high fence that separated the two sectors. The eight policemen responsible for watching over the fence were outnumbered and left the situation to call for reinforcements from outside the stadium.[7] The Liverpool fans were free to embark on a series of consecutive charges, armed with bottle-necks, sticks, stones, belts and bent cans as knuckledusters. Every charge was followed by a brief retreat and then another assault to occupy a further portion of the Juventus end. With a high fence blocking any escape on to the pitch, the charges of Liverpool fans drove the terrorized Italians to the end of the terrace and against a wall, about seven feet in height. One fan remembered that he 'got all my bones crushed by iron bars, they (the policemen) halted us while the English, those damned, were charging us'.[8]

At 7.30 p.m., 45 minutes before kick-off, the wall at the end of Z block collapsed under the pressure of the crowd with fatal consequences. Between the collapsed wall and the central stand was a narrow hollow space into which people fell, pushed by the pressure of the crowd behind them. The fence between the terrace and the athletic track also collapsed under the pressure of the retreating crowd. For some this was a sudden relief, giving them entry to a safer place, but, for those directly against the fence, it was a death sentence. Some were crushed on the ground by the crowd behind them; others were killed by the iron bars of the collapsed fence. One fan remembered, 'I was right in the worst place on the terraces when the troubles broke out, I trod over some people too, I stepped over two people with wide-open eyes. I wondered: am I a piece of dung or a man?'[9] Another recalled, 'We survived because we resisted the charges. Then we got away stepping over the mass of Italians that had been knocked down. Everybody was panicking, everybody was shoving. Some people died to save other people.'[10]

As the tragedy unfolded a decision needed to be taken as to whether to play the match or not. UEFA officials, representatives of the two clubs and the Belgian authorities held an emergency meeting to decide whether to play a game of football in the wake of so many deaths. They were joined by the Italian Government's Minister of Foreign Affairs, Gianni De Michelis, who was present at the stadium to watch the match. Some days later he told the *Corriere della Sera* what happened at that meeting:

> I immediately realized that there was a situation of absolute uncertainty. Finally the Belgian authorities arrived: the burgomaster of Brussels, the head of Gendarmerie, and a high-rank police officer … After a little while there was utmost confusion.

Everybody was standing and shouting, trying to stick to his guns; there is a Babylon of languages: who speaks French, who speaks Italian … The point was: to play the match or to call it off? The discussion lasted almost one hour in a nightmare situation, because every one of us realized that the disaster was going on in the terraces – only then we were told that there were more than 30 people dead – but it may have been nothing in comparison to what could happen yet. We had to take the right decision. Now and again somebody popped in to tell us that out there the tension was reaching a peak, that there were a lot of policemen but they could not manage the situation.

The Juventus party did not want to play. The Liverpool one said that they were available to play. In the meanwhile, the burgomaster kept talking about what had happened before, about what had caused the troubles, trying to justify the action by police and Gendarmerie. I interrupted him: excuse me, we will talk later about what has happened before, would you please tell us whether you can guarantee a safe evacuation from the stadium? He got upset: 'Who are you?' I replied: 'I am a member of the Italian Government.' 'Shut up, or I'll get you arrested!' Then he calmed down, and admitted: 'No, we are not able to guarantee the spectators to safely get out of the stadium.' It was the most dramatic moment. Who could take on the responsibility to announce to a sixty-thousand-crowd in a state of utmost tension that the match has been called off, without the serious risk of a new wave of violence and panic? The question was: how can we avoid other deaths? We realized that the situation could become really unmanageable. I thought to myself: anything could now happen. Finally, the UEFA officials took the decision: the match would be played.[11]

Outside the charges of the Liverpool fans had stopped and the Juventus supporters from Z block were pouring onto the pitch, treading over bodies. Police reinforcements, some on horseback, had arrived, but their intervention had been useless, if not counterproductive. Not only did they not help the evacuation from Z block, but also the police even started hitting the people who had spilled on to the pitch with batons.

At that moment the situation might have exploded. Some Juventus supporters on the opposite terraces, who had helplessly witnessed the tragedy unfold, tried to take the law into their hands, invaded the pitch and headed towards the Liverpool end. Some advanced with scarves masking their faces and brandishing sticks, others moved forward with a banner with the writing 'Reds Animals' on it. One man in a green jacket brandished a gun and fired into the air, only later was it known that the shot was a blank. Somehow, the Belgian police managed to avoid a physical clash between the more excited and violent factions of the two opposing sides.

The trouble seemed to end suddenly. Some of those who had invaded the pitch, probably not realizing the actual dimensions of the tragedy, start kicking around a football. The police and the army descended on the stadium; the fire brigade and the Red Cross began to organize a rescue operation. A camp-hospital was arranged in front of the central stand and a tent mounted to shelter the corpses, and then a second one and then a third. The megaphones poured out an endless series of names. It was unclear if these were the missing, wounded or dead. Amongst the crowd black and white shirts were spotted, worn not by supporters but by the Juventus players themselves who had decided to go out, irrespective of any danger to themselves, in order to placate the anger of the fans. In its own small way, the attempt was successful.

It was 9.30 p.m. when the two team captains, Neal and Scirea, were taken to the announcer's room to read the following message to the public: 'The match will be played in order to allow the police to carry out the evacuation from the stadium; do not reply to any provocation and keep calm. We are going to play for you.' At 9.40 p.m. the two sides, led by Swiss referee André Daina, took to the pitch, and at 9.42 p.m. the match kicked off, late by 87 minutes and 39 dead.

'HOW MANY DEAD ARE THERE?'

The Juventus players were on their way to the pitch for their pre-match warm-up when they were told of the troubles on the terraces. From the tunnel they could see barefoot people in torn clothing roaming around the pitch, begging for help. These people tried to convey to the players what was happening, but they were too excitable, distressed and confused to provide a meaningful account.[12] The club president, Boniperti, was already at the meeting being held to decide what to do, and the Juventus manager Trapattoni went to and from the meeting to get the latest news. Edoardo Agnelli, executive of the club and son of its owner, stood on the pitch, staring at the scenes on the terraces. The players waited for news in the dressing room. Paolo Rossi, the centre-forward, was devastated: 'We can't play, can we? What are we doing here, is there any sense in talking about football in a night like this? Please, tell me, I want to know: how many dead are there?'[13] Goalkeeper Stefano Tacconi later recalled, 'We were resigned not to play, we all thought it would be impossible in that situation'.[14] Although, the players were forced to comply with the decision taken to play the match, the club released a statement to UEFA:

> Juventus FC, notwithstanding the tragic situation which has arisen through causes attributable neither to this club or to its supporters, and which has caused the deaths of dozens of Italians, accept with discipline, even though with the heart full of anguish, the decision taken by UEFA, which has been communicated to our president, to play the match for reasons of public order.[15]

The statement was a clear indication of where Juventus FC felt the blame for the tragedy lay.

The Juventus players had already displayed courage by going out and talking to fans to try and calm the situation. Tacconi recalled, 'There were 30 dead already, but the supporters had been told there were only four: they were outraged and we had to tell them pitiful lies, that there were just a few wounded'.[16]

The actions of the Juventus players were sullied, in the opinion of many observers, by their jubilation after Platini's decisive penalty and the resulting victory. Such celebrations were considered by many to be out of place in such a nightmarish scene. Boniperti tried to defend the players by declaring to the press that:

> the players had strived to calm our supporters down before the game. At the end they wanted to thank and to greet them, getting back in the psychology of the tragic situation immediately afterwards. There has been no celebration party: after dinner everybody went to bed. A great number of them did not manage to sleep a wink, wandering like automatons around the hotel 'til dawn.[17]

Platini himself tried to justify the jubilation after the decisive goal: 'I celebrated the goal because when you are on the pitch you forget everything else. I was happy. In show-biz when something bad happens everything goes on.'[18] Tacconi said of the celebration on the pitch after the cup had been presented to skipper Scirea in the dressing rooms (rather than on the pitch): 'We celebrated to honour our supporters who wanted to touch us, to hug us, and in exchange for it they were attacked by police clubs. We tried to defend them by pushing away the policemen, who were now a small army, too late.'[19] Two Italian MPs criticized the club heavily for playing the match and accepting the cup, which they asked Juventus to give back. Boniperti replied curtly:

> Give the Cup back? No way! Juventus FC will keep it because it has been won by the players on the pitch. The politicians who talk were at their home that night, but those of them who personally lived through that dreadful experience understand everything.[20]

There were rumours that the result had been 'arranged' during the meeting to decide whether to play the match or not, a meeting which the referee had apparently been present at. Boniperti was indignant at such suggestions:

> This is absolute madness! There were about 30 people at that meeting ... Now I realize how heedless UEFA were to award Belgians the organization of the final. They put such absurdities in circulation just to divert attention from their own heavy responsibilities.[21]

The most significant words on the players' behaviour came from the players themselves a few days later in a communiqué that aimed to put an end to any discussion:

> We would rather avoid any technical comment on a game that was played primarily for security reasons. And, in any case, any technical comment would be absurd due to the tragic context. We did not want to play, to honour our compatriots that had died. We, and Liverpool FC, had to play because of UEFA and the Belgian Police authorities forced us to do so. Once we were on the pitch, especially when we scored, we understood that the crowd, the Italians especially, were completely unaware of the scale of the tragedy. We therefore had to play for all the people in the stadium bearing a huge weight on our shoulders, to avoid any further and worse troubles. And our situation was made even heavier by the inexplicable absence, particularly after the final whistle, of those same international authorities that had ordered us to play. An example of this is the fact that we were given the trophy by UEFA delegates only in the dressing rooms. We did not know what to do. To honour the dead? To go where the troubles had broken out, risking making things even worse? Or to play our role until the end? At the end of the day this was what our supporters, unaware of the scale of the disaster, wanted. But we did it unwillingly. We do hope that never again will we be asked to do something like that. Never ever. But now the only thing to do is to send our thoughts and our feelings to our

dead, our wounded, the families of the victims, their anguish, their pain and their problems.[22]

Juventus FC did not forget the victims of the disaster. The players assigned part of their win-bonuses to the relatives of the victims, and they paid visits to the survivors in Belgian hospitals. Tardelli later commented: 'I do hope everybody around the world will always remember Brussels.'[23]

TO DIE 'LIVE' ON TELEVISION

The Italian television audience for the final on Rai-2 peaked at 19.1m viewers (81.3 per cent of that evening's total audience). In other circumstances these would have been extraordinary figures for a sports broadcast, but they were not related to the match specifically but rather to the 'live' broadcast of the unfolding disaster. The television broadcast from Brussels started at 8.13 p.m., but there had already been, a few minutes earlier, a brief audio report during the evening news. This report let viewers know that they would not see any football, but this was not sufficient to transmit to the viewers the sense of horror that was about to strike them. If the first pictures were as surprising as they were appalling, the last ones, showing Juventus players celebrating their victory while an on-screen message gave out numbers to call for information on the victims, left a feeling of hollow dismay.

Neither the pictures nor the commentaries managed, despite their realistic harshness, to immediately convey the scale or causes of the tragedy. The first pictures broadcast were of Juventus supporters clashing with Belgian policemen on the pitch and gave the viewers the impression that the troubles had been caused by Italian supporters. The actual events and causes became more apparent with explanations from the commentator and the broadcast of pre-recorded pictures of what had happened in Z block before the live transmission began. The climax was reached at 8.55 p.m., as far as the Italian television broadcasting was concerned, when Pizzul, the commentator, horrified, yet dutifully carrying out his role as a journalist, reluctantly had to communicate the number of victims: 'Unfortunately there is news that I have to give you. It's official, the source is UEFA itself: there are 36 dead [long pause]. It's really something shuddering, shameful.'[24] This was surely Pizzul's most difficult commentary in a 30-year-long career.

There were criticisms of his commentary. Some viewers were annoyed by its coldness. One wrote to *Corriere della Sera* complaining of 'the detachment of the commentator, who in the dying moments of the match deliberately ignored what had happened before and kept talking of an "unforgettable night", of a "game played with perfect tactics", of a "target finally reached after 11 unlucky attempts", was really absurd, shivering'.[25] Almost ten years later, journalist and politician Walter Veltroni defended the professional and human quality of that commentary:

Pizzul was wonderful throughout the commentary. He was a lone man on the top of a tragedy. He had been responsible, measured, rigorous. The serenity, the future, even the life of many people and families were depending, in those moments, on his voice, on his tones, on the hints of his words. He never exaggerated, he never shouted any rage. He seemed prostrated, emptied and knackered by the astonishment that things had gone that far.[26]

Pizzul himself defended his work to the press a few days after the game:

I tried to be as calm as possible, in order not to sound apprehensive. There were millions of people listening to my commentary; my duty was to inform them gradually about the tragedy, to prepare them for the worst, not being too harsh. As long as I was not given the actual figures I could not imagine the real dimension of the catastrophe. It was the first time I experienced such a situation. It's not easy to talk 'live' about dozens of deaths without sounding pathetic. I hope I will never have to experience something like this ever again in the future. I even thought of interrupting the commentary by saying 'these pictures don't need any explanation', but then I plucked up courage and kept going … The players are to be admired because they played even though they were not in the mood … I could not put any blame on them, it wouldn't have been fair. I instead tried to avoid any kind of technical comment by using a descriptive commentary. I think I managed.[27]

The horrifying but indelible pictures were broadcast to millions of viewers in 29 different countries.[28] Most of all, the pictures brought panic and dismay amongst watching relatives and friends of the Juventus fans present at the stadium. A woman confessed to *Corriere della Sera*, 'I've seen my husband being assaulted on TV. I've seen my son waving his hand to be pulled off the crowd as the fence in Z block collapsed, then the camera changed shot. I feared the worst. I was panicking.'[29] This woman's husband and son survived but forgetting the pictures seems impossible, especially for those who lost loved ones. How could anyone forget the pictures of the desperate calls for help of people being crushed and the corpses lined up on the athletic track?

'WHOSE FAULT IS IT??'

'Whose fault is it?' a crying Giampiero Boniperti, Juventus president, wondered while roaming around the corpses. The catastrophe surely had more than a single cause. In the immediate aftermath the accusing finger was unanimously pointed at the Liverpool supporters. Allegations of negligence were also levied against the Belgian authorities. At best they had shown immense naivety in preparing security for a game that had been assessed by many as high-risk. However, they were most culpable for their inability to understand and manage the emergency situation inside the stadium. The football authorities (UEFA and the Belgian FA) also came in for intense criticism both for having chosen such a decrepit and crumbling stadium to host the showpiece game of European club football and then deciding not to call the game off in light of what happened in the stadium.

From the late 1960s football hooliganism was a well-known social problem in Britain. By the 1970s the 'English disease' was being exported to Europe's biggest games. The 1972 European Cup-winners' Cup final at Barcelona between Glasgow Rangers and Feyenord, the second leg of the 1974 UEFA Cup Final in Rotterdam featuring Feyenord and Tottenham Hotspur, and the 1975 European Cup Final in Paris between Leeds United and Bayern Munich had all witnessed incidents of football hooliganism. Brussels itself had hosted the 1984 UEFA Cup Final between Anderlecht and Tottenham Hotspur, which saw 200 English supporters arrested and one death. In Italy, however, British football hooliganism was often considered more of a myth than a reality. Italy had experienced British hooliganism on its own soil in 1980 when England played Belgium in Turin during the European Nations Championships. But, there was thought to have been no significant trouble at the 1984 European Cup final in Rome between AS Roma and Liverpool.[30] It took the experience of Heysel to make Italians aware that British hooliganism was not just a myth.

Gianni Agnelli, the Juventus owner, exclaimed on the day after the game, 'What incorrigible thugs! The only cure would be to forbid English people to go abroad to support their clubs',[31] echoing the thoughts of many of his compatriots who had no doubt that the Liverpool supporters were to blame and must therefore be punished. For Italians their indignation turned to hate: there were outpourings on television, full-page newspapers headlines and discussions in parliament; British tourists were verbally and physically abused; British institutions in Italy were attacked with graffiti and petrol bombs. Such rage quickly subsided, at least partly thanks to the clear admission of responsibility made by many in positions of authority in Britain. Margaret Thatcher, the British prime minister, said, 'British supporters are to be blamed. These hooligans are killing football.'[32] The *Financial Times* wrote, 'There are no excuses. British supporters' behaviour can be defined only as barbarity', while *The Economist* commented, 'We have to ask ourselves not what is wrong with football, but with Britain as a whole'.[33] Even within British football there was no dodging the blame. 'We have become a nation of hooligans, an ill nation' exclaimed the Birmingham City manager Ron Saunders.[34] The sympathy towards the victims and their families exhibited by some in Britain also helped ease the rage in Italy. Here, pictures of a Liverpool fan, trying desperately to pull as many people as possible out of the crush, played an important role.[35]

The first arrests made by Belgian police before and after the game were carried out almost grudgingly. The 16 men detained by the police (12 English and four Italians) were accused of vandalism and insulting a public official; only six of them (five English and one Italian) were kept in detention pending trial before being sentenced to a couple of months in prison for acts of vandalism. None of them were accused or sentenced for what had happened inside the stadium. The inquiry held by Belgian magistrates in order to identify those responsible for the massacre, led by Mrs Stephane Copleters Wallant and carried out mainly on the evidence of pictures from the television broadcast, proceeded to a slow succession of arrests (26 in the end), and to an even slower extradition procedure. The scandal, however, was that so many of those responsible were not brought to justice, despite Thatcher's desire to put them 'in front of a court to be severely sentenced, because this must not happen again in the future'.[36] When the first legal process came to an end, in late April 1989, only 14 out of the 26 English supporters arrested and extradited to Belgium were found guilty. To the astonishment of the relatives of the victims, they were sentenced to only three years. The sentences were considered 'a scandal' in Italy but 'harsh and unfair' by the relatives of the guilty.[37] One year later, the Court of Appeal increased the sentence of 11 of the convicted to five years.

The Belgian authorities had been completely unable to manage the emergency and, even more seriously, had underestimated the security required for such a delicate and potentially incendiary event. Thus, after the initial rage at the behaviour of English hooligans, Italian and international public opinion began to point fingers at the Belgian police and Gendarmerie and at the Minister of Interior, Mr Charles-Ferdinand Nothomb. The police were accused of mistakes in the deployment of forces in the crucial hours before the game, with a subsequent lack of communication among the units, and of poor professional behaviour in the face of the emergency. They were felt to have used both arrogant and unnecessary degrees of force, and sudden and undignified retreats when faced with real trouble. As one eyewitness told the press, '[T]here were small groups of four or five English boys which were charged by the police only because they were chanting. When these groups were backed up by other supporters then the police would reverse and escape with unbelievable speed.'[38] If the second charge might be understood, even though not justified, it is the first one that could not, and cannot, even today, be forgiven. The first major mistake was a poor security control policy at the point of entry of Liverpool supporters in Belgium. Another mistake was the lack of coordination between Gendarmerie (Belgian national police) and the local Brussels Police force, the latter probably being more worried about looking after city-centre shop windows than the security at the stadium. They had also overlooked ticket-touting, which meant that thousands of Italians gained entry to sectors of the ground that were meant for a neutral public. The Belgian authorities also provided insufficient security controls at the gates of the stadium, which should have avoided the introduction of alcohol and implements that could have doubled as weapons. They were also guilty of an imprudent, if not criminal, dispersion of forces, with 400 policemen outside the ground and only around 100 inside. Finally, it should not be forgotten that there was a grave deficiency in communication between the units allocated outside and inside the *Heizelstadion* (allegedly the head of police had to look for a public phone to call for reinforcements[39]). This contributed to the police intervening in the rioting much too late. These are heavy charges. The Belgian police headquarters, after a series of attempts to shift the blame on to the 'unforeseeable' behaviour of Liverpool supporters, had to admit their responsibility, especially after a special parliamentary committee of inquiry, led by opposition leader Antoinette Spaak, was set up. The Belgian police had been warned of the very likely risks and advised by the Dutch Police on how to attempt to prevent trouble, after the latter had successfully ensured public order at the Cup-Winners' Cup Final between Everton and Rapid Vienna held in Rotterdam a fortnight earlier. Given their experiences of the 1984 UEFA Cup final, held in Brussels between Anderlecht and Tottenham Hotspur, the Belgian authorities should have been more prepared. On that occasion there were 400 policemen on the terraces to separate the opposing supporters. Despite all these precautions two people were killed, one outside the stadium and one on the terraces.

When questioned by the committee of inquiry, General Robert Bernaert, head of Belgian Gendarmerie, had to admit:

> The threat had been taken lightly … The Gendarmerie reacted too late: this is understandable, but inexcusable. The 40 gendarmes that were supposed to watch over Z block were no longer there when the troubles broke out: they had been called to back up the units outside the stadium, where other troubles were feared.[40]

The Head of the Brussels police, Michel Kensier, caused a sensation during his testimony to the same committee. He admitted that he only found out about the troubles at 7.30 p.m., half an hour after the disorder had started, not through communications from his men at the ground, but by turning on the television set in his office to watch the evening news. 'Now everyone says they felt something was going to happen, but when I questioned my men who were on the spot they told me they didn't see anything peculiar', he added.[41] A member of the committee of inquiry exclaimed: 'television viewers knew more about the events at the Heysel stadium than the police!'[42]

Despite such evidence the inquiry did not make any drastic decisions, limiting their actions to the removal of the three officers in charge of the gendarmes inside the stadium, Colonel Alfons van der Borcht, Captain Johan Mahieu and Kensier. Mahieu was put on probation for six months by the Brussels court for 'criminal negligence'. It has to be said that the Gendarmerie considered these removals 'routine rotation', part of the 'annual promotions and demotions',[43] and not a disciplinary action based on the outcome of the inquiry. General Bernaert was exempted from any responsibility.

Charles-Ferdinand Nothomb, Minister of the Belgian Interior, declared himself clear of any blame, in spite of the parliamentary committee of inquiry, the media, public opinion and even some members of his own Government accusing him of being the political culprit of the tragedy. Such accusations were rooted in his responsibility for poor security planning by his cabinet and by the national police. Mr Nothomb let the charges slide off him. Nothing managed to make him resign from the position he had taken the very day after the disaster, when, availing himself of the British prime minister's words, he shifted all the responsibility on to the behaviour of English supporters:

> Mrs Thatcher accepted the responsibility of the tragedy. We will take drastic measures against English football clubs and their supporters. The Belgian people are horrified by this tragic situation. We have nothing to reproach ourselves with as far as security at the stadium is concerned. We cannot turn Belgium into a police state. On this occasion every limit has been exceeded, as well as any reasonable forecast of troubles.[44]

In shifting the blame from himself, Nothomb's favoured scapegoats were, in order of preference: the British hooligans, the local Brussels police, and the system of local self-management of police forces in Belgium. He never admitted his political responsibility, even when the government, led by Wilfried Maertens, was forced to dissolve in a crisis fuelled by parliamentary talks on the disaster and criticisms from the usually silent King Baudouin on the government's role in the tragedy. The political crisis was also aggravated by the position of Jean Gol, Minister of Justice, who had threatened his resignation if neither the government nor parliament took action against Nothomb. Both Gol and Nothomb remained ministers in the new government constituted in autumn 1985, as personal and political interests took precedence over the Heysel recriminations.

On the eve of the first anniversary of the tragedy, Nothomb released a long-awaited report on stadium safety after Heysel. The various recommendations included: stronger fencing to keep rival fans apart; improved control of access and exit points; better coordination between the police and visiting clubs; and a ban on alcohol. Failing to ban the sale of alcohol on the day of the final was another charge that had been levelled against the authorities. 'Nobody forced us to close, nor even suggested it', the owner of a bar in the Heysel area told the press in defence of himself and his peers.[45] The only precaution taken by the authorities had been the distribution of a flyer in which supporters were naively warned that Belgian beer was stronger than British beer. In contrast to his refusal to shoulder political responsibility for the mistakes at Heysel, Nothomb resigned in October 1986, following the failure of his attempts to defend a provincial administrator who had been removed for his position on multilingualism in Belgium.

The football authorities, UEFA and the *Union Royale Belge de Football*, did not escape their share of the blame. UEFA had made a terrible mistake in picking the Heysel stadium to stage the European Cup Final. The Belgian FA should have demanded and verified, both from local and national political and police authorities, that every requirement needed to guarantee a peaceful game had been carried out.

The *Heizelstadion* was an appalling choice of venue to stage the final. Built in the 1930s, it was in an awful state of disrepair and although it had already staged six international football finals, it was now almost universally considered inadequate to host high profile matches. In particular, the terraces were old and worn. It was the bad condition of the walls and floors of the terraces that supplied the hooligans with stones and lumps of plaster to use as missiles. In the aftermath of the disaster, security experts, journalists and football administrators immediately pointed out the inadequacy of the Heysel stadium. The inadequacy of the venue becomes clear when one considers the words of Juventus president Giampiero Boniperti who recalled some years later that: 'At noon [on the very day of the disaster] we made the inspection of the ground and we all tore our hair: it was old, decrepit and it looked like a scrap yard. There were wooden boards all over the place, they looked like cudgels.'[46] Nonetheless, UEFA president Jacques Georges was cleared of any wrongdoing and remained in post until the end of his term of office in 1990.

More culpable than UEFA were the Belgian football authorities for their organization of the event. They had not taken into proper consideration the possibility that tickets for the buffer Z Block might end up in the hands of Italian supporters. Was it really so unpredictable that those tickets, which were poor quality and very easy to forge, might be bought by the thousands and thousands of Italian emigrants in Belgium, either legally or through touts? This was not the only thoughtlessness within the general organization of the match. There was not a single first aid or resuscitation unit at the ground. Most of the deaths were caused by suffocation and thus the presence of oxygen bottles, resuscitation units and similar equipment would have been enough to avoid a considerable number of losses. The National First Aid Service told the parliamentary committee of inquiry that the Belgian FA had never contacted it whilst preparing for the final.

Another absurd organizational fault was pinpointed by Brussels Fire-Brigade, which had promptly joined the police and the army in the rescue operation. According to the testimonies of some of its officers, at least ten emergency exits at the stadium were locked shut by padlocks for which nobody seemed to have keys. All three emergency exits in Z block were locked and turned into death traps, attracting the fleeing crowd but becoming actual 'dead ends'. Due to this series of careless mistakes, the head of the organizing committee of the event, Belgian FA general secretary Albert Roosens, was sentenced to six-months suspended sentence by a Belgian court.

The last page of the official match programme, personally edited by Roosens, made a series of requests to the crowd:

> To ensure that the cup final proceeds in an atmosphere worthy of the occasion, spectators are kindly requested to:
>
> ● refrain from bringing bottles of any kind into the stadium
> ● not throw any objects

- not encroach upon the interior part of the stadium under any circumstances either before, during or after the match
- keep their expressions of joy or disappointment within the limits of normal good sporting behaviour
- help the stadium security officials in carrying out their duties
- prevent an unruly minority from spoiling the enjoyment of the majority who have come to see good football.[47]

Everything that actually happened on the terraces of Heysel had been, at least in theory, foreseen by the Belgian football authorities in these recommendations. So why was it so difficult to avoid the troubles? Did they really think that those recommendations would be enough to convince the 'unruly minority' to desist 'from spoiling the enjoyment of the majority'? For many Italian supporters, that the Belgian FA did not give due care to these issues and instead placed responsibility for them on the fans was simply shameful and unforgivable.

CONCLUSION: THE DEBRIS OF HEYSEL

Out of the debris of Heysel, the football authorities themselves took a number of actions. UEFA banned English clubs from European competitions for a period of five years, with Liverpool FC receiving an additional two-year ban. Juventus' home ground received a two game ban. These actions did not stop football hooliganism but were a strong statement that gave public opinion, especially in Italy, some satisfaction.

In regard to stadium security, the main effect of the Heysel disaster was the signing, on 19 August 1985, of the European agreement on violence and excesses of spectators. This agreement encouraged cooperation between football authorities and police during the organization of sporting events, underlined the importance of the separation of opposing supporters (as well as of more careful security controls at the entrances of stadiums), of bans on alcohol sales, and of the prohibition of items which might potentially be used in a dangerous way inside grounds. The agreement pinpointed the necessity of building new stadiums that guaranteed the safety of spectators, with entry and exit points that would facilitate the quick intervention of security units and rescuers in the case of an emergency. The agreement also provided for international collaboration to identify more easily those who caused riots and to facilitate international transmissions of judicial acts, so as to quicken proceedings and extradition whenever required. The most visible effect of this agreement was the use of CCTV at football stadia, as well as the presence in the stands of stewards responsible for the reception of spectators, escorting them to their seats, and for spotting any potential troublemakers and identifying them to the police.

In Italy the most obvious effect of the Heysel disaster was the greater attention paid to football fandom and hooliganism by the media and many academics. In football itself security and safety measures were tightened, with, in some case, an actual 'militarization' of stadiums. Many leaders of organized groups of supporters did not welcome this. These groups thus immediately split up, bringing an end to the Italian tradition of large organized sets of fans and the creation of several short-lived mini-groups, which were more anarchic and less controllable by club boards and police authorities. As Fabio Bruno says, the 'Heysel tragedy represented a watershed in the *ultrà*[48] movement, which since then evolved following criteria that were completely different from the original ones'.[49] The criteria that followed a sort of code of honour were now to be replaced by more anarchic and instinctive misbehaviour, and the new organized groups absorbed only the more superficial and aggressive aspects, attracted by the negative publicity given to the *ultrà* movements by the media.

Beyond these actual consequences, it is impossible not to dwell upon what cannot be actually 'quantified': the bitterness for a disaster that could, and should, have been avoided, the rage towards all those who were, in Italian eyes, responsible for the catastrophe but never punished adequately, and the general sense of alienation from their most loved sport experienced by everyday people. These were probably the deepest, and saddest, consequences of the Heysel disaster in Italy.

Paolo Rossi and Giampiero Boniperti have recently published their biographies.[50] They talk about the night with words of unchanged grief, despite the fact that almost 20 years have passed. Michel Platini never entered that stadium again. When asked by a journalist why he would not attend any of the Euro 2000 matches played at the new *Koning Boudewijnstadion* in Brussels (the old *Heizelstadion* had been completely refurbished and inaugurated on 23 August 1995 under the new denomination 'King Baudouin Stadium'), he replied: 'for me football is fun, and there is no fun in going back to that place'.[51]

The first Italian side to play at the Heysel stadium after 29 May 1985 was AC Milan, on 7 March 1990, in a European Cup quarter-final against Mechelen. On that occasion, to some boos from Belgian supporters, captain Baresi laid a bunch of 39 red roses on the terraces where 39 supporters had died. This gesture was repeated in the now refurbished and renamed stadium on 14 June 2000 by Paolo Maldini, captain of Italian national team, before a match against Belgium during the European Championships. That gesture was made in order to honour the victims and to keep alive the memory of their deaths. In contrast, UEFA had not arranged any official remembrance event, preferring to forget the disaster, probably, and wrongly, believing that a new name for the stadium and a few more comfortable seats on the stands would be enough to brush the memory of that tragic night away.

Juventus FC finally won the 'cursed' European Cup in 1996, after a hard game against Ajax that was decided by a penalty shoot-out. The club had won an 'authentic' and deserved cup at last. A cup that allowed the glorious 'old lady' to replace that bloody trophy, a cup that journalist Marino Bartoletti had defined as a 'ghost made of silver and blood that somebody pretended to see in the club's showcase'.[52]

NOTES

1. I would like to thank Andrea Linfozzi for his help with the account of the troubles of that night. He was actually on the terraces of the Heysel Stadium on that night, and supplied me with the short unpublished novel he wrote about the tragedy.
2. Quoted in *La Stampa*, 5 June 1985.
3. www.liverpoolfc.tv/lfc_story/heysel.
4. *La Stampa*, Turin, 26 May 1985. All quotes from Italian newspapers are translated by the author.
5. *Corriere della Sera*, Milan, 31 May 1985.
6. Ibid.
7. The Belgian authorities claimed there were a further 30 policemen undercover on the terraces. It is still a mystery where they were exactly and what they did when the riot broke out.
8. *Corriere della Sera*, 30 May 1985.
9. Ibid.
10. *Corriere della Sera*, 31 May 1985.
11. *Corriere della Sera*, 1 June 1985.
12. As reported in *Corriere della Sera*, 30 May 1985.
13. *Corriere della Sera*, 30 May 1985.
14. *La Stampa*, 31 May 1985.
15. Ibid.
16. Ibid.
17. *La Stampa*, 1 June 1985.
18. *La Stampa*, 31 May 1985.
19. Ibid.
20. *La Stampa*, 1 June 1985.
21. Ibid.
22. Ibid.
23. Ibid.
24. Quoted in Walter Veltroni, *I programmi che hanno cambiato l'Italia* (Milan: Feltrinelli, 1994), p.122.
25. *Corriere della Sera*, 1 June 1985.
26. Veltroni, *I programmi*, p.122.
27. *Corriere della Sera*, 2 June 1985.
28. Only Germany and Switzerland-German speaking television networks refused to broadcast the game.
29. *Corriere della Sera*, 31 May 1985.
30. At least at the stadium and in the surrounding areas. There was some trouble downtown, before and after the game. In the afternoon before the match, gangs of drunk English fans damaged bars and shop windows, while in the immediate aftermath of the Liverpool victory there were, allegedly, some assaults by Roma fans against supporters of the opposite side. But the troubles were not comparable to other contemporary incidents of football hooliganism.
31. *Corriere della Sera*, 31 May 1985.
32. *La Stampa*, 31 May 1985.
33. Quoted in *Corriere della Sera*, 1 June 1985.
34. *Corriere della Sera*, 31 May 1985.
35. That fan was later identified as John Welsh, 27, barman.
36. *La Stampa*, 31 May 1985.
37. *The Times*, 29 April 1989.
38. *Corriere della Sera*, 1 June 1985.
39. *The Times*, 28 May 1986.
40. *Corriere della Sera*, 8 June 1985.
41. *The Times*, 21 June 1985.
42. Ibid.
43. *The Times*, 4 Jan. 1986.
44. *La Stampa*, 31 May 1985.
45. *La Stampa*, 1 June 1985.
46. *La Repubblica*, Milan, 22 May 2003.
47. 'Coupe des Clubs Champions Européens 1984/85 – Programme official' (Brusells, 1985).
48. *Ultrà* is the common denomination of the most inveterate supporters in Italy.

49. Fabio Bruno, 'Storia del movimento ultrà in Italia', in EURISPES, *Ultrà. Le sottoculture giovanili negli stadi d'Europa*, in www.eurispes.com/eurispes/201/5par3.
50. See: Paolo Rossi, *Ho fatto piangere il Brasile* (Arezzo: Limina, 2002); Giampiero Boniperti/Enrica Speroni, *Una vita a testa alta. Cinquant'anni sempre e solo per la Juventus* (Milan: Rizzoli, 2003).
51. Quoted in www.soccerage.com/it/13/23651.
52. In www.calcio2000.com/italy/dialoghy/heysel.

6

Not Just A Game: The Kayseri vs. Sivas Football Disaster

YİĞİT AKIN

The 2003–2004 Turkish football season began with heated discussions about the removal of crowd control fences around domestic football stadia. Those who supported the idea argued that Turkish football fans had reached a sufficient level of maturity to follow the game without potentially hindering players and referees. However, the football authorities disagreed with this position. Whilst they acknowledged that the feeling of imprisonment created by the fences provoked fans and potentially raised the overall level of aggression, they emphasized the lack of an established football culture in Turkey and pointed out a number of possible dangers. Openly stated or not, both sides in this discussion had serious doubts about the reactions of fans towards fenceless stadia. Consequently, only two First Division clubs removed their fences.

The major motivation underlying the reluctance to remove fences from Turkish football stadia was a fear of increasing hooliganism. For different reasons, including intensified social and economic problems in major cities, hooliganism has increased markedly in Turkish football during the last few decades. Hooliganism has even mushroomed in the remotest parts of the country where football is yet to emerge as a mass spectator sport. Derbies played between the major teams of Istanbul, namely Galatasaray, Fenerbahçe and Beşiktaş, and also derbies played between the teams of Izmir, Karşıyaka and Göztepe, have seen the most intense levels of hatred and violence. Even when extraordinary preventative measures have been taken before matches, violence and even death has not been kept away from football grounds. In the 2003-2004 football season, for example, a Karşıyaka fan was murdered during the first match (Karşıyaka vs. Göztepe) of the TSYD Cup (Turkey Sports Writers' Association Cup). On 22 February 2004, fans of Gaziantepspor set a stand on fire during a match between Fenerbahçe and Gaziantepspor. On 24 February of the same year, Adanaspor fans attacked rival fans, injuring 19 of them, and earlier in the month Göztepe fans clashed with security forces during the derby with Karşıyaka, resulting in a large number of injuries. In the wake of these incidents, and in the hope of overcoming vandalism and violence in sport contests, a draft bill entitled 'The Proposal on the Prevention of

Violence and Disorder in Sports Contests' was prepared by the government and put out for consultation.

Although deaths and violent incidents at football matches date back to the early years of modern sport in Turkey, it was only in the 1960s when football hooliganism began to be regarded as a serious issue around the game. With the spread of football throughout the country, news about quarrels between rival fans, players and administrators were frequently reported upon in local and national newspapers. Whilst most clashes resulted in few injuries and little material loss, some led to disastrous conclusions that were later to become etched into public memory. This study concentrates on one of the most catastrophic events in Turkish sports history: the football match held on 17 September 1967 between the teams of two major Anatolian cities, Kayseri and Sivas.

The Kayseri vs. Sivas football disaster is perhaps one of the most defining events to affect Turkish society during the late 1960s. For the first time in Turkey, a football match ended in multiple deaths and injuries: 42 people were killed and more than 300 were gravely wounded. The effects of the disaster were not limited to the two cities that were immediately involved. In every part of Turkey, people who became acquainted with football via this disaster thereafter regarded the sport negatively. In the decades that followed, Turkish football has continued to be inextricably linked with the sorrowful events that occurred at the Kayseri vs. Sivas match.

The primary purpose of the study is to outline the social, economic and political influences that lay behind one of the most significant football disasters in Turkish history. It also aims to introduce the reader to the specific dynamics of the disaster, and reactions to the events that happened. The continuing significance of the disaster in Turkish football and Turkish culture will also be analysed.

SOCIAL AND CULTURAL BACKGROUND OF THE DISASTER

The following section outlines the social, economic and political circumstances that facilitated the development of football in Turkey in the post-war period. It will show how sport and physical education developed during the early Republican years with a special emphasis on the educative, reformative-reproductive character of sports, and on the degenerating effects of football.[1] The Kayseri vs. Sivas football disaster occurred during a time of unstable social conditions in the country. Whilst the disaster was a sudden incident that cannot be attributed to one specific reason such as ethnicity, local pride or historical animosities, changing social and economic determinants certainly shaped the context in which it occurred.

The single-party era in Turkey came to an end with the elections of 1950, when the Republican People's Party (RPP), the founding party of the Turkish Republic, relinquished power to the Democratic Party (DP). The liberalization process in the economy had already begun with the introduction of the Marshall Aid

Program in 1947. Despite their financial and fiscal weakness, the Democrats pursued liberal economic policies and, to a certain extent, succeeded in modernizing Turkish agriculture and developing the industrial sector. Thanks to mechanization and irrigation projects, the amount of cultivated land increased dramatically, resulting in a sharp rise in farmers' incomes. During the early 1950s, the economy as a whole grew at a rapid annual rate of 12 per cent,[2] and total investments rose by 256 per cent. State investments were concentrated on a nation-wide network of roads, the construction industry and agro-industries. These economic developments found their reflections in everyday life as new forms of social dynamism emerged.

With economic development, Turkey was transformed by deep social changes during the 1960s, and social mobility occurred on an unprecedented scale. Mass migration into cities such as Istanbul, Ankara, İzmir, Adana, Mersin, Kayseri and Denizli accelerated, mostly due to new opportunities in industry and the mechanization of agriculture which created high rates of unemployment in rural areas. Approximately one million people left their lands and tried to make lives for themselves on the outskirts of the major cities. It was not possible for the developing industries to absorb this growing unskilled labour force, and, as a result, most of the migrants became casual labourers, street vendors or remained unemployed. The number of students and industrial workers rose in the major cities, along with political radicalism. Public life gradually became dominated by this radicalism and society became polarized between leftist and rightist ideas. In addition to a rate of unemployment that exceeded 10 per cent, this political fragmentation led to violence in society on a daily basis. Toward the end of the 1960s, this tension permeated all levels of society.

Interrupted by an economic crisis at the end of the 1950s that resulted in high inflation rates, the economy continued to grow impressively by an average annual rate of 6.9 per cent during the 1960s; a decade in which Turkey adopted a new mode of economic developmentalism. As the Turkish economy lacked native capital until the end of the 1970s, successive governments sought to create an advanced Turkish industrial sector through the strategy of import substitution. Governments stimulated the growth of indigenous industry through subsidies, tax rebates, import restrictions and high tariffs on American and European goods. Pursuing populist policies, the governments allowed high prices to be set for agricultural products, and encouraged high wages for industrial workers. Entrepreneurs made excessive profits, and real incomes rose by an average rate of 20 per cent.[3]

Prompted by development plans that facilitated the spread of industrial investment into the rural parts of the country, small and medium entrepreneurs in the countryside began to utilize the advantages of economic development. In some regional centres, the wealth that was gained through populist policies, such as financial support for rural farmers, started to be transferred to industrial investments. These investments created a large number of new jobs for local people, including unskilled workers. In addition to these developments, some structural steps were taken by successive governments to increase agricultural efficiency. For instance, large dams and a number of irrigation projects were completed in the southern and eastern parts of the country. Moreover, in these years, the money transfers of Turkish workers who had migrated to countries throughout Europe – especially to Germany as *Gastarbeiters* (guest workers) – began to contribute to domestic economic development.[4] These trends led to the accumulation of economic surplus in the countryside, especially in the local centres of the rural regions. A provincial bourgeoisie that had close ties with the government mushroomed in the developing cities of Anatolia.

Beyond its local leisure function, football appeared as a symbol of the rise of the provincial bourgeoisie. This rise was marked by the tension between the Istanbul bourgeoisie and the provincial bourgeoisie. Although the provincial bourgeoisie benefited from the growth of post-war wealth, deep fissures opened between them and representatives of the Istanbul elite, who were assumed to have absorbed the greatest part of the economic surplus. This unequal situation in the economic sphere was echoed in Turkish football. In its early years in Turkey, football had been played only in the major cities. It had taken on the character of a mass sports only after the inauguration of the 'Law for Professionalism in Football' in 1951 and after the formation of the National League. Thanks to developments in the sports media and in football itself, such as new legislative arrangements, the emergence of educated sports personnel, and the improvement of sports fields, the provincial masses as well as the urban populations became familiar with the game and began to play it at the local level in increasing numbers. With the establishment of the Second Division in 1963, football reached new heights of popularity. However, the provincial teams were not particularly successful at a national level. Three powerful Istanbul teams – Galatasaray, Beşiktaş and Fenerbahçe – continued to dominate Turkish football, as they had had since its early years. After the inception of professional football in 1951, the domination of the Istanbul clubs – based on their popularity, financial and administrative strength – was consolidated. It was only in the mid-1970s that a team from an Anatolian city was able to become champion of the First Division.[5]

Until the mid-1960s, the provincial bourgeoisie was deprived of any effective means to express and, more importantly, to challenge the domination of Istanbul, both economically as well as in football. When the conservative Justice Party came to power in the 1965 elections, the weight of the rural areas began to be felt in the political, economic and social life of Turkey. Under these conditions, the provincial bourgeoisie began to manipulate football at the local level as a challenge to the hegemony of the Istanbul clubs. They began to establish new teams and mobilize their collective financial resources to bring success on a national scale.

Richard Holt's argument for Britain, that football's appeal was rooted in its ability to articulate civic/local pride through success on the pitch, is also true for Turkey.[6] As a result of the rise of the peripheral bourgeoisie in the mid-1960s, almost all of the Anatolian cities established football teams with high hopes of success. After 1967, this tendency began to affect the major provinces, whose social and economic conditions were better than those of most cities. The Football Federation also encouraged the establishment of new teams in the countryside. Football teams were usually established under the names of cities and elicited great levels of support from local people. The usual method of establishing a provincial team was the union of local and amateur teams in a single city. As a sign of the identification of the team with the city, the mayors usually became presidents of the teams. These developments represented a significant transformation in the provincial areas. Football helped to create a certain level of social integration in these newly developed cities as people who migrated to these areas adopted new urban identities. Football brought about a sense of belonging to the city that had previously been unimaginable.

However, football teams were more than tools in the challenge of the provincial cities to Istanbul's hegemony. They also contributed to symbolic forms of rivalry between the mid-sized cities, which competed to be regional centres. With the establishment of the Second Division, violent and sometimes bloody events at football games emerged and became a serious problem throughout the country. In cities such as Bolu and Afyon, physical confrontations broke out between fans, some of whom were injured. Conflict was more intense between cities like Kayseri and Sivas. Since the early years of the Turkish Republic, these two neighbouring cities had competed to be the social and economic centre of Central Anatolia. Kayseri was more developed and wealthier than Sivas. Moreover, merchants of Kayseri origin dominated the economy of Sivas. Therefore, while football matches represented for Sivas the idea of challenging the traditional hegemony of Kayseri, for Kayseri it meant resistance to this challenge. Prompted by this strained social and economic background, several fights broke out between the amateur teams of Kayseri and Sivas. Many players and spectators were injured in a match between Elvan Sümerspor and Kayseri Şekerspor in 1965 and between Kayseri Havagücü and Sivas Sümerspor in 1966.

As in other fields, Sivas, unlike Kayseri, was a latecomer to football. A football team, which would represent the city on the national level, was only established in 1967. As the Second Division was established in the season 1963–64, quotas allocated to the teams had already been well set and filled when Sivas football team was founded. Therefore, the Football Federation at first resisted the introduction of Sivas to the Second Division. This sparked large-scale demonstrations in the city. Also, 12 local teams boycotted their matches in the nationwide amateur championships, and all local representatives of sport federations resigned from their positions. Under this pressure, the Football Federation agreed to accept Sivasspor into the Second Division on 1 July 1967.

The representation of the city for the first time at national level became the hottest topic on the local agenda. Notables of the city collected 307,000 Turkish Liras (approximately 34,000 US$) to support the team financially. More than two-thirds of this money was spent on transfer expenditures. Many famous players, most of whom had never been to Sivas before, were brought to the city to play for the new team. A former national player, Hilmi Kiremitçi, was appointed as the coach of the team. The new team were lauded as local heroes who would break the 'hundred year old misfortune' of the city.

BEFORE THE MATCH

On 21 August 1967, the Second Division started in two groups. Both Kayserispor and Sivasspor were among the leading teams of the 'red' group, each having won their first three matches. The game between these two teams was awaited with special excitement and tension, as it would be a clear expression of the deep-rooted rivalry between the two cities. The fans on each side expressed their hatred of the other team via slogans written on the cars of the train running between the two cities.[7]

The day before the match, fans of Sivasspor arrived in Kayseri in a convoy almost ten kilometres in length. Forty buses, 20 minibuses and a train carried approximately 5,000 fans to the game.[8] In the short history of the Second Division, such a crowd of supporters going to another city to support their team had never been seen before. The Sivas fans filled up all of the hotels in Kayseri, and even the local brothels. In the brothels and at other locations throughout the city, quarrels broke out amongst small groups of Sivas fans and the inhabitants of Kayseri. According to the police reports, four Sivas fans were seriously injured and 50 were arrested in pre-game clashes.[9]

DURING THE MATCH

Nearly 21,000 people attended the first league meeting between Kayserispor and Sivasspor, a quarter of whom were fans of the travelling team. Thousands of people who could not enter the stadium crowded the roofs of nearby buildings, disregarding their personal safety. Because of the tension between the fans of the two teams, security at the entrance of the stadium was strict; many weapons, including knives, cudgels, chains and pocket-knives were confiscated.

The match began in a strained atmosphere. In the twentieth minute, the striker of Kayserispor, Oktay, scored. After the goal, some players from both sides began to fight for an unknown reason. The referee of the match showed a red card to one of the players of Kayserispor, but after strenuous objections he changed his decision and allowed the player to remain on the field. As the level of tension escalated, fans began to throw rocks at each other, first individually and then in groups. A group of people on the Sivas side, seeking to escape from the rocks, rushed toward the field and the exit gates. Those who tried to enter the field were met by police batons and turned back. In a panic, thousands of Sivas fans pressed towards the nearest gates, crushing their fellow supporters against the fencing at the front of the terrace. When the human wave drew back, the scene was horrific: 40 people were dead and at least 300 were injured.

As the violence on the ground grew, the referee cancelled the match. The players of both teams fled into the dressing rooms in fear of their own lives. All of the members of the Sivas team were locked in their dressing room and a policeman was charged with guarding them. Yusuf Ziya Özler, one of the of Sivasspor players, is sure today that if the Kayseri fans had seen that only one policeman was guarding the team, they would have been killed mercilessly.[10]

AFTER THE MATCH

Once the Sivas fans had made their way out on to the streets, they destroyed around 60 private cars and the city's gymnasium.[11] They then left Kayseri in a convoy, but 50 kilometres out on the Kayseri-Sivas highway they stopped and began to set fire to cars, buses and trucks whose license plate numbers indicated that they were from Kayseri. The Sivasspor team was kept in Kayseri until midnight and were then returned to Sivas in official vehicles. When the fans and players reached Sivas, they found that news of the match, severely distorted, had arrived before them. It had been said that none of the Sivas fans remained alive. At the city entrance, thousands of people surrounded the vehicles that carried the players asking the fate of their fathers, brothers and sons. Hysterical, they blamed the players and the managers of the team. In the ensuing days, all of the players fled the city and were able to return only after a few weeks had passed.

Following the arrival in Sivas of the news of the disaster, thousands of people set off in buses, trucks, private vehicles and even on foot toward Kayseri. They blocked the highway between the two cities and fought with security forces.[12] Back in Sivas, the disorder and violence was most pronounced in the city centre, where the people rushed into the bazaar of the city and began to plunder the shops, hotels and offices owned by people of Kayseri origin, who, as mentioned above, dominated the economy of the city. The police, who mostly shared the feelings of the people of Sivas, hesitated to intervene. After plundering, shops, hotels and houses were set ablaze, and the fire brigade, trying to extinguish the fires, came under violent attack.

To some observers, these events between the two cities had a religious dimension. Claims were made that the events could be read as a reflection of the traditional hostility between the fundamentalist Sunni Muslims and Shiite Alevis, who typically were affiliated with the political left.[13] Therefore, the wave of hatred was strengthened by myths rooted in folkloric-religious rumours. To explain the violence against the Sivas fans by the Kayseri fans, religious allegories were utilized. According to one, the sons of the caliph Ali, the holy figure of the Alevis, were murdered by their enemies and their heads were kicked around like balls.[14] Now, the Kayseri fans were said to have played with the heads of the Sivas fans.

101

During the riots in Sivas, the plunderers did not come face to face with any of the shop owners. This strengthened the rumours that the disaster in Kayseri had been planned beforehand and organized carefully. Therefore, the plundering was considered revenge for the deaths of the Sivas fans.[15] Local religious leaders preached that plundering the property of those 'sinners from Kayseri' was a prerequisite of Islam.

Hysteria gripped Sivas. Many people were accused of either being from Kayseri or having relatives from Kayseri. Those under suspicion began to stick their identity cards on their windows in order to prove their origins.[16] Although the police arrested 110 locals, two more people died and the violence and plundering lasted almost a week.

REACTIONS TO THE DISASTER

To prevent the continuing spread of violence associated with the match, military units were brought in to block the Kayseri-Sivas highway and hinder movement between the two neighbouring cities. Police took measures to prevent the spread of problems to major cities such as Istanbul and Ankara, where migrants from both Kayseri and Sivas lived, and to high-school dormitories where students from these cities were housed. Despite these precautions, beds and other personal goods of students from Kayseri were set alight in the dormitories.[17] Students of Kayseri origin who were attending boarding schools in Sivas and vice versa were transferred to other cities. To prevent any further violence, the official opening of the education year was postponed for two weeks in Sivas and Kayseri. Similarly, for the sake of their personal security, some local officials of Kayseri origin were transferred to other cities.

Due to the disaster, local mourning was proclaimed in Sivas and almost all of the shops and entertainment centres were closed. Three days after the tragedy, an official funeral was organized for the fans who were killed in Kayseri. Not surprisingly, the funeral turned into a ceremony of revenge. The dead people were proclaimed martyrs and sanctified as if they had died in the holy fight for Islam. Impressive dirges were written to keep their memory alive.[18] Following the events, civil groups from Sivas expressed their reactions to Kayseri representatives and state officials via different organizations. For example, the Sivas Youth Organization published a declaration calling Kayseri 'Murder City'. Blaming the governor of the city, they brought a donkey in front of the governor's office and pronounced it the 'governor'.[19] The *muhtars* (village headmen) of 1,283 villages around the city of Sivas published a common declaration and announced that they would no longer trade with livestock merchants from Kayseri.[20] Moreover, the inhabitants of Sivas organized a comprehensive boycott against shop owners of Kayseri origin. The residents of a ward called *Kayserikapı* (Kayseri gate) changed the name of the ward to *Şehitler* (the Martyrs).

Ankara, the capital city, watched these events in stunned silence. The Prime Minister, Süleyman Demirel, postponed an official trip to Russia for one day. The Council of Ministers gathered immediately and the Second Division was suspended. The Minister of Interior Affairs, the Commanding Officer of the Gendarme, the Minister of Health, and the General Director of Physical Education went to Kayseri to conduct an official inquiry. Whilst the plundering still raged on, these officials who also went to Sivas had the aim of calming the angry reaction to the disaster. Although the Minister of Internal Affairs, Faruk Sükan, called for the people to stop, no one listened. Sükan was faced with an angry crowd shouting slogans such as 'Murder Sükan!' He also received much criticism for having visited Kayseri first, despite Sivas's much more tragic loss of 38 people. When Sükan was unable to complete his speech, one of the well-known lawyers of the city, Ali Take, tried to calm down the crowd. He was attacked, however, and security forces were barely able to save him from the hands of the angry crowd.

Following the disaster, a committee was appointed in Ankara and three doctors from the Medical Jurisprudence Institute were assigned to investigate the reasons for the deaths. According to the report based on the official autopsies, most of the victims had been between the ages of 20–30.[21] The majority had died in the first three to four minutes from asphyxia, heart attack and myocardial infarction. They did not encounter any injuries caused by knives or guns. The report stated that while rocks had injured some of the dead, these injuries had not been fatal. The main reason for the deaths was that the stadium gates had opened in towards the football ground instead of opening out.

There are conflicting views on how the bloody events that occurred in the stadium began. According to Rasim Adasal, a member of the administrative board of the General Directorate of Physical Education, the failure of the referee to send off Oktay, the Kayserispor striker, was the main reason for the escalating tension in the stands.[22] According to another view, after the goal two children had moved towards Sivas fans and started to provoke them.[23] When the Sivas fans had pelted them with rocks that had been concealed from the police at the entrance, the children had tried to escape. However, they had got caught between the iron fence and panicking Kayseri fans and had been crushed to death. It was suggested, then, that between 7,000 and 8,000 Kayseri fans had attacked the Sivas stands, which had led the Sivas fans to panic.

Whereas in news reports and in articles in the national press the Kayseri fans were blamed for the disaster, the chief of police of Kayseri accused the Sivas fans of not being able to stand the loss of the match.[24] In his report, the official observer of the match stated that the events had begun with the throwing of rocks by Sivas fans. In the final conclusion of the official inquiry, the players were found not guilty. There was no problem between the players of the two teams. The lack of administrative measures was declared to be the cause of the events.[25] If there had been sufficient security forces, and if they had intervened at the correct time, the bloody events could have been avoided.[26]

The security measures taken by the local administrators after the match drew severe criticism from the press and opposition parties in parliament.[27] The Union Party attempted to submit a motion of no confidence against the Minister of Interior Affairs. In response to criticism that the safety measures and controls at the entrance had been inadequate, the Minister of Health stated that there had been 237 police and gendarmes on duty at the game.[28] Actually, the numbers were as low as 30 policemen and 15 gendarmes.[29] It should be noted here that warnings made before the match by the administrators of Sivasspor had been ignored to a large extent. Consequently, the governor and the chief of police were found to have failed in suppressing the events and were removed from office. Likewise, the governor of Kayseri, and the chiefs of police and their deputies in Kayseri and Sivas were removed from office and demoted.

THE IMPACT OF THE DISASTER

The Kayseri disaster stimulated different reactions in intellectual circles. Some leftist writers related the events to the decadence of Turkish society caused by American imperialism and the government of the Justice Party. They argued that the partisanship pursued by the Justice Party had split society into two different camps in every aspect of life. Football was no exception.[30] Other intellectuals related the events to the traditional conservatism of Turkish society. According to them, Turkey had still not become an 'open society', and from time to time displays that reflected its feudal past were inevitable.[31] Some went one step further and correlated the events to fanatical 'regionalism', which equated failure with hurting the pride of the people who lived in that region.[32]

The impact of the Kayseri disaster was something that had not been experienced in the history of Turkish sport. In this atmosphere of hostility and violence, the sports authorities discussed radical solutions. For instance, the State Minister responsible for sports affairs, Kamil Ocak, argued that the Second and Third Divisions should be abolished. The General Director of Physical Education, Ulvi Yenal, agreed and stated that the Second Division had not been established with the aim of increasing hostility between the beautiful cities of Anatolia: 'On the contrary, the Second and Third Divisions were established with the aim of improving the friendship between the cities, resuscitating domestic tourism and maintaining the development of Turkish football as a whole.'[33] The authorities generally shared the idea that it was too early for the establishment of the Second and Third Divisions, and that people in the countryside had not reached a high enough level of mental maturity to be able to tolerate this competition.

These events in turn brought forward ideas for legislative changes, especially with reference to punishing football clubs for not controlling their supporters. State officials and the sports press called for a strict set of legislative measures with severe penalties for non-compliance. For instance, Burhan Felek, a leading sports journalist, stated that the reason for these events was the lack of a strict penalty regulation.[34] On 20 September 1967, the Football Federation organized a meeting attended by sports authorities, journalists, sociologists and criminologists. After this meeting, a number of commissions were organized to revise the Penalty Regulations. The governors of cities were equipped with extra powers, such as the suspension or cancellation of games if there was a risk of violence. Moreover, weekend leave for security personnel was to be cancelled for important games, and all higher-rank security officers of the province were charged with the duty of following games and organizing preventive measures against violence. The commissions also made the decision to demote any club found to be involved in violent incidents.[35]

One week after the disaster, the state officials of physical education and sports gathered representatives of the sports clubs from the Second and Third Divisions in Ankara. For the first time in the history of Turkish sport, the state asked for guarantees of compliance from the teams to continue their matches. During this meeting, representatives of the clubs blamed the disaster on the anxiety that the clubs felt about potential relegation to a lower division. According to the representatives, such events could not be prevented unless the threat of relegation was abolished for at least three years.

Faced with the potential breaking up of lower league football in Turkey, a number of sport authorities agreed on the vital importance of the existence and development of new clubs in the Second Division. The head coach of the National Football team, Adnan Süvari, argued that some populist politicians had pressed for and promoted the development of Second Division football, regardless of the level of preparedness of these regions to manage a new football culture. However, he clearly emphasized the necessity of the Second Division.[36] The Syndicate of Professional Football Players published a declaration stating that the abolition of the Second Division would prevent the players from earning their livelihoods.[37] In the face of these arguments, the council of ministers made the decision to continue the Second Division matches, but with much stricter regulations.[38]

After these meetings, both Kayserispor and Sivasspor were announced as legally defeated by the decision of the Administrative Board of the Federation, and were penalized with five months prohibition from playing matches in their home cities. The match between the two teams was repeated on 10 March 1968 in Ankara. Kayserispor won the game by 1-0. To keep the memories of the disaster victims alive, the name of the busiest street in Kayseri was changed to Sivas Street. Two music records, namely *Kanlı Gol* (Bloody Goal) and *Öldüren Gol* (Murderer Goal), were released by local singers Rıza Aslandogan and Selim Atakan respectively.[39] The tragedy continued to occupy a central place in the culture of the fans of the two teams until 1990. Prior to this, the two teams did not have the opportunity to play against each other as they had been assigned to different groups in the Second Division. In 1990, the Football Federation decided that the two clubs could be in the same group of the Division. The first match played between the clubs in 23 years attracted great attention from the media and fans of both sides. But this time, the game was played in a friendly atmosphere.

CONCLUSION

In many ways, the Kayseri disaster can be read as one of the most significant milestones in Turkish sports history. It is difficult to argue, however, that it led to the drastic changes that resulted from other football disasters such as those that occurred at the Hillsborough and Heysel stadiums. Despite all of the legislative measures introduced after the tragedy, violence and vandalism were not erased from Turkish football grounds. Fights between rival football teams continued to break out at different times and in different locations. For example, just two years after the Kayseri vs. Sivas disaster, three people lost their lives in April 1969 following violence related to a match between Kırıkkale and Tarsus İdmanyurdu. Similarly, matches between the teams of Eskişehir and Bursa, and Siirt and Adana saw violence that year, although deaths were avoided.

Whilst the Kayseri disaster did not stop violence at Turkish football matches, it did influence many Turkish people's opinions towards the game. Football maintains a special place in the hearts and minds of many Turkish people, and especially amongst the young. However, many older people, who were brought up with a certain suspicion of football, could never closely associate with the game after the events of 1967. The same can be said for many Turkish women: at the very mention of football, the mothers and grandmothers of the nation often remember the 42 victims of the disaster. The Kayseri disaster also resulted in changed opinions towards football in political circles. Since the events of 1967, governments and politicians seeking to increase their popularity no longer supported the development and spread of football, especially in rural areas of the country. Similarly, the Football Federation started to make efforts to implement special measures on the spread of football in the countryside and pursued a much more careful development strategy.

The Kayseri disaster continues to be a permanent reference point in Turkey during discussions of crowd disorder in football stadiums. Even today, 35 years after the disaster, if a violent fan-related event takes place in the context of Turkish football, the authorities will refer back to the Kayseri disaster without hesitation. However, many within Turkish football seem to forget that, as with other football disasters, the events at Kayseri took place under certain circumstances that were determined by the social, cultural and economic developments of the day. Although a small spark initiated the bloody events, they reached the level of a 'disaster' thanks to numerous external conditions.

In recent years, safer and more comfortable stadiums have been built in Turkey. Moreover, sport professionals dealing with crowd-control issues have been educated to a higher level, and the government has produced severe legislation against domestic football hooliganism. However, the battle against football-related violence in Turkey has been concentrated too much on simple criminal measures. Lessons on the external factors that contributed to the Kayseri disaster seem to have been ignored. Despite all recent developments in Turkish football, football hooliganism continues to be a significant problem under increasingly exacerbated social and economic conditions (as outlined at the beginning of this chapter). If the authorities continue to ignore these conditions and insist on solving the problems only through police interventions, there is no reason to be hopeful about the removal of violence from Turkish football grounds. In such a climate, a repeat of the Kayseri vs. Sivas disaster remains a distinct possibility.

NOTES

1. For a critical history of sports and physical education during the early Republican years see Yiğit Akın, *Not Just A Game: Sports And Physical Education In Early Republican Turkey (1923–51)*, Unpublished MA Thesis submitted to Atatürk Institute for Modern Turkish History, Boğaziçi University, 2003.
2. Erik J. Zürcher, *Turkey: A Modern History* (London: I.B. Tauris, 1998), p.235.
3. Ibid., p.263.
4. These workers' cash remittances increased eight-fold in one year between 1964 and 1965. Douglas A. Howard, *The History of Turkey* (Westport: Greenwood, 2001), p.142.
5. Until today, 40 out of 46 championships have been won by these three Istanbul teams.
6. Richard Holt, *Sport and the British: A Modern History* (Oxford: Oxford University Press, 1989), chapter 3.
7. Ekrem Kiracıoğlu, 'Futbol Sahası Harp Meydanına Dönmüşrü', ('Football Ground Had Turned Into a Battle Ground') *Fotospor*, 54, 18 (Sept. 1967), 8.
8. *Cumhuriyet*, 18 Sept. 1967, p.1.
9. Ibid.
10. Hakan Dilek, 'Makus Talihi Futbolun', ('Unfortunate Football') http://www.ntvmsnbc.com/news/228797.asp.
11. *Milliyet*, 18 Sept. 1967, p.1.
12. *Cumhuriyet*, 19 Sept. 1967, p.1.
13. İlhan Selçuk, 'Gerçek Bir Facia' ('A Real Disaster'), *Cumhuriyet*, 19 Sept. 1967, p.2.
14. Zeki Coşkun, 'Yiğidoların Tarihsel Yenilgisi-İç Anadoluda Büyüklük Rekabeti ve Sivas', ('The Historical Defeat of Yigidos: The Competition for Seniority in Central Anatolia and Sivas') in Roman Horak, Wolfgang Reiter and Tanıl Bora (eds), *Futbol ve Kültürü (Football and its Culture)* (İstanbul: İletişim Yayınlari, 1993), p.361.
15. Ibid., p.360.
16. Dilek, 'Makus Talihi Futbolun' ('Unfortunate Football') .
17. *Milliyet*, 20 Sept. 1967, p.8.
18. Hüseyin Gülmez, *Kayseri'de Şehit Düşen Sivaslıların Destani (The Epic of the Martyrs From Sivas Who Died in Kayseri)* (Sivas: Esnaf Matbaasi, 1967).
19. *Cumhuriyet*, 19 Sept. 1967, p.9.
20. *Cumhuriyet*, 21 Sept. 1967, p.7.
21. *Milliyet*, 19 Sept. 1967, p.8.
22. Dilek, 'Makus Talihi Futbolun'.
23. Mustafa Gümüşkaynak, *Cumhuriyet*, 18 Sept. 1967, p.1.
24. *Cumhuriyet*, 18 Sept. 1967, p.7.
25. Ibid.
26. *Cumhuriyet*, 19 Sept. 1967, p.9.
27. For press declarations of the RPP (Republican People's Party) and the NP (Nation Party) see ibid., p.7.
28. Ibid., p.7.
29. Kiracioğlu, 'Futbol Sahasi Harp Meydanina Dönmüşrü', 8.

30. İlhan Selçuk, *Cumhuriyet*, 19 Sept. 1967, p.2.
31. Ecvet Güresin, *Cumhuriyet*, 19 Sept. 1967, p.1.
32. Halit Deringör, 'Beklemek Gerek'('We Have to Wait'), *Cumhuriyet*, 21 Sept. 1967, p.9.
33. *Cumhuriyet*, 18 Sept. 1967, p.9.
34. Burhan Felek, *Cumhuriyet*, 21 Sept. 1967, p.4.
35. *Maç Spor*, no.643, 21 Sept. 1967, p.3.
36. *Cumhuriyet*, 22 Sept. 1967, p.9.
37. 'Profesyonel Futbolcular Sendikasının Bildirisi', ('Declaration of the Syndicate of Professional Football Players'), *Cumhuriyet*, 22 Sept. 1967, p.9.
38. *Cumhuriyet*, 27 Sept. 1967, p.1.
39. Mehmet Ö. Alkan, 'Kırılsaydi Ayağım Atmazdım Golü', ('Was My Leg Broken, I Would Not Kick the Goal'), *Toplumsal Tarih*, 121 (Jan. 2004), 120–1.

7

'Like Cows Driven to a Dip': The 2001 Ellis Park Stadium Disaster in South Africa[1]

PETER ALEGI

On Wednesday 11 April 2001, Kaizer Chiefs and Orlando Pirates took the field at Ellis Park stadium in Johannesburg, South Africa, for a derby with the league championship at stake. As the 8 p.m. kick-off time approached, the 62,000-seat stadium was bursting at the seams with more than 80,000 fans squeezed into every seat, aisle, and access way. Outside the arena, thousands of fans pressed to get inside to watch the country's two most popular clubs. A portion of this massive crowd in the north-eastern corner of Ellis Park surged forward. A suffocating crush ensued. Veli Mpungose, his nine-year-old daughter Londiwe and 13-year-old son Siphiwe were trapped at the top of a steep stairway. 'I felt something push us away. We were scared. We thought the stadium had collapsed', Mpungose said. 'I was trying to rescue Londiwe and when I reached for Siphiwe, there were … big guys lying on top of him. I felt his pulse and I couldn't feel anything. He was dead already.'[2] Media images captured the heartbreaking scene of Mpungose and Londiwe kneeling in tearful prayer over Siphiwe's limp, lifeless body on the pitch.

In the end, 43 people died and 158 were injured in South Africa's worst-ever sport disaster.[3] Drawing on interviews, government documents, newspapers, video footage and a visit to Ellis Park in August 2003, this study analyses the causes, consequences and legacy of the tragedy. This analysis of the disaster reveals that conditions beyond the control of fans were primarily to blame for transforming Ellis Park into a landscape of death and destruction. These included fundamental organizational flaws, contempt for spectator safety, and incompetence and dereliction of duty on the part of security personnel. Under South African Football Association guidelines for high-risk matches, responsibility for spectator safety lay with the home side, Kaizer Chiefs, the Premier Soccer League (PSL), and, to a lesser extent, Ellis Park stadium management. A critical examination of the governmental commission of inquiry into the tragedy notes the limitations of the investigative process and questions the official interpretation of the events. While South African football's main powerbrokers emerged unscathed from the public probe, the victims of Ellis Park have lapsed from national memory. The study also demonstrates that South African soccer has failed to learn lessons from the past in relation to spectator safety.

THE CRUSH

In an immediate sense, overcrowding, an ill-timed announcement that the stadium was full, the use of teargas, and unruly spectator behaviour caused the Ellis Park disaster. Video footage supports the estimates of informants, who said that attendance on 11 April might have exceeded stadium capacity by as much as 25 per cent. This dangerous scenario had presented itself several times since the stadium opened in 1982. On 2 August 1986, for example, an estimated 100,000 people attended a miraculously incident-free second leg of the John Player's Special knockout final between Kaizer Chiefs and Moroka Swallows.[4] More recently, a dangerously oversold Chiefs-Pirates duel on 10 October 1998 saw police fire rubber bullets into the crowd as rioting broke out. This incident caused extensive damage to the stadium and several injuries, but luckily no deaths.[5]

The gargantuan size of the Ellis Park crowd on the night of 11 April overwhelmed security personnel and police units. Approximately 45 minutes before the game was due to kick off, security staff made an impromptu public announcement outside the stadium that the arena was full and that fans who had yet to gain entry should leave immediately and return home. Stunned by this news, people with and without tickets suddenly feared being shut out of the match. More aggressive fans knocked down portions of the perimeter fence and broke through gates. In an ill-advised last-ditch attempt to defuse the situation, security personnel at the southern entrances ordered thousands of fans to go around to the northern side. Chiefs supporter John Matibe of Pretoria recalled how 'as soon as this announcement was made that tickets had run out, the people that were already in the queue started looking for another way to get into the stadium'.[6] This movement 'created a wave of people the security personnel could not stop'.[7]

For the next hour or so chaos reigned at Ellis Park. The throngs from the south side arrived at the north end only to find an impenetrable human wall. Thousands of people were stuck in wooden channels near Gate 4; these were temporary structures built the previous day to control crowd flow.[8] According to eyewitness accounts, security guards in this area yelled: 'whether you have a ticket or not, go in through that gate [4] ... we followed, like cows driven to a dip'.[9] Members of Wolf Security, a private contractor hired by Ellis Park management, then fired teargas into the helpless crowd of people trapped in this horribly congested space.

This senseless act caused the crowd to panic, as people were pushed forward and crushed. John Matibe said that 'At this [north-east] gate I hurt my right knee during the pushing. It was there that the pressure from all the angry fans resulted in many people falling over. The worst thing was when that heavy steel gate fell on top of the people already lying on the ground.'[10] Fourteen fans died in the vicinity of Gate 4. Siyabonga Mkhwanazi, a reporter for *The Star*, was called to the scene soon after the tragedy. Having been forced to abandon his car in the massive traffic jam around Ellis Park, Mkhwanazi arrived at the stadium on foot. He could not believe his eyes. 'There were bodies outside [Gate 4]. I saw a young woman holding her boyfriend's hand; he was just lying there on the ground. She was pleading with him not to go. Then he died.'[11] Autopsies later revealed that the victims died from suffocation, crushed lungs, fractured skulls, broken lower limbs and various internal wounds. Eleven-year-old Rosswin Nation was the youngest victim; his father, Roy, had surprised him at the last moment by taking him to Ellis Park to see Chiefs vs. Pirates. 'When they did the autopsy', Roy Nation said, 'they found that he was wearing his pyjamas under his clothes.'[12]

THE MATCH GOES ON

At kick off, thunderous cheers smothered the screams of the dying.[13] Few of the 80,000 spectators realized the extent of the problems in the northeast grandstand.[14] The two sides, similarly unaware of the tragedy, played thrilling, end-to-end football. In the 14th minute, Chiefs' supporters erupted in celebration when Nigerian striker Tony Ilodigwe scored the game's first goal. Two minutes later, with rescue operations underway behind the advertising billboards to the left of Chiefs' goal, Benedict Vilakazi drew Pirates level. The young midfielder raced towards the corner flag and raised his arms triumphantly, coming to a stop a few meters from where rescue workers administered cardiopulmonary resuscitation to dying fans. 'That's when I realized things were worse', remembered Chiefs goalkeeper Brian Baloyi, who assumed that the medics behind the billboards were treating victims of fights in the stands. 'For the first time, I saw people were lying on the ground receiving treatment from the paramedics. Then I saw more people coming. My concentration on the game dropped after that', Baloyi said; 'I kept looking back at what was happening behind me, and then looking to the referee.'[15]

Nevertheless, the game continued. Twenty minutes into the first half an emotionally distraught television reporter roaming the sidelines confirmed the death of two people. For the next dozen minutes the hard-fought match took on an increasingly surreal quality, as emergency workers and volunteers from the crowd brought more and more bodies from the stands onto the pitch near Baloyi's goalposts. From the confines of the South African Broadcasting Company's television booth, play-by-play announcer Michael Abrahamson and analyst Thabiso Thema oscillated, schizophrenically, between business-as-usual commentary and sober acknowledgment of fatalities.[16] In the 33rd minute, Abrahamson blurted out that it had been a 'very, very good derby so far. Very unfortunate the incidents that are happening amongst the crowd. But the players are oblivious to it – they've got a job to do.'[17] Thirty seconds later, however, Premier Soccer League (PSL) chief Robin Petersen stopped the game; the growing number of casualties could no longer be ignored.

Twenty-nine people had lost their lives in the north-eastern corner of the grandstand, overwhelming rescue workers. Mathapelo Mansi, a nurse from the emergency services said: 'The medical personnel never expected such a disaster to happen, which is why untrained people volunteered and tried to help. It was very frustrating', Mansi continued, 'because when we called up others from nearby hospitals and clinics they could not come because of the traffic jam.'[18] A helicopter landed on the pitch to evacuate critically wounded spectators. Putco Mafani, Chiefs' public relations officer, took the microphone and announced that 47 [*sic*] people had died. Then the two teams held hands around the centre circle, paying their respects to the dead with a prayer. The chairmen of Chiefs and Pirates, Kaizer Motaung and Irvin Khoza, the mayor of Johannesburg, Amos Masondo, and the Minister of Sport, Ngconde Balfour, expressed their condolences and pleaded for calm. The stunned, mournful crowd began to file out of Ellis Park. PSL Media Officer Clinton Asary recounted, 'I never heard 80,000 people be so quiet'.[19] In the aftermath of the tragedy, the stakeholders participated eagerly in public displays of sympathy. Players together with club and league officials visited injured fans at hospitals and attended memorial services and funerals.[20] Chiefs, Pirates and the PSL also established the Ellis Park Disaster Trust Fund to benefit families of the victims, which eventually received about R1.5 million in charitable contributions from the public.[21]

THE NGOEPE COMMISSION

On 20 April 2001, South African President Thabo Mbeki established a Commission of Inquiry into the disaster, chaired by Transvaal Judge-President Bernard M. Ngoepe. Mbeki's creation of the commission expressed the government's desire to find out what had happened and asked for recommendations to prevent similar tragedies in the future. 'The South African public want transparency, they want honest findings. We don't want findings by a commission which is set up to suit certain people', warned August Makalakalane, an ex-professional and media commentator. 'Officials who were responsible for the disaster have to come clean. We owe it to the families of the 43 people that died.'[22] However, prior to the investigations, comments by President Mbeki and other political leaders cast doubts on the extent to which the truth would be revealed. A Johannesburg city councillor, for example, told the press that 'it is imperative that we refrain from apportioning blame for this catastrophe'.[23] Mbeki's statement to the media that the commission 'mustn't point fingers' aroused great concerns that 'heads won't roll over the Ellis Park tragedy'.[24]

Indeed, the Ngoepe commission functioned as a truth-searching body that skilfully avoided apportioning blame on powerful soccer officials and stadium

112

owners. The commission's work began on 16 July 2001 and continued for ten weeks. Forty-seven witnesses testified at public hearings. Judge Ngoepe and Advocate I.A.M. Semenya, the second member of the commission, visited Ellis Park and also travelled to the United Kingdom, 'to learn from their experiences' of coping with football disasters.[25] The Commission compiled an interim report on 4 February 2002, which the government released to the public on the first anniversary of the tragedy. The commissioners signed the 130-page final report on 29 August 2002 and it appeared in print and electronic form a month later.[26]

The final report established important facts that helped to understand more clearly what led to the deadly stampede at Ellis Park. Specifically, the commission highlighted 14 contributing factors:

- poor forecast of match attendance
- failure to learn from the lessons of the past
- failure by the role players to clearly identify and designate areas of responsibility
- absence of overall command of the Joint Operation Centre
- inappropriate and untimely announcement that tickets were sold out
- failure to adhere to FIFA and SAFA guidelines
- unbecoming spectator behaviour
- sale of tickets at the venue and unreserved seating
- the use of teargas or a similar substance
- corruption on the part of certain members of security personnel
- dereliction of duty; failure to use the big screen
- inadequate public address system
- failure by the Public Order Police Unit to react timeously and effectively.[27]

'No single factor', the final report concluded, 'can be said to have been decisive: the disaster was the result of a combination of all of them, each having contributed to a lesser or greater extent.'[28] Based on these findings, the Ngoepe commission made numerous recommendations to prevent future disasters in South Africa. These prescriptions included both voluntary initiatives by league and clubs, and mandatory changes to improve the safety and security of spectators at high-risk matches.[29] In his final report, Justice Ngoepe recommended the professionalization of safety and security staff and that pre-event planning should be taken more seriously. A wide-ranging voluntaristic scheme encouraged advance ticket sales and use of reserved seating. It underlined the need for traffic control and adequate parking outside stadia. In highlighting the importance of ensuring the safety of supporters, the report called for an adequate public address system, use of a big screen outside the arena, body searches, preventing dangerous containers and weapons from entering the stadium, and keeping access ways clear at all times. In addition, the establishment of a central operations centre, the report advised, would guarantee proper crowd monitoring. Finally, Ngoepe recommended the creation of a PSL Safety Committee, to be headed by an experienced and independent (of soccer authorities) national safety officer. Together

113

with a concerted drive to educate crowds and improved fixture scheduling, these voluntary changes, Ngoepe argued, would make protecting spectators a primary interest of soccer bodies.[30]

The report did not stop at advocating self-regulation by clubs and the league; it also recommended the introduction of government legislation to regulate high-risk football matches in South Africa. The commission did not draft legislation, but limited itself to 'suggesting the framework, objectives and some of the aspects which need to be covered in the bill'.[31] The report noted how this Act must:

- identify the role players responsible for the safety and security of spectators
- certify stadia as suitable for high-risk matches
- create an inspectorate to certify and inspect stadia according to specific criteria
- make 'minimum security enforcement facilities' for stadia compulsory
- regulate employment and accountability of security personnel
- categorize matches according to the level of risk
- empower security personnel to remove unruly spectators and criminalize certain acts
- prohibit ticket 'scalping'
- enforce provisions and punish offenders.[32]

In other words, the proposed regulatory system for South African football – modelled on British football's post-Hillsborough reforms – emphasized accountability, standardization of safety standards and a tougher law-and-order approach with unruly fans.

The commission's major shortcomings were a conveniently relativistic explanation of the disaster and the disempowerment of victims' families. By focusing on the microscopic details of the event, it neglected to analyse the broader socio-economic and historical context of the tragedy. This extraordinarily narrow approach enabled the commission to give roughly equal weight to multiple causal factors rather than prioritizing specific individual and organizational responsibilities. Most importantly, the Ngoepe report found no criminal or civil liability, thereby shielding the Premier Soccer League, Kaizer Chiefs and Ellis Park management from prosecution. Some families threatened a civil suit but later abandoned the idea, probably due to lack of funds.[33] This was due in no small part to the fact that relatives received modest compensation payments from the Ellis Park Disaster Relief Fund, which amounted to roughly R15,000 for funeral expenses and a 'Christmas gift' of R2,500.[34]

Not only was the commission's analysis flawed, but the procedure for collecting evidence also came under scrutiny at the time of the investigation. Three days before public hearings began, for instance, very few of the bereaved knew about the official proceedings.[35] Some individuals aware of the inquiry found it extremely difficult to testify. Most notably, two survivors submitted sworn affidavits to the commission 'claiming they had been prevented from making submissions to, or even attending, the inquiry by staffers of the disaster fund'.[36] In the end, several survivors and relatives of the dead did speak before the commission. Veli Mpungose and others gave voice to their 'traumatic experiences'.[37] Alina Gwala of Sasolburg gave a harrowing account of how she anxiously tried to reach her husband on his cellular phone that night. 'I had been calling continuously when the mortuary worker [at the Hillbrow morgue] picked up Mfana's cell phone and asked me to describe what he was wearing. He then told me that he was no longer with us.'[38] These emotional contributions lent some legitimacy to the investigative process. Nonetheless, a legacy of bitterness towards the organizers of the match suggests that some victims' relatives, as well as football insiders, believe the commission delivered truth without justice. The Ngoepe report documented the immediate factors leading to the stampede, but these catalysts provided at best a partial explanation, one that deflected blame from those responsible for the death of 43 people.

BEYOND OFFICIAL INTERPRETATIONS

Despite the Ngoepe commission's absolution, the Premier Soccer League (PSL), which represented the South African Football Association (the country's supreme football authority), and Kaizer Chiefs, the home side, bear tremendous responsibility for the carnage. The decision by the PSL and Chiefs to stage such a crucial game mid-week at Ellis Park reflected, at best, a shocking lack of foresight and, at worse, sheer callousness. Chiefs vs. Pirates duels have long captured the country's imagination. South African football's greatest rivalry originated from a fractious split. Legendary Pirates striker Kaizer Motaung and flamboyant team manager Ewert 'The Lip' Nene, broke away from the parent club to form Kaizer XI in January 1970, renamed Kaizer Chiefs in 1971.[39] Distinctly separate supporter identities fuelled antagonism between the heavyweight clubs from Soweto. The skull-and-crossbones of Pirates seemed an apt symbol for a club often seen as thuggish by opposing fans.[40] Instead, the Amakhosi (Chiefs in Zulu) faithful adopted the V peace symbol and became known as 'hippies'.[41]

Historically, Chiefs vs. Pirates matches have been marred by disorder and unrest. The most deadly disaster in South African football before Ellis Park took place on 13 January 1991 at a packed Oppenheimer stadium in Orkney, where Chiefs and Pirates staged a pre-season friendly in front of 23,000 spectators. Forty-one people died as fans trampled and battered each other while fleeing knife-wielding thugs in the stands.[42] An internal league investigation conducted by R.D. Sishi, Cyril Kobus and Leon Hacker recommended that 'stairways, access ways and landings should be kept clear at all times' and that due to the 'fanatical support that Kaizer Chiefs and Orlando Pirates enjoy, it is essential to employ adequate numbers of security personnel ... [which] should always be visible to the spectators ... [and] monitor the [crowd's] behaviour'.[43] In the aftermath of the

Orkney disaster the recommended changes were not made. Overall, security at football matches in South Africa did not improve, probably owing to organizers' lack of concern for the safety of spectators.[44] More recently, there were the afore-mentioned problems at Ellis Park in October 1998. Disorder spoiled a Wednesday night match at FNB stadium on 29 November 2000, when 15,000–20,000 specta-tors made their way into the arena by tearing down perimeter fences and forcing gates open. That same month, a missile-throwing incident forced the abandon-ment of the Women's African Nations' Cup final between Nigeria and South Africa at Vosloorus stadium.[45]

Given the history of crowd trouble at marquee matches and the intense rivalry between Chiefs and Pirates, staging a dramatic contest with the league title on the line on a Wednesday at Ellis Park was an extraordinarily poor decision. This facil-ity could not handle such a huge crowd of people arriving at the end of the work-day with less than two hours to buy tickets and enter the arena. With the benefit of hindsight, current PSL boss Trevor Philips admitted that 'the game should never have been played on a Wednesday night'. Phillips went on to explain how 'they tried to have this game played mid-week at Ellis Park when I was first PSL chief [1998–2000], but I refused. "Not on my watch" I said, it's [Ellis Park] just too small and there's not enough time to get everybody in.'[46] However, the inex-perienced PSL chief at the time, Robin Petersen, who had held the position for about six months, decided to approve the mid-week evening derby. With the rela-tively safer, 80,000 capacity all-seater First National Bank stadium, located between Soweto and Johannesburg, available to house this game the choice of venue appeared at first glance to be questionable. However, this venue was ruled out by Chiefs because they believed that Pirates' magicians had 'treated' it with potent *umuthi* (propitiatory medicine).[47]

If the choice of date and venue seemed remarkably infelicitous, then the organizers' misjudgement of attendance was inexplicable. According to the Ngoepe commission, 'such a gross underestimation of possible attendance, must be seen as the fundamental cause of the tragedy'.[48] 'Everyone had to get there', reported *The Star*, 'if you missed this game, you had missed the lifeblood of soccer itself.'[49] People came from Gauteng (Johannesburg and Pretoria area) and from provinces several hundred kilometres away, such as KwaZulu-Natal, Mpumalanga and Limpopo. Predictably, trains, mini-buses and cars simulta-neously emptied legions of fans into the narrow streets of gritty Doornfontein, the neighbourhood that envelops the Ellis Park sports complex. Passion for the game inspired 34-year-old Gideon Mudau, a Sundowns supporter, to travel more than 300km from Kromdraai, Limpopo to Johannesburg that ill-fated evening. 'Soccer was a religion, and he laid down his life for it', said his brother Nkhitheni Mudau.[50]

Transcripts of three pre-game safety meetings that took place on 27 March, 3 April and 10 April acknowledged the high-risk nature of the match and expressed concerns about potential attendance figures.[51] But not all of those responsible for spectator safety took the discussions seriously.[52] The fact that neither PSL officials nor Public Order Policing representatives were present at the meeting on 3 April suggests a desultory interest in safety and security issues. Be that as it may, Ellis Park security paid special attention to patterns of crowd congestion at gates 4, 5 and 6 on the north side of the ground. At each of the pre-match operational meetings, stadium management and security companies suggested bringing a large mobile screen from neighbouring Johannesburg Stadium to Ellis Park. Apparently, live telecasts outside the arena had mollified people shut out of previous marquee games. At one of the pre-game security meetings, Ellis Park General Manager George Stainton warned how 'it makes sense to have the screen, but it will have a cost implication for Kaizer Chiefs'.[53] Putting profits before fans' safety, Chiefs refused to pay their half of the R50,000 cost. 'The idea of using the big screen', the Ngoepe report stated, 'was abandoned because of cost implications to Kaizer Chiefs.'[54] And so no screen was used.

Spectator safety ranks low in the priorities of South African football. As the Ngoepe commission pointed out, the long-standing tradition of having a general admission policy (rather than assigned seating) has complicated crowd control efforts and led to the over-selling of tickets at big matches. The Ngoepe report also chastised stadium security teams for not coordinating their efforts. PSL staff (lacking basic equipment such as two-way radios), contracted security and the South African Police Service did not communicate with each other. George Stainton told the Ngoepe commission, for example, that 'the match referee had no way of communicating with PSL officials and would not have been aware of the security situation at the time the match was to have started'.[55] People entered the stadium without tickets through some unmanned entry points. As the crowd swelled in size and tension rose outside the arena, security companies and PSL employees (without safety training) panicked and abandoned their posts. Inside the stadium, many PSL security men focused on the match instead of watching the crowd, which caused them to overlook or ignore distress signals from spectators in the stands.[56] An empty Joint Operations Centre, the lynchpin of crowd control and enforcement efforts at Ellis Park, symbolized a lack of centralized decision-making, as well as dereliction of duty on the part of security staff.

The undignified treatment of football customers at Ellis Park revealed a racial dimension to the events of 11 April 2001. Black spectators felt intimidated by stadium security, which included members of apartheid-era law enforcement agencies in its ranks. 'The ones wearing black uniforms and white helmets are the ones who caused the whole disaster', said Ntebaleng Shongoane, who attended with his brother Rakgabo, who died.[57] 'They were holding the electric shock batons and they were using them to intimidate people. I felt it and it was very, very painful and I understand why it made people get angry and push to get away.' Other testimonies reveal that this pattern of abuse was seemingly common at Ellis Park. 'The white securities are racists', said Shongoane, 'they treat a black man like a pig. At other venues you do not see this bad behaviour.'[58] In his testimony before the Ngoepe commission, Veli Mpungose, who lost his son Siphiwe, gave a deeply moving account of such racism. 'As we left the stadium after the stampede, the Wolf Security guards at the gates laughed at me and said I was lucky because I was able to see a Good Friday.'[59]

Compounding the problems caused by incompetent and derelict security staff, PSL gate attendants took cash bribes from fans. This behaviour is a regular feature of marquee matches in South Africa. A representative comment on what happened at Ellis Park came from Soweto resident Thapelo Ralesema: 'I arrived at the stadium at 19:35. I did not have a ticket, but I was positive that I would get inside.'[60] From previous experience, Ralesema knew he would find a way to get inside. He recalled how 'I was very very hungry for the game. I tried to force my way by pushing as I heard that there were no tickets available, but the securities denied me entry – until I popped out R40 and gave it to a security man as a bribe because I was very desperate to watch the game.' Ralesema added that 'the securities helped me get in, together with about six or seven supporters who had also bribed them'. Kaizer Chiefs, the PSL and the managers of Ellis Park all share responsibility for disregarding spectator safety and maintaining a climate of disorder and unaccountability.[61]

In addition to faulty organization of the sporting event itself, a social and political context plagued by material poverty and South Africa's racist past influenced the events of 11 April. Before the 1990s, the political and economic climate surrounding domestic football in South Africa made it impossible for clubs to own their grounds. As a black-dominated sport, soccer struggled to overcome apartheid barriers, which included laws preventing Africans from legally accumulating capital and from purchasing land in urban areas. The heavy burden of the past explains in part why – a decade after the onset of democracy – top sides like Chiefs and Pirates rent world-class stadiums from white-dominated rugby bodies. Ellis Park – home of the Transvaal Rugby Football Union – typifies this pattern. As renters, Kaizer Chiefs have few incentives to spend money on safety improvements; why invest capital on rented property? It can also be argued that Chiefs may prefer this arrangement because it allows the club to dodge responsibility and avoid liability if necessary.

Another palpable effect of a century of state racism and economic deprivation can be found in the limited disposable income available to black working-class supporters, a legacy which produced a tradition of purchasing tickets at the stadium on the day of the match.[62] The insecurity of living day-to-day makes it difficult for people to purchase tickets in advance. On weekends this propensity to buy tickets at the last minute poses fewer safety problems because spectators filter through the gates over a period of six or more hours. But for the game on Wednesday 11 April 2001, Chiefs sold less than 4,000 tickets in advance, which meant that more than 100,000 people expected to gain admission to a 62,000-capacity stadium in less than two hours.

THE LEGACY OF THE ELLIS PARK STADIUM DISASTER

Has football safety improved since the disaster of 11 April 2001 and, if so, to what extent? Senior league officials Bafana Dlamini and Ronnie Schloss have offered assurances that a system based on centralized command and greater accountability is being put into effect.[63] In their view, the coordination of security has improved, especially after the decision to put the highest-ranking officer from units of the South African Police Services or South African National Defence Forces in charge of overall security operations at big matches. This change could be significant in light of the tragic events of 11 April because the PSL, Chiefs and Ellis Park management had sharply diverging views on who was supposed to be responsible for security that evening. According to league sources, existing Joint Operation Centers have been refurbished and expanded and are manned at all times. The PSL believes that Chiefs' recent introduction of a policy of advance ticket sales through the club's official fan clubs around the country will assist in preventing future disasters. Finally, the PSL recently launched a Safety Committee, which established a new working relationship with Ellis Park stadium management in order to attenuate tensions between law enforcement contractors and predominantly black soccer crowds.

Many knowledgeable members of the local media, as well as players and fans, disagreed with this portrait of a voluntarily transformed approach to spectator safety. Veteran reporter Billy Cooper, who described covering the Ellis Park disaster as 'the worst experience of my life', seemed unsure about present-day conditions for football audiences: 'I pray it has improved'.[64] Anecdotal evidence compiled during the research for this study strongly suggests that the PSL continues to employ temporary male workers without training them in basic safety and security procedures. Siyabonga Mkhwanazi claims that the PSL 'pays them R50 and gives them a bib. That's it'.[65] The author's experience whilst attending the Telkom Charity Spectacular at FNB stadium on 2 August 2003 authenticated Mkhwanazi's observation. At this four-team one-day tournament, PSL stewards either failed to search fans at the gates or did so cursorily. Inside the arena, there was no reserved seating, fans blocked stairways, and security personnel watched the action on the pitch instead of monitoring the 60,000-plus spectators. Communication problems transpired when it took more than 15 minutes for stadium staff to fulfil a request by league officials to switch on the floodlights.

Sloppy organization and incompetent security have also marred recent international matches. On 30 April 2003, for instance, about 20,000 people attended a South Africa-Jamaica friendly at Cape Town's Athlone stadium.[66] A ticket policy of unreserved seating, combined with scarce signage and lackadaisical event planning, led to dangerous congestion outside the gates, especially at the main grandstand. Unprepared security personnel failed to communicate properly with fans. On at least two occasions, police officers fired tear gas to disperse an increasingly frustrated and rambunctious crowd. In the end, many ticketed spectators endured hour-long delays to gain access to the arena, thereby missing portions of the first half.

There have been other indicators that lessons have not been learned from the Ellis Park disaster. The much-vaunted PSL Safety Committee, established in the wake of the tragedy, has failed to live up to expectations lacking, as it does, the independent, experienced national safety officer recommended by Justice Ngoepe. In sum, the accumulated documentary and circumstantial evidence strongly suggests that self-regulation, as recommended by the Ngoepe commission, has had little, if any, impact on stadium security in South Africa. In fact, protection of soccer fans and the development of a culture of safety remains a marginal concern for top-flight clubs, football authorities, and the government. As of January 2004, a football safety bill has yet to be introduced in the South African Parliament.

CONCLUSION

From scheduling a high-risk weeknight match at Ellis Park to inept security and widespread corruption, Kaizer Chiefs and the PSL share enormous responsibility for the catastrophic events of 11 April. The extent to which financial motivations tainted decision-making is jarring. Profiteering motivated Chiefs' refusal to pay for the installation of a big screen outside the stadium. The PSL failed to train its security personnel, viewing it as an expensive drain on its financial bottom line. Greed led to the overselling of tickets. And while Kaizer Chiefs earned around R1 million for staging the tragic derby, neither the clubs nor the PSL contributed any money to the Ellis Park Disaster Trust Fund.[67] The unwillingness of Chiefs, Pirates and the league to support the victims' families clearly illustrates the callousness of the organizers. This conduct also calls attention to how the sport's powerbrokers in South Africa exploit fans' visceral passion for the game. Thanks to the Ngoepe commission's careful whitewash, the role players most at fault for the death of 43 people dodged responsibility, received protection from legal action, and swiftly resumed a business-as-usual approach.

The televised Ellis Park disaster stands as a shocking reminder of how South African football repeats mistakes of the past. From the 1991 Orkney tragedy, to the violent incidents at Ellis Park in 1998, FNB Stadium and Vosloorus in 2000, faulty organization and inadequate security have played a larger role than unruly spectator behaviour in causing disorder, damage and deaths at local football grounds. Given football organizers' failure to learn lessons from history, it is hardly surprising that South African fans maintain a cavalier attitude in relation to stadium safety. Simron Tigerls, whose 30-year-old younger brother Danny perished at Ellis Park, captured the resignation of some black fans when he said: 'It was an accident. If it had to happen it happened. I accept it.'[68] As historian Norman Baker astutely pointed out in a study of the 1946 Bolton soccer disaster, this fatalistic response may belie a profound understanding of how the dangerous conditions of black working-class leisure are 'merely an expression of how things were, part of a natural order about which little could be done'.[69]

An official statement released by the ruling African National Congress the day after the disaster affirmed that the deaths of soccer fans in Johannesburg 'will take a long time to be erased from our memories'.[70] But three years later the victims have vanished from memory. Jacob Thabethe, who lost his 23-year-old grand-daughter Thandi at Ellis Park, felt betrayed by the PSL: 'They have totally aban-doned us, hoping that the nation will forget about the event.'[71] On the second anniversary of the tragedy, the PSL, Chiefs and Pirates organized a memorial service without bothering to inform the families of the deceased. During a visit to Ellis Park in August 2003, the author had to strain to catch a glimpse of an austere mural listing the names of the dead on a concrete pillar forty feet above Gate 4. The haunting words of a South African reporter writing in the immediate after-math of the disaster came to mind: 'I wasn't there, but I can still feel the pain, the despair, the anguish. I can smell the blood of hopelessness. I dream of the horror. The suffering permeates my body, my entire being. The screams of terror rever-berate in my head like thudding bullets. And the loss, oh the loss, sets off an explo-sion of anger within my soul. I am angry.'[72] Has South Africa done enough to avoid a disastrous repetition of Ellis Park? According to Mark Gleeson, an expert South African football commentator and correspondent for Reuters and the British Broadcasting Corporation, 'Ellis Park was not even a hiccup. The train of indif-ference continues on its tracks.'[73]

NOTES

1. The author wishes to thank the Eastern Kentucky University Research Committee for funding this study and the following individuals for their support in South Africa: Clinton Asary, Saleem and Shireen Badat, David Coplan, Glenn Cowley, Jermaine Craig, Mark Gleeson, Verne Harris, Richard Maguire, Siyabonga Mkhwanazi, and Rodney and Ayesha Reiners. The paper benefited from comments by Robert Topmiller, Paul Darby, Mark Gleeson, Rodney Reiners and Catherine Foley. I dedicate this piece to the victims of the Ellis Park disaster (see Appendix).
2. *The Star*, 20 April 2001.
3. For in-depth coverage of the Ellis Park disaster and its aftermath see the electronic archive at: http://www.iol.co.za/html/features/ellis_park_disaster/index.php. For intimate portraits of the victims see *The Star*, 20 April 2001.
4. Mark Gleeson, 'History of the Castle League' (manuscript), p.93. My thanks to Mark Gleeson for shar-ing his manuscript with me.
5. Final Report, Commission of Inquiry into the Ellis Park Stadium Soccer Disaster of 11 April 2001 (29 Aug. 2002), pp.23–9 (hereafter the Ngoepe Commission Report). The report is available online at: http://www.gov.za/reports/2002/finalellispark.pdf.
6. *Kick Off*, 14 May 2001.
7. Ngoepe Commission Report, p.53.
8. Ibid., pp.58–64, 78.
9. *The Star*, 12 April 2001.
10. *Kick Off*, 14 May 2001.
11. Interview with Siyabonga Mkhwanazi, Johannesburg, 6 Aug. 2003.
12. *The Star*, 20 April 2001. Another member of the family, Calvin Arnolds (Rosswin's uncle), also perished.
13. This sentence paraphrases a headline in *The Star*, 21 Aug. 2001.

14. Interview with Clinton Asary, PSL Media Officer, Johannesburg, 2 Aug. 2003. Information corroborated by other interviews, video footage and media reports.
15. *Kick Off*, 14 May 2001.
16. South African Broadcasting Corporation, television broadcast of Chiefs vs. Pirates, 11 April 2001.
17. Ibid.
18. *Kick Off*, 14 May 2001.
19. Interview with Asary.
20. *The Star*, 13 April, 20 April 2001.
21. *The Star*, 13 June 2001.
22. *Kick Off*, 14 May 2001.
23. *The Star*, 21 April 2001.
24. Mbeki quoted in *Kick Off*, 14 May 2001. Second quote is by Mike McGrath, *Sunday Tribune*, 14 April 2001.
25. Ngoepe Commission Report, p.7.
26. A detailed analysis of the Ngoepe Commission Report need not detain us here. For the purpose of this brief study, it is more important to weigh its major accomplishments and shortcomings.
27. 'Factors which preceded the event and which led to the tragedy, and mismanagement', cited in Ngoepe Commission Report, pp.65–84.
28. Ngoepe Commission Report, pp.65–6.
29. Ngoepe Commission Report, pp.88–130.
30. Ngoepe Commission Report, pp.99–120.
31. Ngoepe Commission Report, p.121.
32. Ngoepe Commission Report, pp.121–30.
33. Telephone interview with Simron Tigerls whose brother died at Ellis Park, 11 Aug. 2001.
34. *The Star*, 11 April 2003. Simron Tigerls told me that his family had received R22,000 in total.
35. *The Star*, 13 June 2001.
36. *The Star*, 15 July 2001.
37. Ngoepe Commission Report, p.6.
38. *The Star*, 20 April 2001.
39. For more details on the formation of Chiefs see Sekola Sello, *Chiefs: 21 Glorious Years: The Official History of SA's Glamour Football Club* (Johannesburg: Skotaville, 1991).
40. Richard Maguire, 'The People's Club: A Social and Institutional History of Orlando Pirates Football Club, 1937–1973' (BA Hons thesis, University of the Witwatersrand, 1991), p.92.
41. James North, 'Sports: The Kaizer Chiefs', in J. North, *Freedom Rising* (New York: Macmillan, 1985), p.147.
42. Ngoepe Commission Report, pp.22–3.
43. Ngoepe Commission Report, p.23.
44. *Kick Off*, 14 May 2001. In response to requests for access to the 1991 Sishi commission report, the PSL claimed it could not find a copy of the document.
45. 'Brick-hurling fans halt Banyana final', *Sunday Times*, 26 Nov. 2000. Available at: http://www.suntimes.co.za/2000/11/26/news/news02.htm.
46. Interview with Trevor Phillips, FNB stadium at Soccer City, 2 Aug. 2003.
47. For more details on the use of magic in South African football see Peter Alegi, *Laduma! Soccer, Politics and Society in South Africa* (Pietermaritzburg: University of KwaZulu Natal Press, 2004).
48. Ngoepe Commission Report, p.67.
49. *The Star*, 12 April 2001.
50. *The Star*, 20 April 2001.
51. Ngoepe Commission Report, pp.33–47.
52. Ngoepe Commission Report, p.102. Interview with Mark Gleeson, Cape Town, 20 Aug. 2003.
53. Ngoepe Commission Report, p.47.
54. Ngoepe Commission Report, p.81.
55. *The Star*, 18 July 2001.
56. Ngoepe Commission Report, p.57.
57. *Kick Off*, 14 May 2001.
58. Ibid.
59. *The Star*, 28 Aug. 2001.
60. *Kick Off*, 14 May 2001. All other Ralesema quotes in the paragraph come from this source.

61. Ngoepe Commission Report, pp.68–9.
62. Ngoepe Commission Report, pp.76–8. For documentary evidence on South African fan culture in the 1980s see: Papers of the Football Association of Natal and KwaZulu, PC 114/1/8/1: Operations Review of the National Professional Soccer League, Alan Paton Centre, University of Natal, Pietermaritzburg, Aug. 1983.
63. Interviews with Bafana Dlamini and Ronnie Schloss, FNB stadium at Soccer City, 2 Aug. 2003.
64. Interview with Billy Cooper, Johannesburg, 6 Aug. 2001.
65. Interview with Mkhwanazi.
66. George Dearnaley, 'Can We Really Host the 2010 World Cup?' (manuscript). I am grateful to Richard Maguire for giving me a copy of this unpublished essay.
67. *Kick Off*, 14 May 2001.
68. Interview with Simron Tigerls.
69. N. Baker, 'Have They Forgotten Bolton?' *The Sports Historian*, 18, 1 (1998), 120–51. Electronic version accessed on 15 June 2003 at: http://www2.umist.ac.uk/sport/baker.html.
70. *The Star*, 12 April 2001.
71. *The Star*, 9 April 2002.
72. *Cape Argus*, 19 April 2001.
73. Interview with Gleeson.

8

A Context of Vulnerability: The Zambian Air Disaster, 1993

PAUL DARBY

INTRODUCTION

In the introduction to this volume the editors explored the difficulties associated with establishing what actually constitutes a 'disaster'. It was argued that this conceptual problem can be overcome by classifying disasters in qualitative rather than quantitative terms. This makes it less problematic to define single events involving relatively small numbers of deaths, such as those described throughout this volume, as disasters. However, in Africa or at least sub-Saharan Africa, difficulties in defining loss of life in football-related settings as 'disasters' remain. The term disaster, when used in the African context, is usually synonymous with tragedies that have brought about a loss of life and suffering on an almost unimaginable scale. These include the famine in Ethiopia in 1984–85 which resulted in almost one million deaths, the genocide in Rwanda in 1994 which claimed around 800,000 lives in just over 100 days and the AIDS pandemic currently sweeping the continent which left an estimated 2.4 million dead in 2003 alone.[1]

In purely quantitative terms it may appear absurd and perhaps even obscene to apply the same descriptor to incidents in football-related contexts in Africa involving losses of life that 'only' reach double figures. Furthermore, in a continent where life expectancy is relatively short and the value of human life, at least outside the immediate family circle or local community, appears to be so cheap, the levels of mourning, media coverage and analysis that such events generate seems incongruous. This raises questions about the validity or legitimacy of the process whereby events in or around football matches in Africa that result in multiple deaths and injury are regarded, described and constructed as disasters in the popular imagination in the locales where they occur and far beyond. My argument here is that it is appropriate and accurate to describe such tragedies as disasters in the African sense of the word because they are on the same causal continuum or are at least linked to the same economic, social and political processes that have contributed to other, quantitatively larger African 'disasters'.

At the core of many African disasters in the post-colonial period has been the difficult transition from European colony to independent state and the, at times, debilitating legacy of European colonialism. Flagrant misuse of political power by often autocratic heads of states, corrupt regimes, weak economic and administrative infrastructures, massive foreign debts, near bankruptcy, rampant inflation, parochial ethnic and cultural attitudes and tensions, and spiralling population growth have not only been characteristics of post independence African nations, but have also loomed large as the context to many African disasters. Whilst the combination of ingredients underpinning disasters in Africa has varied according to specific locales and time periods, many have involved variants of a similar recipe.

As the first half of this study demonstrates, these characteristics or ingredients have featured, to varying degrees, in an increasing number of incidents leading to loss of life within African football stadia. However, football-related disasters in Africa have not only been confined to the stadium. On 28 April 1993, 18 members of the Zambian national football squad along with a number of technical staff and football administrators were killed when the aeroplane carrying them to a World Cup qualifying game in Senegal crashed into the sea off the coast of Gabon. An analysis of the context to, and aftermath of, this particular disaster constitutes the focus of this study. Although the air crash led to a relatively small number of deaths, even in comparison with some of Africa's other football-related disasters, its place in this book and its classification as a disaster is justified by the fact that its causes are rooted in the same context as other African disasters. The fact that the Zambian national team were travelling to their match on a military *cargo* plane reveals that the causes of this crash cannot glibly be put down to technical problems, human error or accident. Indeed, as the narrative contained in this study reveals, the types of broader economic, political, administrative and structural problems that have underpinned stadium-based tragedies in Africa as well as many other larger, African disasters, were as much a cause of the Zambian air crash as any mechanical or human failings that occurred on the plane.

ANALYTICAL FRAME

Now that the status of the Zambian air crash as an 'African' disaster has been established, it is necessary to say something about the analytical frame specifically employed in this study. The analyses here adopt a liberal and inclusive conceptualization of 'disaster', which classifies a disaster in qualitative terms and as being an event that is not restricted to a particular place or time, but rather as something that has phases of development. The traditional conception of disaster is that it is an unforeseeable and uncontrollable act of God. As the field of disaster studies has developed and become more sophisticated, alternative conceptions of disaster have emerged which explain them as long-term processes involving contexts of political, social and economic vulnerability or predisposition.[2] This approach has been particularly evident in some of the key academic analyses of sport and leisure disasters. For example, Hartley's assessment of the 1989 Hillsborough and *Marchioness* disasters[3] demonstrates that the causes of these events extend well beyond the surge of football fans onto terracing or the moment of impact between a pleasure boat and a dredger. As her work shows, any accurate reading of what led to these tragedies must account for the 'broader political, economic contexts of vulnerability or predisposition' that existed prior to the actual incidents.[4] Scraton *et al.*'s work on the Hillsborough disaster and its aftermath[5] extends this notion of disasters as having phases of development, and identifies eight stages ranging from: historical context; immediate context; immediate circumstances; the moment; rescue and evacuation; immediate aftermath; short-term aftermath and the long-term aftermath. This study adopts the analytical approach of Hartley and Scraton *et al.* by explaining the Zambian air disaster as an event that had phases of development. Although the moment and post-moment phases are discussed here, this study focuses on the broader context of vulnerability or predisposition that precipitated this event.

The central argument of this study is that the administrative, financial and structural problems afflicting Zambian football in the period leading up to the plane crash rendered the national team at worst predisposed, or at best vulnerable, to the events that transpired on 28 April 1993. The first half of this article deals exclusively with the context that led to the disaster and, in doing so, covers the first two elements of Scraton *et al.*'s stages of a disaster (historical context and immediate circumstances). The second half deals with a series of issues that can be located within the remaining stages of Scraton *et al.*'s model. Thus, the *moment* of the disaster is described and the immediate and short-term aftermath is accounted for by assessing the response of the Zambian football authorities, the Zambian government and the Zambian people in the days, weeks and months following the disaster. The long-term aftermath of the disaster is analysed by examining the ways in which the government dealt with the official inquiry into the plane crash and explores the unsatisfactory manner in which the victims were commemorated and their families compensated for their loss. However, before turning to these specific concerns, it will be useful to explore the extent to which the notion of context of vulnerability or predisposition can be employed to explain some of the other disasters that have blighted African football.

THE MANAGEMENT AND DEVELOPMENT OF AFRICAN FOOTBALL: A CONTEXT OF VULNERABILITY?

There have been events resulting in serious injury and loss of life within the African game since the 1970s. In the most serious of these early disasters, 48 spectators were killed when a barrier and wall collapsed as they were attempting to enter a match at the Zamalek stadium in Cairo, Egypt.[6] During the last decade of the twentieth century incidents involving significant loss of life at football matches throughout the continent became increasingly common and over 70 spectators are known to have died at various African football venues in this period.[7] Important lessons on managing large and excitable groups of football fans inside stadia were clearly not learned by those charged with ensuring the safety of spectators, and in the opening years of the twenty-first century, the continent witnessed some of its most serious football disasters.[8] In Africa's worst football tragedy, 130 people died on 9 May 2001 when over-zealous policing involving the indiscriminate firing of tear gas canisters into the crowd led to a stampede for the *locked* exit gates at a match at the Accra Sports stadium in Ghana between local rivals Accra Hearts of Oak and Asante Kotoko. That disaster brought the total number of people killed at African football stadia between April and May 2001 alone to over 180. Although all of the disasters that have blighted African football since the 1970s have each had very specific causes, the underdeveloped nature of football's infrastructure in Africa combined with poor management and financial constraints have been common factors in the majority of these disasters. As such, underdevelopment, administrative malaise and economic difficulties in African football can be described as the context of vulnerability or predisposition within which these events have occurred. Thus, in keeping with the analytical premise set out at the beginning of this study, any attempt to understand the causes of football-related disasters in Africa, including the Zambian air crash, must be cognisant of this context.

At the same time that Africans were losing their lives in football-related disasters, the continent's top national teams were making significant progress at the very highest levels of the international game. African players were increasingly plying their trade in the elite leagues of Europe and were widely acclaimed for their performances.[9] African football administrators were also making advances and their lobbying for greater democratization and equality within the context of FIFA was bearing significant fruit.[10] Superficially at least, it appeared that African football was in a relatively healthy state. However, a more penetrating analysis of football development on that continent reveals that progress on the field of play and in FIFA's corridors of power may only have served to deflect attention away from the many problems afflicting the African game. Indeed, the fact that Africans were dying in football-related contexts with increasing and alarming regularity highlights that below the veneer of success in the international playing and administrative arena, the game in Africa was seriously underdeveloped in terms of infrastructure, organization and funding. This is a view subscribed to by Emmanuel Maradas who, in the aftermath of the Ellis Park and Accra Sports Stadium disasters in 2001, argued that,

> The crisis (in the African game) was for a long time hidden by the success of Africa's professional footballers, playing for the most part for clubs in Europe. But it has been brought starkly into perspective by the series of tragedies that shook the African game in April and May (2001).[11]

The development of football in Africa has been affected, to varying degrees, by factors over which those responsible for the African game have had little control. Chief amongst these has been the precarious state of many African economies. Massive economic disparities between the first and the third world and weak and unstable economies have long had a deleterious impact on African football. This is a point encapsulated by Bobby Charlton, the ex-England international, who has been involved in a number of football development programmes in the third world:

> The only problem with African football is money. Just that one word. It is their downfall because they just don't have enough of it. And because of that, their best players leave home to play in Europe. On top of that, the national sides do not have the money to afford to travel and play the games that they would like.[12]

One by-product of this state of affairs has been an inability on the part of African football federations to invest the finances necessary to rectify the poor state of repair of many African stadia, particularly those within sub-Saharan Africa. Without adequate financial investment it has proved extremely difficult to provide an entirely safe environment in which to watch football matches and, as highlighted above, this has had grave consequences for African football spectators.

Despite the financial problems that are faced by African football federations, it would be erroneous to claim that the difficulties that have confronted the African game are solely a consequence of external pressures. Internal administrative malaise has long been one of the key constraining factors in the development of African football and has, by implication, had a negative impact on the extent to which national federations have been able to ensure spectator safety. According to Faouzi Mahjoub, the respected Moroccan sports journalist, the organization and management of African football, at all levels, has suffered from what he describes as a 'culture of mediocrity'.[13] Mahjoub elaborates on what he means by this by arguing that 'imperfection is a fact of life in African soccer. It is accepted to the point of institutionalisation, and nobody takes up cudgels to fight it.'[14] In the discourse surrounding some of the more recent stadium disasters in Africa evidence of such 'imperfection' and its 'institutionalisation' is stark. For example, in various journalistic accounts of the Accra Sports and Ellis Park stadium disasters, poor stadium management and crowd control, lax ticketing arrangements, indifference to safety, neglect, ineptitude and disinterest on the part of football authorities were cited as contributory factors in the 173 deaths that occurred as a consequence of these incidents.[15] Indeed, in his assessment of the causes of these and other disasters in 2001, Mark Gleeson, the eminent South African football journalist, partially attributed the deaths to an 'administrative malaise which continues to retard the progress of African soccer'.[16]

Of course, the types of administrative deficiencies on the part of football authorities that potentially place the safety of football fans in danger are not exclusive to Africa, and it would be Eurocentric to say that they are. Indeed, as this collection illustrates, at the root of virtually every football-related disaster in the twentieth century there has been varying degrees of ineptitude and inertia on the part of those charged with ensuring fan safety. However, there are a number of issues that are more specific to the African context, or that have at least been more keenly felt there, that have not only hampered the development of the game but have also reduced the capacity of those involved in the running of the game to assure the safety of football fans and players. The most significant of these have been corruption and government interference in the administration of the game.

In recent years the levels of income that African football federations have been able to generate from football-related activity have increased markedly. Sponsorship of national competitions has become much more apparent and the levels of direct financial subsidies to African federations from the world governing body have increased, particularly since the election of Sepp Blatter as FIFA President.[17] It might have been hoped that these developments would go some way towards forging the type of economic footing necessary to improve stadium safety and management. However, the extent to which these funds have been used for these purposes has not only been undermined by the need to invest in other aspects of football development, but also by the endemic corruption that invariably characterizes the administration of the African game. As Sugden and Tomlinson have argued:

> quite often the money which should be spent on football development ends up in the pockets of corrupt administrators and government officials ... We could present material in support of this claim for almost every sub-Saharan African country.[18]

The debilitating effect that the instability of Africa's economic situation and the well-documented presence of corruption have had on the African game is augmented by government interference in football administration. Although most governments in Africa provide financial subsidies for the game and thus argue that they are entitled to play a central role in its running, the influence of leading politicians often creates havoc for the football authorities and destabilizes African football.[19]

As noted earlier, each particular football disaster in Africa has had its own specific causes. However, an unstable or weak economy, financial impropriety, government interference and a general 'culture of mediocrity' remain a central part of the context of vulnerability within which football-related disasters in Africa have occurred. This context of vulnerability is particularly evident in the Zambian air disaster and any reading or understanding of this tragic incident must take account of this context. Thus, this study now turns to assessing the broader financial, administrative and structural problems that afflicted Zambian football in the period leading up to 1993.

A PREDISPOSITION TO DISASTER? THE DECLINE OF ZAMBIAN FOOTBALL

The need to understand the longer-term context in which the Zambian air disaster occurred becomes clear when one considers the words of Mussa Kasonka, former treasurer of the Zambian Football Federation. He suggests that:

> The period from 1980 to 1993 was a difficult time for Zambian football. Economically it was not good and we also wrestled with administrative problems: Corruption and politicians who interfered with football matters ... the period turned out to be a build up to the saddest moment in our history.[20]

Although Zambia has never won the African Cup of Nations, nor qualified for the World Cup Finals, the national team was widely recognized as the main football force in southern Africa, at least until the return of South Africa to the world game.[21] Part of the reason for this was the support that the national team received from Dr Kenneth Kaunda, President of Zambia between 1964–91. Kaunda, like other leaders of fledgling independent African states, recognized the value of sport, and particularly football, in mobilizing popular support for their regimes and projecting themselves on the international stage.[22] Football rapidly acquired a prominent place in the priorities of the governments of these new states and, as a way of registering their status as liberated, fully independent nations, membership of the Confédération Africaine de Football (CAF) and the Fédération Internationale de Football Associations (FIFA) was sought quickly.[23] Thus, almost as soon as Kaunda was elected President in 1964, the Football Association of Zambia (FAZ) became affiliated to both CAF and FIFA. Such was his association with the Zambian team that the national side soon became popularly known as the 'KK Eleven'[24] and with his reputation linked to their progress, financial and technical support was made readily available to them. Prior to the mid-1980s the domestic club game in Zambia was also in a healthy state, with the lucrative state-owned copper mining industry,[25] particularly the conglomerate Zambia Consolidated Copper Mines Ltd (ZCCM), supporting teams financially and effectively running them as a social service. While this situation prevailed, FAZ and the clubs were able to invest in football development, and the structures that were put in place produced a steady stream of talented young footballers who went on to represent the national team at various levels.

With the stability of the Zambian game so clearly linked to the economic viability of the country's mining enterprises and the support of Kaunda's authoritarian regime, it is clear that if these companies experienced financial difficulties and/or Kaunda's leadership of the country was threatened then football would also suffer. This is exactly what happened. In the late 1980s Zambia experienced monumental political transformation and a downturn in economic fortunes. With the winds of democratic change blowing throughout the African continent in the late 1980s and early 1990s, Zambia found itself on the verge of its first democratic elections since 1963. When these elections took place in 1991 Kaunda was defeated by Frederick Chiluba, and Chiluba's Movement for Multiparty Democracy (MDD) replaced the previous regime in government.

When Chiluba came to power his most pressing task was the need to arrest an alarming economic slump that had seen Zambia become one of the poorest countries in Southern Africa.[26] Almost immediately Chiluba's government embarked on a programme of financial austerity that saw budget cuts and decreases in public expenditure. In such an environment it was unlikely that the government would sustain the same levels of investment in FAZ and the national team as had occurred in the Kaunda era. With the International Monetary Fund pressing for the privatization of the mining industry as part of Zambia's recovery programme, the domestic game's key funding stream was also threatened. Indeed, when privatization was first mooted and gradually introduced in the 1990s the industry saw little benefit in continuing to support football clubs, and those companies that had previously been happy to bankroll the club game scaled down their levels of investment. As a result the domestic game quickly went into a state of free fall. For example, in the 1992 season 16 clubs withdrew from the national league because of financial difficulties and ZCCM announced that the five professional teams that it supported would be reverting to amateur status for the 1993 season.[27] With limited opportunities for earning a living from the game, the most talented Zambian footballers began to migrate to other national leagues in the region, which further contributed to the underdevelopment of the domestic game.[28] Provision for youth football, which had previously been organized through a schools football programme and was supported by the mining industry, also suffered under Zambia's economic and political transformation and it too experienced financial cut backs.

Although Zambian club teams struggled to keep pace with their African counterparts in intercontinental competition, the impact of these financial and structural problems appeared to be less sharply felt by the national team which continued to more than hold its own in international fixtures. The key reason for this was the fact that the last generation of players to come through the old youth programmes were a particularly talented group of individuals. Indeed, by the early years of the 1990s, Zambia had a team that was not only capable of consistently taking on and beating the best in Africa but was also on the verge of World Cup qualification. However, in much the same way that the success of elite African football countries in recent years has masked the problems inherent in the running of the game throughout Africa, the continued strength of the Zambian national team on the field of play only served to deflect attention away from the mounting difficulties faced by FAZ. By the beginning of 1993 these difficulties reached a crisis point when the weakness of the Zambian currency, the Kwacha, in foreign exchange markets, and the government's decision to significantly reduce levels of expenditure on football, left FAZ in an extremely precarious position.

The timing of this economic crisis could not have been worse for FAZ because the national team's quest to reach the African Cup of Nations was reaching a conclusion and they were about to embark on the second phase of their World Cup qualifying campaign. Successful qualification for the continent's most prestigious tournament and for the international game's most lucrative competition were crucial for the future sustainability and development of the Zambian game. What was needed in this period was a strong, competent and stable administration that was able to explore and implement ways of coping with the financial pressures on Zambian football. However, the types of administrative deficiencies that constrain the game in many African countries have also featured prominently in Zambian football, and this made it difficult for FAZ to respond to the crisis of the early 1990s. Chief amongst these difficulties was a lack of stability and continuity at the highest levels of football administration. For example, since 1975 successive FAZ boards have been unable, largely due to government interference, to conclude a single term of office. These same problems coupled with financial impropriety raised their head again in August 1992 when the FAZ chairman, Jabes Zulu, along with his deputy, Wilfrid Monani, were suspended for alleged misappropriation of funds raised from Zambia's participation at the South Korea President's Cup in July.[29] The situation that Zambian football found itself in, and the reasons behind this predicament, are aptly summed up by Pongo Liwewe: 'Take an economy on its knees … add administrative incompetence and political interference; put self-interest above the collective good, and season the mixture with despair. That is the recipe that has brought Zambian soccer to its knees.'[30] On the 28 April 1993 these ingredients, this context of vulnerability, conspired tragically to cause one of Africa's worst football-related disasters.

THE ZAMBIAN AIR DISASTER AND NATIONAL MOURNING

Two days after beating Mauritius to move to the top of their African Cup of Nations qualifying group, the Zambian national team began their ill-fated journey from Lusaka to Dakar where they were due to face Senegal in the second round of their World Cup qualifying campaign. Unable to raise the funds to fly the team commercially or charter a passenger plane, FAZ arranged for the trip to occur on a Zambian Air force DHC-5D Buffalo cargo plane. Given that the plane was designed for short haul flights, three refuelling stops were built into the schedule. The 18 players, two coaches, team doctor, three FAZ officials, one journalist and five crew that made up the party eventually took off from Lusaka following a six hour delay. The plane touched down in Brazzaville five hours later for the first refuelling stop and a series of technical checks. The journey resumed with a two-hour flight to Libreville, the capital of Gabon from where the plane was due to depart for Abidjan in Cote d'Ivoire before flying to Dakar the following day.

132

During brief technical checks the Libreville ground crew identified a problem with the left engine. The Zambian air crew was informed but, despite attempts to dissuade them from doing so, the plane took off for the penultimate leg of its journey. This failure in crew coordination, a common factor in contemporary air disasters,[31] had dire consequences because minutes after the plane took off it plunged into the Atlantic Ocean killing all on board.[32]

When the official news of the crash broke in Lusaka on the lunchtime news the following day, an atmosphere of shock and disbelief descended throughout the country. As the realization set in that Zambia had lost a group of footballers who were on the verge of continental and international acclaim, a sense of national loss became palpable. Frederick Chiluba cut short a tour of East African states and in an emotional televised address to the country he announced that the deceased would be honoured with a week-long period of national mourning. Following consultation with the families of the dead, it was also decided that a state funeral would replace the norm of private, family-oriented funerals. The growing feeling of national loss and grief was very much in evidence when the bodies of the deceased were brought back to Lusaka from Libreville. The Zambian President was present when the Zambia Airways *passenger* plane bearing the remains of the players and officials touched down at the international airport.

The route from the airport to the Independence Stadium, where the bodies were to lie in state, was thronged with thousands of mourners who had lined the streets to pay their respects to a group of players who had struggled in adversity to bring a sense of national pride and self-respect to Zambian citizens. Thirty five thousand people awaited the bodies of the dead in the national stadium, many of them staying overnight until the state funeral the following day. The funeral itself was an intensely emotional affair and during the seven hour service there were very public expressions of grief from the highest ranking members of the government, from FAZ officials and finally from fans of the Zambian national team. Julio Chiluba, former secretary of FAZ, aptly sums up the scene in the national stadium on the day of the funeral: 'President Chiluba was the most important speaker, but several times his speech was interrupted by tears. Everyone could only stand and weep. This feeling of grief ... was unprecedented in the history of our country.'[33] When the service concluded the bodies were laid to rest at a site just outside the northern end of the stadium.

COMMEMORATING *NATIONAL* HEROES

Burying the victims of the accident in the vicinity of the national stadium was clearly an act of commemoration on the part of FAZ and the government. Further efforts in this regard were evident with the construction of a monument at the site of the graves and the decision to hold an annual memorial service. These acts were aimed at ensuring that the players and coaches would long remain in the consciousness of Zambian football fans and citizens. In the immediate aftermath of the disaster the players and staff were elevated to the status of national heroes who had perished while in service to the country. Indeed, the burial site has since come to be popularly referred to as 'Heroes' Acre'. This status, real or imagined, was clearly central both to the desire to honour their memories and to the collective outpouring of grief that followed the disaster. Whilst the victims remained in the consciousness of the nation, in the months that followed the crash the emotional intensity of the grieving began to wane. This is a natural part of any grieving process and as this process was lived out the extent to which the victims of the plane crash remained at the forefront of the minds of Zambian football fans and administrators declined. The ability of FAZ and the population to come to terms with, and in many ways move on from, the disaster was aided not only by the passage of time but also by the decision to resume Zambia's African Nations Cup and World Cup qualifying campaign so soon after the crash. Following emergency consultations between the FAZ executive and the Zambian Government, a panel of players, built around those who played their club football in Europe and who had not been on the flight to Senegal, was hastily put together. An intensive period of training in Denmark[34] ensued and the new squad remarkably secured qualification for the Nations Cup with a 3-0 home win against South Africa and a 1-1 draw in Harare against Zimbabwe. Qualification and Zambia's subsequent performance in the 1994 tournament where they finished runners-up ensured that Zambians again began to associate football with feelings of pride and self-respect rather than the grief and sorrow that defined their identification with the national team in the aftermath of the crash.

For those who had lost their loved ones in the disaster the success of the newly constituted national team would have done little to alleviate their sense of bereavement. What was more important to the families of the dead was having their questions surrounding the causes of the crash answered and obtaining adequate compensation for the loss of the main earners in their family unit. The words and actions of FAZ and the government in the days and weeks after the crash may have instilled confidence in the families that these things would be forthcoming. However, once the intensity of the initial period of mourning had passed it began to appear that this confidence may have been misplaced and that the air disaster was becoming less of a national priority. The most immediate sign of this was the fact that after the first memorial service, the government informed the families that it was no longer in a position to make a contribution to any future memorials. FAZ also failed to step in with a commitment to take the lead in organizing future events and responsibility for organizing and raising the funds necessary for any subsequent services was passed onto the families and the national team's official supporters association, the Chipolopolo Soccer Fans Association.[35] This failure to adequately support the memorial beyond the short-term aftermath of the disaster was perceived as disrespectful by the families and served to detract from FAZ's and the government's earlier efforts to honour the memories of the victims.[36]

In much the same way that the cause of the disaster can be found in Zambia's broader economic plight, so too can the cause of the government's and FAZ's inability or unwillingness to commemorate the victims of one of the country's most tragic episodes. Chiluba's government simply found itself preoccupied with its macro economic and social reforms as well as its desire to remain in office. For its part, FAZ struggled financially and administratively in the period following the crash[37] and concerned itself in the main with building a national team capable of helping it secure qualification for the game's most lucrative international tournaments. In such an environment, the ability and, perhaps, the desire of FAZ and the government to act in a way that continued to honour the memories of the dead gradually declined. It should also be noted that support from the general Zambian population has also declined since the mid-1990s and attendance at the annual memorial service has dwindled in recent years. The reasons for this are also partially tied up with Zambia's socio-economic condition. Ordinary Zambians, 67 per cent of whom were living below the poverty line by 1997,[38] have found their lives dominated by formidable economic difficulties. Although many continue to have sympathy for the victims of the air crash, their ability and desire to honour the memories of the dead through attendance or financial contributions to the memorial service have simply been replaced by the demands of day to day survival.

OFFICIAL INQUIRY AND COMPENSATION

In the aftermath of the funeral, difficult questions were posed of FAZ and the government by the families of the dead and their legal representatives about the circumstances of the accident and around the issue of why the team had travelled to the game on a short haul military plane. The financial plight of FAZ, combined with the reduced levels of investment in sport by the government in light of Zambia's economic situation, were clearly the key factors in the decision to fly on the DHC-5D Buffalo. Answers surrounding the precise cause of the accident were going to prove to be more difficult to deal with, particularly when it became known that three similar planes in Zambia in the previous ten years had been involved in accidents resulting in 32 deaths.[39] There were also reports that an air controller had raised serious concerns about the air-worthiness of the plane during its refuelling stop in Brazzaville and that these concerns were ignored.[40]

An inquiry involving officials from Zambia, Gabon and the aircraft's Canadian manufacturer De Havilland was launched but progress was slow, largely because of political wrangling between the Zambian and Gabonese investigators. It soon became clear that the families would have a long wait for the sense of closure that might come with the completion of the inquiry and publication of the official report. The report was due to be released in May 1996 but was delayed initially on grounds that the inaccessibility of the wreckage had made it difficult for the investigative team to conclude their work. Disputes about the high cost of paying for the report and the financial contribution of air force investigators led to further delays, and the revised June 1997 date for publication of the findings of the inquiry passed without action. As the ninth anniversary of the crash loomed the government came under increasing pressure from opposition MPs to release the official report whilst the families of the victims took the opportunity of this anniversary to threaten to take the government to the International Court of Justice. Despite this threat the Zambian authorities continued to procrastinate and more than ten years after the accident the relatives still wait to find out the precise cause of the deaths of their loved ones.

In the harsh economic realities of everyday life in Zambia, the issue of financial support has been equally pressing for the bereaved relatives but their quest for appropriate compensation was frustrated for almost as long as their calls for the publication of the report on the causes of the disaster. As part of the initial response to the disaster the government and FAZ agreed that any acts of commemoration should go beyond the symbolic and offer some sort of practical assistance to the bereaved families. Thus, shortly after the crash a trust fund was established to help provide financial support for the families and look after the longer-term interests of the children of the victims. This fund amounted to Kwacha 119.6 million (£140,000), and additional funds were raised through a benefit game organized by FIFA, played in Italy between an African and a Rest of the World select. The government-appointed trustees, Meridien Financial Services Ltd of Lusaka, decided that the best way to distribute the funds was to pay a series of separate instalments to the parents of the victims and their widows. The idea of paying in instalments was to ensure that funds were not misused and it was believed that separate payments to parents and widows would prevent disputes within the families. Two meagre instalments were paid in the summer and autumn of 1993 but the families were told that no further payments would be forthcoming for a further two years. The ability of the families who were based abroad to secure their allocation from the fund was further hampered by FAZ's inability to come up with the finances necessary to fly them to Zambia.[41]

The families responded to the slow disbursement of the trust fund and the failure of the authorities to publish the official inquiry by threatening legal action. In early 1996, 25 of the families signed a letter of consent instructing their lawyers to file a case for damages against the Zambian government. After a series of adjournments the government eventually agreed, in August 1998, to pay compensation but were at pains to stress that this move was not an admission of liability. However, it took another four years of court action before the government was finally ordered to pay the families Kwacha 17,000 million (US$4 million). The actions of the government in stalling over the payment of compensation to the victims' families and the delay in releasing the official report into the causes of the disaster clearly does not tally with the emotional response that leading state officials exhibited during the state funeral. However, as this study reveals, the contradiction between the immediate post-disaster response and subsequent attitudes towards the families of the dead players and officials has not only been evident in the words and actions of the government but also in those of FAZ and the general population. The net result of this is that there has not been sufficient pressure to date on the government to release the report of the official inquiry or to begin to pay the families appropriate compensation.

CONCLUSION

In popular discourse on disasters there has often been a tendency to focus on the actual *moment* of the disaster and the chain of events that immediately preceded it. In the absence of an official report and the failure to complete the official inquiry it has proved impossible to state with any certainty the nature of the technical or human failings that may have precipitated the moment of the Zambian air disaster. However, by adopting a broader view of disaster as a long-term process with phases of development in which risks are created and accumulated, it is possible to identify the more general causal factors of the tragedy. As demonstrated in this article, the historical context in which the disaster occurred was crucial. Put simply, had football in Zambia continued to benefit, to the same extent, from the continued benevolence of the government and the mining industry, it is highly likely that FAZ would have been in a position to organize a safer mode of transport for the match against Senegal. However, the reduction of funding levels for Zambian football in the late 1980s and early 1990s, and administrative and political difficulties within FAZ, combined to create a context of vulnerability around the Zambian game. In the planning stages and management of the ill-fated trip to Dakar this context created a situation in which Zambia's finest footballers were placed in a very precarious position. Not only was it inappropriate that a nation's top football players were required to travel such a long distance on a military cargo plane but it was potentially hazardous to fly them in a make of plane that was designed for short haul flights and had a history of technical failures. Tragically, this potential was realized when the plane crashed shortly after its take-off in Libreville.

In terms of the lessons to be learned from this disaster and ensuring that events of this nature do not happen again, it is essential that FAZ and the Zambian government act on all of the recommendations of the official report, when and if it is published, that deal with the *moment* of the crash. In the meantime, FAZ and officials within Zambian clubs should ensure that players, managers and coaches do not travel to games in inappropriate modes of transport. Beyond these short-term responses it is crucial to adopt a conceptualization of the Zambian air disaster as a long-term process. This might allow those charged with managing and funding Zambian football to work towards ameliorating, if not completely eradicating, the context of vulnerability that continues to impact on the game in Zambia. With the mining industry and the government no longer in a position to bankroll football to the same extent as it did in the past, FAZ must work towards the creation of a self-sustaining development dynamic that will help alleviate the financial difficulties that Zambian football faces. This might be achieved by innovative approaches to club competitions, sponsorship, marketing and development programmes. The administrative malaise that has afflicted Zambian football must also be dealt with. Ensuring that FAZ executives are left alone by the government to get on with their job and are allowed to see out the full term of their office will go some way towards rectifying this. Steps should also be taken to ensure greater accountability in how funds are used and that the types of financial impropriety that have afflicted African and Zambian football are purged.

Dealing with the context of vulnerability in which the Zambian air disaster occurred is something that can only be achieved through long-term strategic planning. However, it should be noted that the success or otherwise of any long-term strategy aimed at eradicating the context of vulnerability embedded in African football is likely to be partly contingent upon factors over which the football authorities and government officials in Zambia and indeed, throughout the continent, have little or no control. These include unfettered economic globalization and continued neo-colonial exploitation, the unpredictable and fragile nature of ethnic relations in many African countries and internal political instability. The same problem faces those charged with dealing with the types of contexts of vulnerability that have given rise to larger scale disasters throughout Africa. That said, it is incumbent on FAZ and Chiluba's government to at least make a start in dealing with the context of vulnerability that still surrounds the Zambian game. Doing so would perhaps provide a more suitable tribute to those who lost their lives in the air disaster than the memorial found at 'Heroes' Acre'.

NOTES

1. J. Vidal, 'The Stakes Could Not Be Higher', in *The Observer, HIV/AIDS in Africa* (Produced by The Observer in association with Concern, October 12 2003), p.1.
2. See Hartley's succinct and thoughtful review of work that adopts such a conceptualisation. H.J. Hartley, *Exploring Sport and Leisure Disasters: A Socio-Legal Perspective* (London and Sydney: Cavendish Publishing Limited, 2001).
3. The Hillsborough Disaster has been covered elsewhere in this volume. The *Marchioness* was a pleasure boat that was hosting a 21st birthday party when it collided with a dredger on the River Thames in London resulting in 51 deaths.
4. Hartley, p.1.
5. P. Scraton, A. Jemphrey and S. Coleman, *No Last Right: The Denial of Justice and the Promotion of Myth in the Aftermath of the Hillsborough Disaster* (Liverpool City Council. The Hillsborough Project Centre for Studies in Crime and Social Justice, Edgehill University College, Ormskirk, Lancs. 1995).
6. In addition to this incident, two spectators were killed in October 1976 following an outbreak of crowd violence after a World Cup qualifying match between Cameroon and the Congo in Yaounde, Cameroon. Fifteen people were killed and 35 were injured at a football stadium in Ghana in 1978 when part of a wall collapsed. A year later, 24 fans died following a stampede in the aftermath of floodlight failure at a match in Nigeria, and in 1982 a concrete roof at a stadium in Algiers, Algeria collapsed killing ten spectators.
7. In January 1991 in Orkney, South Africa, brawls broke out in one of the stands causing widespread panic which resulted in 42 spectators being crushed or trampled to death. In July of the same year one fan died at an African Nations' Cup qualifying match between Kenya and Mozambique in Nairobi. In

June 1996 in Lusaka, Zambia nine spectators died in a crowd stampede following the home team's victory over Sudan in a World Cup qualifying game. In December of the same year two died during a stampede in Zaire's national stadium. In 1997 in Lagos, Nigeria five died in crushes as supporters left the national stadium following Nigeria's World Cup qualifying victory over Egypt. Fans arrived at the stadium exit gates to find that only two of the five gates were open. In 1998 four spectators died at a local derby match in Kinshasa, DRC when troops opened fire. In the same year, nine people were trampled to death and 50 others were injured after a World Cup qualifier between Zambia and Sudan. In the last stadium disaster of the 1990s, 11 died in a stampede in the aftermath of a derby game in Alexandria, Egypt between Korm and Al Ittihad in January 1999.

8. In July 2000 13 died in a stampede in Harare, Zimbabwe following a World Cup qualifier with South Africa. In April of the following year 43 fans were killed as they tried to enter Ellis Park Stadium in Johannesburg, South Africa to watch Kaizer Chiefs play Orlando Pirates (see the study in this collection by Peter Alegi). Eighteen days later, eight fans lost their lives in a stampede at a game in Lubumbashi, Congo.

9. P. Darby, 'The New Scramble for Africa: African Football Labour Migration to Europe', *The European Sports History Review*, 3 (2000), 217–44.

10. P. Darby, *Africa, Football and FIFA: Politics, Colonialism and Resistance* (London and Portland: Frank Cass, 2002).

11. E. Maradas, 'A Time for Reflection and Reorientation', *African Soccer*, 68 (July 2001), 5.

12. Cited in *The Independent*, 11 Jan. 1992, p.46.

13. F. Mahjoub, 'Culture of Mediocrity', *African Soccer*, 1 (Jan./Feb. 1992), 38.

14. Ibid.

15. See Peter Alegi's study on the Ellis Park stadium disaster in this volume.

16. M. Gleeson, 'Disasters Cast World Cup Shadow', *BBC Sport Online*, 10 May 2001.

17. See P. Darby, 'Africa, the FIFA Presidency and the Governance of World Football: 1974, 1998 and 2002', *Africa Today*, 50, 1 (2003), 3–24.

18. J. Sugden and A. Tomlinson, *FIFA and the Contest for World Football: Who Rules the Peoples' Game* (Cambridge: Polity Press, 1998), p.145. They go on to provide evidence of corruption in the administration of football in Zäire, Cameroon and South Africa.

19. See Darby, *Africa, Football and FIFA*, p.178.

20. Cited in M. Broere and R. van der Drift, *Football Africa!* (Oxford: Worldview Publishing, 1996).

21. Zambia has twice been runner-up in the African Cup of Nations (1974 and 1994) and has finished third on three occasions (1982, 1990 and 1996). They also won the Cosafa Castle Cup (the regional Southern African football tournament) in 1997 and 1998.

22. See Darby, *Africa, Football and FIFA*.

23. P. Darby, 'Football, Colonial Doctrine and Indigenous Resistance: Mapping the Political Persona of FIFA's African Constituency', *Culture, Sport, Society*, 3, 1 (Spring 2000), 61–87. See also E. Quansah, 'The Cup to Surpass All Cups', *Africa Today* (Jan./Feb. 1996), 26.

24. A. Versi, *Football in Africa* (London: Collins, 1986).

25. Because of the success of the copper mining industry, Zambian incomes per capita considerably exceeded those of neighbouring African countries in the 1960s and 1970s. In this period the contribution of the mining industry to Zambia's total export earnings was typically around the 90 per cent mark. In addition, until 1970 more than half of Government revenue arose directly from the copper industry. P. Daniel, *Africanisation, Nationalisation and Inequality: Mining Labour and the Copper Industry* (Cambridge: Cambridge University Press, 1979).

26. C. Graham, *Private Markets for Public Goods: Raising the Stakes in Economic Reform* (Washington DC: Brookings Institution Press, 1988).

27. P. Liwewe, 'New Boss – Still No Money', *African Soccer*, 2 (March-May 1993), 30–1.

28. For an assessment of the impact of African player migration on domestic African leagues see Darby, 'The New Scramble for Africa'.

29. It should be noted that in this same period, a culture of corruption pervaded even the highest levels of government. For example, by 1994 almost half of the original Cabinet members of Chiluba's Government were either dismissed or resigned because of corruption-related allegations. Graham, *Private Markets for Public Goods*.

30. P. Liwewe, 'Empty Future', *African Soccer*, 64 (March 2001), 6–10.

31. According to Butcher and Dunn, poor crew coordination practices, which often result from entrenched communication channels between the cockpit and the flight or ground crew, are amongst the typical

contributors to contemporary air disasters. In the absence of the official report on the Zambian air disaster it is impossible to identify the precise nature or causes of the failure of crew coordination on this particular flight. J.N. Butcher and L.A. Dunn, 'Human Responses and Treatment Needs in Airline Disasters', in R. Gist and B. Lubin (eds), *Psychological Aspects of Disaster* (New York: Wiley, 1989), pp.86–119.

32. H. Mba Allogo, 'The View From Libreville', *African Soccer*, 3 (June-Aug. 1993), 11. P. Liwewe, 'Zambia Mourns', *African Soccer*, 3 (June-Aug. 1993), 8–10.

33. Cited in Broere and van der Drift, *Football Africa!*, p.142.

34. As part of a long-standing commitment to development in Zambia the Danish Government financed a four-week training camp for the new Zambian squad.

35. K. Gondwe, 'Zambia Disaster Plans in Disarray', *BBC Sport Online* (www.bbcsportonline.co.uk).

36. E. Djokotoe, 'Remembering Gabon: The FAZ Debacle', *The Lusaka Post,* posted on www.allafrica.com 28 March 2003.

37. For example, in early 1994, the FAZ executive was dissolved following accusations of incompetence and financial mismanagement. P. Liwewe, 'Paying the Price of Success', *African Soccer*, 7 (July-Sept. 1994), 24.

38. Graham, *Private Markets for Public Goods.*

39. Liwewe, 'Zambia Mourns', p.10.

40. It was reported in *African Soccer* (3, June-Aug. 1993, 11) that their correspondent, Jean-Gilbert Foutou had been *obliged* to hand over his tape recording and notes from the interview with the air controller to Congolese Transport Ministry officials.

41. P. Liwewe, 'Trust Fund Troubles Continue', *African Soccer*, 5 (Jan-March 1994), 13.

9

'The Flowers of Manchester': The Munich Disaster and the Discursive Creation of Manchester United Football Club

GAVIN MELLOR

INTRODUCTION

On 6 February 1958, an airliner carrying Manchester United players and officials home from a European Cup quarter-final match against Red Star Belgrade crashed after re-fuelling in the German city of Munich. The incident resulted in the deaths of 23 passengers, including eight of the famous 'Busby Babes' Manchester United team. From the moment that the crash occurred, the British press reported it as a 'disaster' of national and even international significance. *The Times* newspaper called the air crash 'the blackest hand yet set upon sport in these islands',[1] whilst the *Daily Mail* referred to it as 'a black day for Manchester, for football, and for the British people'.[2] International political leaders also shared in this interpretation of the crash. President Tito of Yugoslavia sent Harold MacMillan, the British Prime Minister, condolences over what he described as 'a heavy blow to British sport and to the British people'.[3] Messages of support to those involved were also received from, amongst others, the Argentine Football Association, the French Football Association, the German Football Association, the Indonesian Football Association, the Roman Association of Sporting Journalists in Italy, staff of the *Corriere dello Sport* in Italy, Dukla Prague Football Club, and Real Madrid Football Club. Even Queen Elizabeth II and the Pope felt moved to send their condolences and support to the Lord Mayor of Manchester and to the people of the city.[4]

The depth of feeling elicited by the Munich air crash was in part a result of the high esteem in which Manchester United were held in English and European football in the years before 1958. In 1957, the club reached the semi-finals of the European Cup at the first attempt, only to be knocked out by eventual winners Real Madrid. A year later, of course, they reached the semi-finals again, but lost heavily to AC Milan with a depleted post-Munich team. As an indication of Manchester

United's reputation at the time of the air crash, *The Times* described the club in the following way:

> The irony of it all is that this disaster should come at a time when Manchester United have set English standards even higher on the Continent. Having just reached the semi-final of the European Cup ... their name has never shone more brightly. Whenever they played on the Continent and in America they have left behind a reputation for their skill and their correct behaviour both on and off the field. They have been outstanding ambassadors for England and the debt owed to them is immeasurable.[5]

It was not only United's excellence and on-field achievements, however, which influenced reactions to the Munich air crash. In the days, weeks and months that followed the crash a wide range of discursive interpretations of Manchester United emerged in the British press that served to construct the Munich air crash as a 'disaster'. These also helped to shape and re-define readings of the club's past, present and future.

The aim of this study is to analyse the discourses that developed around Manchester United as a result of the Munich air crash. First, it will consider the immediate aftermath of the air crash in 1958 and the media narratives that helped to construct the event as a disaster. Second, the study will consider the air crash's impact on Manchester United in the late 1960s. It will analyse how Munich became a fixed part of the Manchester United narrative in the 1960s, and how themes of loss and recovery influenced interpretations and 'readings' of the club during their first European Cup success in 1968. Third, the study will consider the continuing influence of the Munich air crash on Manchester United and its supporters. It will comment on the 'consumption' and re-appropriation of Munich by current Manchester United fans, and analyse how Manchester United's close association with the air crash during the 1990s 'negatively' influenced the construction of contemporary narratives around the club.

DISASTERS, COLLECTIVE MEMORIES, MYTHS AND FOLKLORES

Before commencing with a close investigation of the Munich air crash, it is worth spending a little time outlining the theoretical framework for this study and explaining why the air crash should be considered a topic worthy of analysis. Simply put, this study will analyse the Munich disaster, not because of its intrinsic importance as a significant air crash, but rather because of its role in recreating the discursive identity of Manchester United Football Club in the second half of the twentieth century. In line with the work of Gawronski and Olsen on the 1985 Mexico City earthquake, the study will consider the initial 'construction' of the air crash in 1958, and will then study how certain readings of the event helped to create a 'collective memory' of Munich for Manchester United supporters that partially defines who they are and what they represent.[6] The study is, therefore, a consideration of the place of disasters in the construction of 'communities' (football 'communities' in this case), and more specifically an analysis of how the narratives that emerge from disasters serve as important cultural resources in bonding people together.

In theoretical writings on disasters, it is frequently noted that a variety of readings or discourses emerge in the initial period after a disaster to help make sense of events. In fact, the cultural representations that appear in the wake of disasters (for example, newspaper reports and television pictures) are frequently the only ways in which people experience disastrous events, save for those directly involved. As Webb, Wachtendorf and Eyre argue:

> In a practical sense, cultural representations of disaster play an essential role in transmitting knowledge between individuals, groups and generations. Most people in a particular society do not experience disasters first hand. Rather, they learn about disasters through the experiences of others, as told by survivors, expressed by others, or conveyed in a movie or media account. Cultural representations shape a group's understanding of disasters and may influence the way in which that group prepares for, responds to, and recovers from actual disasters.[7]

Disasters are, therefore, socially constructed phenomena around which discourses are created in line with 'specific socio-economic, historical, cultural and chronological contexts'.[8] People do not come into contact with disasters as singular, unambiguous events. Rather, they observe and interpret them through mediated images and texts that often shape feelings in very specific ways.

In the aftermath of a disaster, the discourses that help to make sense of events often become significant 'historical markers' in the memory of people who feel affected by the incident.[9] This is particularly true of people who have a close affinity or connection with the people who died or were injured in the disaster. As historical markers, disaster narratives frequently come to serve as part of the shared culture of collective groups of people (neighbourhoods, communities, regions, nations), and inform people about their pasts and where they have come from. As Webb, Wachtendorf and Eyre suggest:

> The stories of a culture's experience with disaster are often passed on through folklore, remembered through permanent or occasional memorials, relived through dramatised portrayals, and embedded in a group's collective conscience as permanent markers of social time.[10]

If a group has been subjected to a collective trauma in the past, the story of how it happened, how it was dealt with, and how it connects with the present will often be told to say something about group members' collective identities. Narratives about loss and recovery, rising to enormous challenges and overcoming tragedy are frequently evoked to define a group's character and values. These narratives can be re-appropriated by future generations, thereby ensuring that disasters can influence the lives and identities of people who were not even born when they occurred.

The enduring stories of disasters frequently live on through a variety of cultural forms. We are reminded about disasters through mediated literary and visual forms and practices, and increasingly through popular cultural artefacts that can be conspicuously consumed by people who want to associate themselves with disasters or tragedies from the past.[11] This point is particularly significant in the case of analysing the legacy of the Munich disaster for Manchester United supporters. Since social identities became more fluid in Britain in the post-Second-World-War period, some football supporters have been increasingly willing to choose their clubs on criteria other than a traditional sense of place and home.[12] In the process of proving one's allegiance to a football club, practises of consumption have, for some fans, become as commonplace as attending matches and asserting one's geographical heritage. In this way, the 'consumption' of the Munich disaster by new Manchester United supporters has become a key ritual in creating an allegiance to the club and to fellow United supporters.

THE NARRATIVE CONSTRUCTION OF THE MUNICH DISASTER

Before considering the present-day consumption of the Munich air crash by Manchester United supporters, it is important to analyse the range of discourses that emerged around the tragedy in 1958. By doing this, the original construction of the air crash as a 'disaster' can be understood, as can the initial debate about what Munich meant for Manchester United's past, present and future. To gain access to the narratives that surrounded and helped to structure the aftermath of Munich, a range of local and national British newspapers have been analysed.

From studying press reports in the days, weeks and months after the Munich air crash, it can be observed that a number of discourses were created to help make sense of what had taken place. These can be split into three categories. The first aimed to make clear what had happened during the crash, and questioned why it had occurred. The second explained how Manchester United supporters and the people of Manchester were coping with the tragedy. The third analysed what Munich meant for the future of Manchester United and the club's chances of further success. Let us consider these in turn.

In the direct aftermath of the air crash, press reports appeared that inevitably questioned why it had happened, and who was to blame. However, these reports were not particularly numerous. Four days after Munich, *The Times* reported that preliminary investigations by British European Airways and the German Traffic and Transport Ministry had concluded that ice on the wings of the airliner had probably caused the crash.[13] This early interpretation of events appears to have been generally accepted by the British press, with one or two exceptions. The *Manchester Evening News* reported two days after the crash that the pilot of the airliner may be charged over the accident by German authorities,[14] whilst the *Daily Mail* claimed a few days later that the disaster would not have occurred had a house not been located at the end of the airport runway.[15] In fact, the *Daily Mail* was one of the only British newspapers that attempted to create a sense of debate and controversy around the causes of the air crash in the weeks after its occurrence. In a front-page editorial on 16 February 1958, the *Daily Mail* registered its disquiet that the two official inquiries that had been established to investigate the causes of the air crash – one by the German authorities and one by British European Airways – were both to be held in private. The *Daily Mail* challenged the British Government to say to themselves 'this disaster has shaken the British people more than any other of recent years. Let us show by some special investigation that we are aware of it.'[16] The paper also stated that the 'great tragedy' of Munich still had the potential to become 'a great scandal'.

Despite the best efforts of the *Daily Mail*, the causes surrounding the Munich air crash were generally perceived to be far too obvious for discourses of conspiracy, intrigue, blame or anger to dominate press reporting around the disaster in 1958. Instead, the press turned to the effects of the disaster on the people of Manchester as one of the principal foci of their reporting. Here newspapers could report upon the widespread grief that was felt as a result of the air crash, and on the supposed unifying influence that the disaster created for the people of the city. In line with theorists who have argued that greater social cohesion develops in the immediate aftermath of disasters,[17] the British press were keen in the days and weeks after Munich to show how Mancunians, regardless of affiliation to Manchester United, had shared their grief in the wake of the crash. The most remarkable piece of reporting with this focus appeared in the *Daily Mail* two days after disaster. Under the headline 'The Day After: I See a City Draw Breath, Live, Die and Sigh as a City', a *Daily Mail* journalist reported:

> Being in Manchester in the past two days has been like intruding … [into] the heart of the family. This is not an occasion on which dramatic words are necessary, and all I can say is that I have never before known anything like this sensation of awareness that around me a whole city was drawing together, proud, hurt and resentful of strangers in its midst.
> We are often told today that ordinary people can no longer have the same feeling for the large cities in which they live as their forefathers used to have for their villages and country towns. I no longer believe this. In these past two days I have seen a city draw breath as a city, live, die or sigh as a city.
> Gradually, one began to realise that there was hardly one person in Manchester who did not have some feeling of personal contact with the

United team ... But it was not just a question of soccer fans. Wherever one went the subject was at first avoided then suddenly brought into the open and then gloomily discussed. It made no difference whether one was with 'top' or 'bottom' people. Businessmen at the Bodega, top businessmen and headwaiters at the Midland [hotel], top people at the Reform Club, they were no less concerned than the workers at Metro Vickers, no less hurt and feeling no less deprived.

There it is then. The vast city, the centre of the largest conurbation in the country, apparently without personality, shape or unity.

There it is, its personality suddenly cohering so that even a stranger can sense it. Suddenly taking shape before ones eyes. Suddenly united and exclusive.

Where, we are so often asked, is the heart of a large industrial town? What symbol gives one a sense of belonging?

Dare one say it? Dare one say that where the symbol once lay in a village inn, or a church, or 'the big house', it now lies in a football team?[18]

The *Daily Mail*'s reading of the Manchester public in the wake of Munich is notable because of the intensified level of 'community' that the newspaper claimed to have observed in the city. The *Daily Mail* constructed Mancunians as a family, unified regardless of social class, and with identifiable personality characteristics. In this, they were not alone. Many articles appeared in the British press in the days and weeks after Munich that stressed how the disaster had brought people together in Manchester in ways that had rarely been seen before. The *Daily Mail* itself set the tone on the day after the disaster when it offered its observations on the initial effects of the air crash on the people of Manchester:

> Crowds of Manchester United fans hammered on the door at Old Trafford, the club's headquarters, last night asking for more news ... A knot of teenage girls stood sobbing under the shadow of the giant stand ... In the pubs and cafes of Manchester last night, on the buses and on trains, the ordinary people talked about THEIR football team.
>
> The cloth-cap-and-raincoat supporters who paid their half crowns, the tens of thousands who followed United through the sports columns, the people who never saw them play but rooted for them 'because everybody at our house does'.
>
> Everybody knew them – not only the footballers, the sports reporters too.

The *Manchester Evening News* continued this theme when they reported that the bodies of the victims of the crash had been flown back to Manchester from Munich. The paper reported that people had lined the route that the bodies had taken from Manchester airport:

They waited in their thousands at the kerbside to pay homage to the Manchester United players and journalists who died in the Munich air disaster.

Businessmen in their new cars, Teddy Boys, housewives carrying young children, cloth-capped men with cycles, schoolboys, office girls in head-scarves. Along the roads from Manchester airport to Old Trafford they stood bareheaded or wept quietly, or knelt in prayer.[19]

They also reported similar scenes at the first funeral to result from the air crash. The funeral was for racehorse owner and Manchester businessman William 'Willie' Satinoff. Despite not being a Manchester United player or a well-known journalist, the *Evening News* reported the funeral as an occasion for citywide unity. The paper claimed that 'all sections of the city were there ... women with shopping bags, businessmen, barristers, doctors, errand boys'.[20]

The discourse of unity in Manchester that emerged in the wake of Munich extended to industrial, political, cultural and sporting institutions across the city. The *Manchester Evening News* noted that local clothing manufacturers E. Raffles and Company held a minute's silence in response to the disaster.[21] The newspaper also made much of a disaster fund, set up by Manchester's Lord Mayor, which received significant donations from Great Universal Stores, the *Manchester Evening Chronicle*, the *Manchester Evening News*, the *Manchester Guardian* and a number of other large employers.[22] Elsewhere, the *Times* reported that Manchester's Hallé Orchestra had played a special performance of Elgar's Nimrod as an *in memoriam* to the victims of the crash, and that the 1,000 people who attended the concert had stood for a minute's silence at its conclusion.[23] With reference to the sporting community, *The Times* reported that Jack Solomons, a London boxing promoter with links in Manchester, offered to arrange an open-air boxing tournament in the city in aid of the crash victims.[24] The staff and players of Manchester City Football Club were also reported to be sharing in Manchester United's grief. City, who lost one-time goalkeeper Frank Swift in the air crash, were described in *The Times* as being 'Manchester United's brothers' in the wake of the disaster.[25] Later in the *Manchester Evening News*, Manchester City player Bert Trautman explained the club's feelings on what had happened to their near neighbours. He stated: 'it has struck us very hard because although we were possibly United's strongest rivals, we were also neighbours, which meant friends'.[26] The *Evening News* also reported that Manchester City's official message of condolence to Manchester United had included the statement, 'anything we can do to help in any way, we shall do with all our hearts'.[27] Clearly the Manchester press were keen to show that the gravity of the Munich disaster cut across even well-established sporting rivalries.

The strength of the discourse of Mancunian unity that emerged after Munich was such that dissent was not kindly reported upon in the Manchester press. In the week after the disaster, the *Manchester Evening Chronicle* described how commercial and retail organizations in Manchester that had refused to fly flags at half-mast in recognition of the Munich Disaster were being criticized for showing 'a disregard for public feeling'.[28] In response to this report, a number of letters were published that strongly refused to accept the homogeneous response to the air crash that the discourse of unity demanded. A Manchester trader wrote:

> Business people whom [your newspaper] accuses of showing a lack of respect by not lowering their flags to half-mast are not all imbued with the same mass hysteria that causes 'the sheep', for the want of something better to do, to flock to Old Trafford terraces on Saturdays. Everybody deeply regrets the sad deaths of the United players and the sports writers. But every day there are many Manchester citizens who also meet tragic ends by other means.[29]

In the weeks after the air crash, other notes of criticism against the unity discourse were also reported in the Manchester press. On most occasions, these were met with a strong response in the form of editorials or readers' letters. After a series of letters in March 1958, questioning whether it was appropriate for the people of Manchester to continue to grieve for the victims of Munich, Arthur Walmsely, the *Manchester Evening Chronicle*'s sports editor, wrote:

> Manchester, especially its soccer public and its press, is under fire from without and WITHIN. We are accused of prolonging the Manchester United agony beyond the bounds of genuine sorrow and sympathy. We are accused of an unhealthy, mass hysterical support of a football club which violates the borders of sport and trespasses on the forbidden ground of maudlin spirit. Bluntly, we are accused of making a meal of that Munich Disaster by carrying it on through the present United side.[30]

Walmsely defended these criticisms by stating that they were, 'inspired by sour grapes and even an inverted form of envy of the tremendous loyalty displayed by the Manchester public to the United club'. He was later supported by a number of letters to the *Chronicle*. Under the title 'Sour grapes flavour criticism of United', one reader claimed that any decline in the blanket sympathy that had previously existed for United in the press was informed by personal agendas. With specific reference to newspaper reporting that had followed Manchester United's victory over West Bromwich Albion in the sixth round of the FA Cup, the letter stated:

> 'Bubbling cauldron', 'seething crucible' – these are among the highly coloured descriptions of Old Trafford I have seen since the defeat of West

148

Bromwich Albion in the sixth round replay [of the FA Cup]. And the Manchester United supporter – brother, is he popular? 'Loutish legions on the terraces', 'mass hysteria', 'the most partisan crowd anywhere', 'shrieking women midst milling hordes of angry shut-out fanatics', 'howling and inhibited savages'.

Well, well, well!!! Apparently you have all missed your cue in Manchester. Properly fluffed your lines you have. It seems the way the drama SHOULD have unfolded after Munich was one single great demonstration of loyalty, one brave fight by the remoulded team and then a series of shattering defeats. If this had happened, the same critics who see physical peril in even venturing near Old Trafford would have been engulfing us in a treacle of their boundless sympathy.[31]

Clearly, some United fans felt that the continued success of their club in the aftermath of Munich was the real reason why sections of the media and others were questioning the appropriateness of United supporters' feelings of mourning.

The apparent gradual breakdown of the discourse of unity in Manchester in the months after Munich fits with the contentions of social theorists who assert that increases in social cohesion in the wake of disasters are usually temporary. Drabek, for instance, has noted that a 'temporary focus' on a disaster after it has occurred usually 'precipitates a pulling together', but that this phenomenon is often short lived.[32] Old structures and divisions (class, gender, ethnicity, age, territory, affiliation to a football club) begin to assert influence again as people 'return to normal'. In this sense, the unity created by disasters is viewed as being extraordinary and transient and not representative of lasting social change.

If the discourse of unity gradually declined after Munich, a further post-disaster discourse seems to have had a more prolonged influence. This was the debate about where the Munich air crash sat in the history of Manchester United and what it meant for the club's future. In the days after the crash, the British press reflected on the post-1945 history of Manchester United in an attempt to understand how the club would survive its present predicament. In particular, a discourse of 'loss and recovery' or 'tragedy and renewal' was created to explain how United would emerge from Munich as a still great club with a difficult but ultimately successful future. The newspapers explained consistently that Manchester United had gone from being a financially-impoverished club without a stadium at the conclusion of the Second World War (Old Trafford suffered bomb damage during the conflict), to FA Cup winners, League Champions and European contenders in the following 12 years. *The Times* began this line of reporting on the day after the disaster and drew specific attention to the role of Matt Busby, Manchester United's manager, in the development of the club:

> If anyone could ever in the world be said to be solely responsible for success in any field of venture, then in football that man is Mr Matt Busby, the

Manchester United Manager ... He has built the name of Manchester
United out of the ruins of the last war.

To measure the true extent of their achievements, we must look back to
October 22nd 1945, when Mr Busby took over the post of manager. At that
time the Old Trafford ground at Manchester had been reduced to ruins by
German bombs ... With no ground and no money, Mr Busby and his directors faced the future – and what a great future came to pass.[33]

The importance of Busby in the previous development of Manchester United
and his potential central role in the future of the club was a constant theme in the
days after the air crash. *The Times* followed up its initial reflections on the crash
with the following passage:

The strength of Manchester United ... lies in its background. A farsighted
policy, carried over the past years by Mr Busby was based on the belief in
and training of youth. No club in the country can claim a finer, home-grown
nursery ... It is on this young and virile limb that the club must now lean.
Perhaps for the next two or even three years Manchester United may stand
quietly in the shadows. They have done so in the past and risen. They will
do so again, especially if Mr Busby is there to lead them. Meanwhile, they
have given millions something to treasure and remember.[34]

The Times was not unique in this line of reporting. With headlines such as 'From
Ashes to Fame in 12 Years',[35] the *Daily Mail* informed readers that Matt Busby
'built up the side from almost nothing into the most glamorous combination in
League football'.[36] The *Manchester Evening News* also reminded readers of
United's post-war history in its first report on the air crash:

From the ashes of the old pre-war, poverty-stricken Manchester United,
they [the players] had lifted the team sky-high to world fame and were cruis-
ing towards the greatest soccer treble history has known. The Munich air
crash struck the greatest blow at what the world has [come] to recognise as
the greatest club.[37]

In subsequent reports, the *Evening News* continued the theme of loss and recovery. It informed readers that the great United team of the 1950s had been built
from humble and difficult beginnings, and assured them that this would be the
case again. For the *Evening News* and other newspapers, Munich was as much of
a 'beginning' for Manchester United as it was an 'ending':

From the stricken shell of Manchester United will rise another great team.
For the spirit instilled into the world-beating side of yesterday will live
through this grievous Munich tragedy and be inherited by the boys who are
the team of tomorrow.[38]

150

The *Manchester Evening News* also printed a number of letters that reflected this theme of renewal. One suggested that Manchester United should be renamed 'Manchester Phoenix' to reflect the team's forthcoming and inevitable emergence from adversity.[39] Another, sent in by 'a few female supporters', pleaded with the players left at the club to continue their efforts to make the club great again: 'It is now up to all you young players to show the country and the world what you are made of, so come on lads and bring more glory to your club and the memory of your lost teammates.'[40]

The discourse of loss and recovery was particularly evident in the British press at the time of Manchester United's first match after Munich: a fifth round FA Cup tie at Old Trafford versus Sheffield Wednesday on 19 February. Manchester United Chairman H.P. Hardman set the tone for the occasion in a statement released to the press before the match:

> Although we mourn our dead and grieve for our wounded, we believe that great days are not done for us. The sympathy and encouragement of the football world, and particularly our supporters, will justify and inspire us. The road back may be long and hard, but with the memory of those who died at Munich, of the stirring achievements and wonderful sportsmanship ever with us, Manchester United will rise again.[41]

Hardman's wish for a resurgent Manchester United started well in the match against Wednesday. A young, inexperienced and in some cases borrowed United team won the match 3-0, thereby putting United into the sixth round of the Cup. The result was greeted in the press as a sign of the enduring quality of Manchester United and as an indication of the club's rebirth. With reference to the first goal of the match, the *Daily Mail* wrote, 'note the time: 7.58. Note the date: February 19th. Both of these will go down in history of the rebirth of Britain's most famous club.' Later in the same report, the paper continued:

> The fantastic Busby Babes, the incredible Red Devils of Manchester United, arose again in the smoke and the tears and the cheers of Old Trafford last night. As I write, a bright-eyed Manchester boy, Seamus Brennan, is crying in his bath after a sensational first game in which he scored twice to become the first hero of the new Babes.[42]

The *Daily Mail's* report on the Sheffield Wednesday game is notable for its focus on what the match signified for the future of Manchester United. Instead of grieving for the past, the report constructed the match as a new start for the club: an opportunity that would allow players such as Seamus Brennan to establish themselves as first team regulars and United heroes. In this sense, the discourse of loss and recovery came to represent opportunity and excitement as well as bereavement and sorrow. The British press effectively began to report that Munich had forced a new beginning on United. The club now had to prove that it could rebuild itself for a second time since the war, and achieve more than it had during even the 'Babes' era. To do that, of course, United would need to win the European Cup.

RECOVERY: THE 1968 EUROPEAN CUP FINAL

On 29 May 1968, some ten years after the Munich air crash, Manchester United played Portuguese champions Benfica at Wembley stadium in the final of the European Cup. It was United's first appearance in the final and the culmination of a period of rebuilding that had seen the club win the FA Cup in 1963 and the League Championship in 1965 and 1967. Matt Busby was still the manager of United, and two other survivors of Munich, Bobby Charlton and Bill Foulkes, remained as regular members of the team. The raw materials to continue and complete the discourse of loss and recovery were securely in place. If United could win the European Cup, the predictions of those who had asserted that Busby would rebuild the post-Munich Manchester United team would prove to be correct.

The strength of the loss and recovery discourse that surrounded Manchester United in the years after Munich ensured that the press had a clear and common understanding of what the European Cup final of 1968 symbolized. In the build up to the final, the press consistently made references to the fact that Manchester United's quest for the European Cup had begun with the 'Babes' team of the late 1950s, and that the club now had to fulfil this long-standing ambition. The *Daily Mail* described the European Cup as Matt Busby's 'obsessive dream' and evoked the memory of the Munich players as inspiration for United's present team:

> This ... sense of being about to conquer in a competition in which many of them have exhausted their careers, had even lost some of them their lives, will carry United through before their own folk at Wembley tonight.[43]

Other newspapers made similar statements on the significance of the final. *The Times*, noting that a ten-year-long dramatic story would be completed if United won the final, stated: 'if sentiment ... [has] anything to do with the case then Manchester United will kick off with a head start'.[44] The *Manchester Evening News* even called the 1968 Manchester United team 'the Busby Babes', thereby symbolically obliterating the differences between two Manchester United teams from different eras.

Manchester United, of course, won the final 4–1 after extra time to become the first English club to win the European Cup.[45] In match reports on the final, the victory of the United team was placed consistently in the historical context of Munich, thus portraying the club's recovery as complete. The *Manchester Evening News* set the tone of its reporting with an editorial on the day after the team's victory:

Surely the spirits of the men of Munich must have hovered over Wembley last night. Certainly they could not have been far from the thoughts of Matt Busby who survived to tread the long road back from that disaster of 10 years ago. By masterly leadership he communicated his personal brand of courage to this team which he has rebuilt. Never was it more evident than last night when, at the moment when it most mattered, he called forth from his men new heat, new energy, and new skill to carry them through.[46]

The *Manchester Evening News* even reprinted reports, scores and photographs from the 'Babes' 1957–58 European Cup campaign alongside its 1968 final match report.[47] In doing so, they invited readers to forget about United's false starts and failed European campaigns between 1958 and 1968. The paper simplified the loss and recovery discourse to ensure that readers understood the connections between February 1958 and May 1968. The press, therefore, effectively implied that the genesis of United's victory in 1968 had been laid ten years earlier and that the club had now fulfilled its destiny.

The national press similarly constructed an unquestionable link between the Munich disaster and Manchester United's victory in the European Cup. In its report on the final, *The Times* drew attention to the fact that Bobby Charlton, a Munich survivor, had made such a telling contribution to the final with two goals:

> Appropriately it was Bobby Charlton who made two of the decisive strikes … Ten years after surviving the Munich air crash, which destroyed the 'Busby Babes', Charlton and Matt Busby, United's manager, have reached the one pinnacle of European football which had always eluded them.[48]

Elsewhere in the newspaper, longstanding *Times* football writer Geoffrey Green shared his reflections on the final. In his description of what the event meant for the survivors of Munich, he wrote:

> With that other warrior Bill Foulkes … Charlton typifies the loyalty that inspired this great Manchester club. Together they are two of the few who survived the Munich crash, and last night at Wembley I am certain each of them played as devotedly for that lost past as for the living present.[49]

Green's sentiments were reflected in many reports on the final. A number of journalists speculated that Charlton and Foulkes, and manager Matt Busby, saw the final as a specific opportunity to reflect on the past and pay their debts to those who died. This made the final more than a football match: it was presented as a cleansing, quasi-religious experience that would afford the Manchester United club, manager and players the opportunity to fulfil the promises made by the press on their behalf in the days, weeks and months after Munich.

The quasi-religious properties of the final were further constructed in Geoffrey Green's comments in *The Times* on Matt Busby. In a clear statement on how the final fitted with the discourse of loss and recovery, Green wrote:

> He [Busby] has learned that the man who never gets lost will never find. Because he himself has been both to heaven and to hell and back again, been tempered in the fires and remained true to his principles, he is what he is: someone to be respected and admired.[50]

For Green, it was clear that Busby would not have succeeded at United had he not endured the pain and loss of the Munich disaster. It was the destruction of his young team in 1958 that drove Busby to continue to seek his ultimate goal. It was his unshakable belief in his 'principles' and methods of working, even when faced with the most harrowing of circumstances, which enabled him to fulfil his and his club's ambitions.

In constructing the narrative of the 1968 European Cup final in this way, Geoffrey Green and others refined the original loss and recovery discourse that had emerged in the wake of the Munich disaster. The 'opportunity' that was presented to Manchester United by the air crash was now slightly recast with specific reference to Matt Busby's career as Manchester United manager. In fact, Busby and United became synonymous as his leading role in the reconstruction of the United team in the years after Munich made his and the club's 'stories' indivisible. Busby, of course, had been part of the original discourse of loss and recovery in the immediate aftermath of Munich: his role in rebuilding Manchester United in the post-war period made sure of that. For some time in 1958, however, it was not known whether Busby would make a full recovery from the air crash, or whether he would want to return to football management after such an ordeal. The fact that he did recover and did return to lead United to European Cup success made sure that he ultimately played a more central role in United's discourse of loss and recovery than would otherwise have been the case.

THE CONTINUING IMPORTANCE OF THE MUNICH DISASTER FOR MANCHESTER UNITED SUPPORTERS

The fact that Manchester United won the European Cup in 1968 ensured that the discourse of loss and recovery entered into the 'folklore' of the club. Whilst other readings of the Munich disaster, such as the discourse of Mancunian unity, had dissolved fairly quickly after February 1958, press statements on how the Munich disaster fitted with the past of Manchester United and what it meant for the club's future ultimately proved to be correct and, therefore, unshakable. In the final section of this study, the meaning of the Munich discourse for Manchester United and its supporters today will be explored, together with contemporary interpretations of the 'the Munich story' by other clubs' supporters.

Matt Busby's death in January 1994, aged 84, brought new attention to Manchester United's discourse of loss and recovery. Busby had continued to hold a variety of roles at United from 1968, and was eventually made Club President. In the press reporting that followed his death, it was clear that Busby would be remembered principally for the periods of loss and recovery that had occurred at Manchester United between the end of Second World War and 1968. The *Manchester Evening News* reminded its readers that:

> United was on its uppers when Matt arrived home from the war in 1945 to be appointed to his first and last job in management. Old Trafford was blitzed and the club was virtually bankrupt...
> His resilience in football was unparalleled, recovering as he did from his injuries and the calamity of the Munich air disaster to create more fine teams with players who became household names.[51]

Specifically on the years before the Munich disaster, the paper also contended that:

> Matt Busby ... was the man who lit the torch of hope and inspiration that led a city out of the post-war gloom after 10 years of depression and six wars. The legendary Busby Babes brought pride and respect to the bomb-shattered streets, the pre fabs and the council estates through the austere years.[52]

In its comments on the crowds that gathered at Old Trafford to lay tributes to Busby on the day of his death, the *Evening News* also cast its comments in terms of the story of Munich:

> Nobody spoke as they walked the familiar journey down ... Sir Matt Busby Way to the famous stadium. The ghosts of Sir Matt's first all-conquering team walked with them. Silent in thought, the fans remembered the courage of Sir Matt, clinging to life in an oxygen tent after the shattering blow of the Munich air disaster on February 6th 1958. Twice Sir Matt was given the last rites and twice he fought back determined to rebuild his life and his team to fulfil his dream of winning the European Cup ... Yesterday, the light that had guided three great teams to glory was finally extinguished.[53]

The national press similarly reminded readers of the loss and recovery discourse in its obituaries and comments on Busby's death. *The Times* gave the following account:

> Munich had ended the lifespan of the two great United teams created by Busby. Simply, he began and built a third ... It meant a patient wait, but

only until 1963 for a victory in the FA Cup and until 1965 and then 1967 for the League Championship. There were setbacks in failures to snatch the European trophy that Busby felt he owed to himself and to his dead team. But that finally came in 1968 when, in extra time at Wembley, Busby rallied a tired team to beat Benfica. Twenty years to get there, the one thing that mattered most.[54]

The paper also commented on the important fact that Manchester United and Matt Busby had gradually become indivisible and indistinguishable in the post-war period:

> Sir Matt became synonymous with Manchester United, a club that he led out of the Second World War, through the Munich air crash in 1958, to become, in 1968, the first English club to win the European Cup.[55]

The *Daily Mail* told an analogous story. By drawing attention to the key years between 1958 and 1968, the paper constructed the life of Busby very much in terms of loss and recovery:

> Sir Matt's strong but sporting manner was the [mark] ... of a side that in the late fifties and sixties was the pride not only of Manchester or of Britain, but of the footballing world. They were known as the Babes ... and so it was that when the aircraft in which they were flying home crashed at Munich airport, Sir Matt effectively lost his 'other family' ...
> But the gravel voiced Scott was a battler. His personal fight for survival gripped the nation ... A decade later this remarkable man had rebuilt his life and assembled another brilliant team. On an unusually hot May evening at Wembley the transformation was complete.[56]

By constructing the life of Matt Busby according to this discourse, the press secured a reading of Busby's career as being born of occasional adversities that drove him and Manchester United on to greater victories.

The press coverage that accompanied Busby's death did not end with comments on his role in building the successful Manchester United teams of the 1940s, 1950s and 1960s. Attention was drawn to the legacy of Busby's years as team manager, and to the links between his success and the success that the club was enjoying in the early 1990s. In both the *Daily Mail* and the *Manchester Evening News*, stories were told of parents taking children to Old Trafford after Busby's death to explain the significance of the man to the history of Manchester United.[57] Through these stories and others it was suggested that Busby had laid the foundations for Manchester United's present-day success through the revival that he inspired after Munich. It was, therefore, posited that the club could still be read according to the discourse of loss and recovery.

156

The proposed link between the Busby era and the success and status of Manchester United in the 1990s does not appear to have been lost on Manchester United supporters. Fans of the Old Trafford club would, of course, have referenced the Busby years in the construction of their shared support throughout the 1970s and 1980s: Busby was still a physical presence at the club during those decades and represented 'better times' to people who were perpetually disappointed by the performances of United during a relatively unsuccessful period. However, since the 1990s it appears that a fresh regard for the discourse of Munich and the 1968 European Cup has developed amongst Manchester United's supporters. This has seen new cultural practices emerge at the club that act to restate and re-enact the links between Manchester United in the present and the club's story in one specific period of its past. In recent years, Manchester United fans have continued to sing 'we are the Busby boys', despite their clear devotion to present manager Sir Alex Ferguson (who has also led the club to a European Cup victory). They have also hung a semi-permanent banner in the Old Trafford stadium that references the date of the Munich air crash and describes the Munich victims as 'The Flowers of Manchester'. In fact, this banner draws on another recent cultural practice that has developed at United, namely, the singing of the late 1960s song 'The Flowers of Manchester' by supporters who gather at the Munich memorial at Old Trafford every year on the anniversary of the air crash.[58] Through these practices and many more, United supporters display the continuing resonance of the Munich loss and recovery discourse in their fandom.

A particularly extreme form of remembrance from Manchester United supporters around the Munich disaster could be observed on the club's pre-season tour of the United States of America in the summer of 2003. Before the club's match in New York, a banner was hung in the city bearing the legend 'Munich 6th February 1958 – New York 11th September 2001 – United in Grief – Lest we Forget'. By inviting comparison between the Munich air crash and the attack on the New York World Trade Centre, the group of United supporters who were responsible for the banner received a great deal of criticism, not least from fellow United supporters who felt that they were overstating their case.[59] However, this extreme example was employed by rival supporters to draw attention to what has long been perceived to be an 'exploitation' of the Munich disaster by Manchester United and its fans for the club's commercial gain. Supporters of clubs with a particularly sharpened sense of rivalry with Manchester United, such as Leeds United, Liverpool and Manchester City, have for many years claimed that the discourse of Munich is kept alive by Manchester United Football Club to draw new supporters to the club. They believe that the mysticism and mythology of Munich is the main reason why Manchester United emerged as a 'super-football-club' with supporters drawn from around the globe, and claim that the club continues to market the disaster for its own ends.[60] In fact, some Manchester City supporters now routinely refer to Manchester United supporters pejoratively as 'Munichs' to register their criticisms of this process.

The contest over the meaning of Munich as a mythologized discourse of loss and recovery indicates its centrality to the identity of Manchester United Football Club and its supporters. For many Manchester United fans, keeping the memory of 'the Munich story' alive, in the specific way in which it was constructed by the British press in the late 1950s and 1960s, is central to their supporting practices regardless of criticisms from rival supporters. Their mutual belief in the loss and recovery discourse is a central part of their shared fandom: it is the story that defines the history of 'their' football club, and thereby helps fans understand where their club came from and where it is going. In this sense, the Munich disaster is much more than an historical event for many Manchester United supporters. It is a living cultural practice that needs to be learned and 'consumed' as part of 'becoming a United fan'.

CONCLUSION

The evidence presented in this study shows the enduring importance of death, disaster and tragedy in the creation of collective identities. Indeed, it indicates the lasting influence that disastrous events have on 'communities' (communities of football supporters in this case), and shows how disasters add fresh meaning to institutions from which people derive shared experiences. Manchester United was effectively defined by the discourse that emerged in the wake of 6 February 1958, and the club continues to be redefined by the same event to this day.

The role of disasters in building communities is especially noteworthy at this particular historical juncture. In much recent writing on community, it has been noted that the old ties that bound people together, such as class, gender, locality, ethnicity and nationality, are no longer as relevant as they once were. In place of communities built around these 'old' affiliations, writers such as Giddens, Lash and Maffesoli have claimed that people now increasingly associate themselves with 'communities of taste' or 'elective communities' that are established via consumption, ritual and the reflexive project of identity construction.[61] If this is correct, then Leeds United, Liverpool and Manchester City supporters should not be surprised that the Munich disaster is constantly re-evoked by Manchester United supporters and 'marketed' by the club for consumption by contemporary fans. Many football supporters in England and elsewhere have been routinely choosing their clubs on grounds other than locality for much of the post-war period,[62] and, therefore, are willing to assert their fandom through ritual and consumption, as well as through more 'traditional' means. In this regard, it is entirely unremarkable that the discourse of Munich continues to be such a visible marker of Manchester United's identity. In fact, it would be more remarkable if it were not.

NOTES

1. *The Times*, 7 Feb. 1958.
2. *Daily Mail*, 7 Feb. 1958.
3. *The Times*, 7 Feb. 1958.
4. *Manchester Evening News*, 8 Feb. 1958.
5. *The Times*, 8 Feb. 1958.
6. V.T. Gawronski and R.S. Olson, 'Tapping Collective Memory of Disaster: Getting "Inside" the 1985 Mexico City Earthquakes', *International Journal of Mass Emergencies and Disasters*, 19, 3 (2001), 297.
7. G.R. Webb, T. Wachtendorf and A. Eyre, 'Bringing Culture Back In: Exploring the Cultural Dimensions of Disaster', *International Journal of Mass Emergencies and Disasters*, 18, 1 (2000), 7.
8. T. Horlick-Jones, 'Modern Disasters as Outrage and Betrayal', *International Journal of Mass Emergencies and Disasters*, 13, 3 (1995), 306.
9. Gawronski and Olson, 297.
10. Webb, Wachtendorf and Eyre, 5.
11. Ibid., 6–7.
12. For an extended discussion of this point with specific reference to Manchester United see, G. Mellor, 'The Genesis of Manchester United as a National and International Super-Club, 1958–68', *Soccer and Society*, 1, 2 (2000), 151–66.
13. *The Times*, 10 Feb. 1958.
14. *Manchester Evening News*, 8 Feb. 1958.
15. *Daily Mail*, 16 Feb. 1958.
16. Ibid.
17. For a debate on this issue see, S. Sweet, 'The Effect of a Natural Disaster on Social Cohesion: A Longitudinal Study', *International Journal of Mass Emergencies and Disasters*, 16, 3 (1998), 321–31.
18. *Daily Mail*, 8 Feb. 1958.
19. *Manchester Evening News*, 11 Feb. 1958.
20. Ibid.
21. *Manchester Evening News*, 7 Feb. 1958.
22. *Manchester Evening News*, 8 Feb. 1958. See also *The Times*, 9 Feb. 1958.
23. *The Times*, 8 Feb. 1958.
24. *The Times*, 8 Feb. 1958.
25. *The Times*, 10 Feb. 1958.
26. *Manchester Evening News*, 11 Feb. 1958.
27. *Manchester Evening News*, 8 Feb. 1958.
28. *Manchester Evening Chronicle*, 11 Feb. 1958. This quote and others relating to conflict within Manchester over the Munich disaster have previously been used in G. Mellor, '"We hate the Manchester Club Like Poison": The Munich Disaster and the Socio-Historical Development of Manchester United as a Loathed Football Club', in D. Andrews, *Manchester United: A Thematic Study* (London and New York: Routledge, 2004).
29. *Manchester Evening Chronicle*, 26 Feb. 1958.
30. *Manchester Evening Chronicle*, 5 March 1958.
31. *Manchester Evening Chronicle*, 15 March 1958.
32. T.E. Drabek, *Human System Response to Disaster* (New York: Springer-Verlag, 1986), pp.181–2.
33. *The Times*, 7 Feb. 1958.
34. *The Times*, 8 Feb. 1958.
35. *Daily Mail*, 10 Feb. 1958.
36. *Daily Mail*, 7 Feb. 1958.
37. *Manchester Evening News*, 6 Feb. 1958.
38. *Manchester Evening News*, 7 Feb. 1958.
39. *Manchester Evening News*, 8 Feb. 1958.
40. Ibid.
41. *Daily Mail*, 20 Feb. 1958.
42. Ibid.
43. *Daily Mail*, 29 May 1968.
44. *The Times*, 29 May 1968.
45. Glasgow Celtic were the first British club to win the European Cup in 1967.

46. *Manchester Evening News*, 30 May 1968.
47. Ibid.
48. *The Times*, 30 May 1968.
49. Ibid.
50. Ibid.
51. *Manchester Evening News*, 21 Jan. 1994.
52. Ibid.
53. Ibid.
54. *The Times*, 21 Jan. 1994.
55. Ibid.
56. *Daily Mail*, 21 Jan. 1994.
57. *Daily Mail*, 21 Jan. 1994 and *Manchester Evening News*, 21 Jan. 1994.
58. I have observed these practices on visits to Old Trafford. I thank my colleague Adam Brown for draw-ing attention to the singing of 'The Flowers of Manchester' at Old Trafford on anniversaries of the Munich disaster.
59. A long debate about this banner occurred between football supporters on the football supporters' website *The Pride of Manchester* in August 2003. Go to: www.network54.com/Hide/Forum/180216.
60. For more on this see Mellor, 'We hate the Manchester Club Like Poison', and C. Brick, 'Can't Live With Them, Can't Live Without Them: Reflections on Manchester United', in G. Armstrong and R. Giulianotti (eds), *Fear and Loathing in World Football* (Oxford: Berg, 2001), pp.9–21.
61. See, for instance, A. Giddens, *Modernity and Self-Identity* (Cambridge: Polity Press, 1991); S. Lash, 'Reflexivity and its Doubles: Structures, Aesthetics, Community', in U. Beck, A. Giddens and S. Lash, *Reflexive Modernization: Politics, Tradition and Aesthetics in the Modern Social Order* (Cambridge: Polity Press, 1994); and M. Maffesoli, *The Time of the Tribes: The Decline Of Individualism in Mass Society* (London: Sage, 1996).
62. See Mellor, G., *Professional Football and its Supporters in Lancashire, circa 1946–1985* (PhD thesis, University of Central Lancashire, 2002), chap. 7.

10

Political and Social Fantasies in Peruvian Football: The Tragedy of Alianza Lima in 1987[1]

ALDO PANFICHI, VÍCTOR VICH

*Anyone who has not felt grief in Football
knows nothing about grief.*
– Julio Ramón Ribeyro

THE TRAGEDY

Following the first round matches of the 1978 World Cup, the Argentine magazine *El Gráfico*[2] described the Peruvian team's midfield players (César Cueto, Teófilo Cubillas and José Velásquez of the Alianza Lima team) as the best in the world. The blue-and-white-shirted Alianza team had won the national championship that year for the second year in a row. Subsequently, however, the team had had a barren spell that seemed never-ending. Indeed, 18 years went by before the Alianza Lima team was able to relieve the suffering of its fans by winning the national championship in 1997.

This 18-year wait would, in all likelihood, have been significantly shorter had it not been for the events of 8 December 1987. By 1987 – nine years after their last national title – the team had been totally renewed and was comprised of a new generation of stars. These players, commonly referred to as *los Potrillos* (the colts) because they had come from Alianza's minor divisions, were considered the new hope for Peruvian soccer. Seven of that squad had already been called up to the national team, and were seen by the fans as replacements for the great players of the 1970s, who could help Peru qualify for the 1990 World Cup in Italy.[3] With three games remaining in the 1987 national championship, *los Potrillos* were in first place. However, before they could clinch the Peruvian title the entire team drowned as a result of a tragic air accident.

On 8 December the team played its final game in the Peruvian jungle against Deportivo Pucallpa, which Alianza won 1-0. According to one media report, the players acted in a strange manner on the day of the match as was evidenced when they did not celebrate the goal that had brought them to the verge of the league championship. It is said that after the match, they returned to their hotel, bathed, picked up their belongings and without wasting any time, went to the airport in order to return to Lima as soon as possible. Such was their haste to return to the capital that the club had chartered an airplane from the Navy (a Fokker F-27 A-560) to fly them back to the capital city that same day.[4] The plane left Pucallpa at 6.30 p.m. and at 8.15p.m., shortly before the scheduled landing, the crew reported an emergency on board. That was the last contact made with the control tower in Lima before the plane plunged into the Pacific.

A problem with the instrument panel in the aircraft's cockpit appears to have been the cause of the accident. Lima was blanketed in heavy fog when the airplane began its descent that evening. Alarmed at being unable to confirm whether the landing gear had dropped into place, the pilot contacted the control tower so that they could check whether this had occurred. The technicians assured him that there was no problem and that he could land. According to Juan Parra, the air traffic controller on duty, the aircraft was losing altitude when, in an attempt to turn around to return to the airport, its right wing hit the ocean. The impact proved to be fatal.[5]

The death toll amounted to 43 and included 16 players, five members of the coaching staff, four managers, eight fans, three officials and seven crew members. The pilot (Navy lieutenant Edilberto Villar) was the only survivor of this tragedy. The dead included the team's star player, Luis Escobar, who made his debut in the team at 14 years of age (he was 18 when the accident occurred) and had become the sensation of Peruvian football. Also lost were Francisco Bustamante (age 21) and José Casanova (age 22) who had earned much acclaim and had already been called up to the national team. The outstanding striker, Alfredo Tomasini, (age 22) and the defenders Daniel Reyes (age 21) and Tomas Farfán (age 21) perished in the crash. Marcos Calderón, recognized as the best Peruvian coach of all time, also died in the accident, as did Jose Gonzáles Ganoza (age 33), popularly known as 'Caico', the legendary goalkeeper who had defended the Alianza goal for 14 years. As mentioned previously, it was the general consensus of the press that this talented young team represented the renewal of Peruvian soccer and the conviction that success and glory were imminent.

Mourning the Victims

Unsurprisingly, the tragedy made headline news for several consecutive days, kindling and keeping alive the distress and sorrow that swept through the capital city and far beyond. Radio and television stations started broadcasting the news very early on the day after the crash. People were taken aback by the news and a general feeling of sadness spread throughout the country. Spontaneously, relatives, fans and friends made their way to the beaches of Ventanilla or to the Club's stadium in the district of La Victoria to obtain further news and express their sorrow in a communal fashion. In the following days, collective expressions of suffering were repeated as bodies began to appear in the Pacific Ocean. Multitudes participated in dramatic religious ceremonies, attended fervent football matches in honour of the deceased players and bid their idols farewell in sorrowful pilgrimages from the players' original neighbourhoods to the Matute stadium in the district of La Victoria and from there to the General Cemetery. Needless to say, special press issues on the crash as well as memorabilia such as photographs, jerseys and posters of the departed players quickly sold out to Alianza fans. According to a popular saying prevalent at the time of the tragedy, the Alianza party had gone from 'Victory to Glory' (in reference to La Victoria, the club's original district).[6]

Elite groups in Peruvian society, as well as political leaders, also made their presence felt in this period of public mourning. Alan García, President of Peru at the time, Cardinal Juan Landázuri Ricketts and several State Ministers attended the main public services for the victims of the crash and the majority of them claimed to have been Alianza fans since childhood. The Municipal Council of La Victoria ordered everyone in the district to fly the Peruvian flag and declared three days of mourning in honour of the dead. Teófilo Cubillas, who had retired from football the previous year, announced that if Alianza needed him, he would wear the shirt again. This was a promise he kept, turning out for the team three weeks later when the national championship resumed. From London, Bobby Charlton publicly expressed his sorrow at the news of the tragedy, recalling the air accident suffered by the Manchester United club on 6 February 1958.[7] Likewise, Peñarol of Montevideo (Uruguay) played the finals of the Intercontinental Cup in Tokyo wearing black arm bands as a sign of solidarity with their Peruvian counterparts.[8]

THE POLITICAL-ECONOMIC CONTEXT OF THE DISASTER

The above is a brief account of the circumstances of the crash and the outpouring of grief and mourning that followed it. This section will examine the context of the disaster. In order to do so, it is important to understand some general traits of Peruvian football as well as the exceptional circumstances of mid-1980s Peru. Historically, Peru's professional football teams have been characterized by limited resources and extremely unstable income flows, with no support from the state and only limited commercial income. This means that the Peruvian Football Federation has always been in the difficult position of balancing the expectation level of Peruvian football fans, and the realities of organizing the sport in a context of poverty. However, this precarious balancing act became much more difficult after 1985, when a populist government and an increasingly powerful military intervened in this sphere.

In 1985, the newly elected government of Alan García Pérez responded to long-standing historical demands by enacting a series of measures promoting the political and economic decentralization of Peru. In response to these moves, a range of institutions in civil society followed suit. In such an environment the

Peruvian Football Federation felt it was a political necessity to have teams from all regions represented in the First Division, which to date had been dominated by Lima-based clubs. To this end, the Federation decreed that as of 1986 there would be decentralized, regional championships involving clubs on the coast, the highlands and the Amazon jungle. Practically overnight, this decision increased the number of first division teams from 17 to 44 (with the two best in each region going through to the finals). Given the number of clubs and regions involved, the cost of organizing this new championship would be much higher. For example, in 1986 the costs of team travel were often greater than the income generated from the games, and the clubs tried to save money by taking informal flights rather than commercial airlines, without much concern for the risks this involved.[9]

These risks were made worse by the deplorable state of the country's commercial aviation system in the mid-1980s. Half of the 200 planes registered for commercial use in Peru were paralysed due to a lack of replacement parts. The inability to rectify this situation was rooted in the general economic crisis of the 1980s. Another deficiency in the Peruvian aviation system was the increasing involvement of the military in air transportation. Taking advantage of an outdated air transport law that did not prevent military involvement in commercial air travel, the armed forces began to offer their cargo planes for charter flights at lower prices than private companies. Despite the potential safety irregularities associated with this, the government tacitly accepted the military's involvement in the Peruvian air transport, not least because it was a mechanism for generating additional income for the military during a period of budgetary constraint and serious political instability.

In this context, therefore, it is important to note that it was a Navy aircraft that plunged into the ocean that night, having been chartered by the Alianza Club to fly to Pucallpa. The plane had no formal permission to fly, it had not been reviewed by the civilian authorities and the pilots had not been subjected to any checks. Although the Alianza club bears responsibility for taking such a risk, the fact that they did so reveals the weak financial situation of organized sports and the armed forces in this country. In other words, the backdrop to this crash is that of a poor nation with weak institutions, whose airplanes crash and whose most popular clubs rely on informal channels to make ends meet.

Although there was much press speculation regarding the cause of the crash, the Navy said little in the days immediately following the disaster. Its announcements regarding the accident were scant and straightforward and demonstrated little in the way of sensitivity towards the relatives of the dead. Indeed, on 9 December, the written press reported tense arguments between the distraught relatives and the security guards at the navy base where the former had gone in search of news and more information.[10] Three witnesses – two leading sports journalists and one Alianza official – also claim that shots were fired into the air as a warning for them to leave.[11] The Navy's reluctance to disclose information was obvious and became even more radical when it prohibited the relatives of the victims from participating in the search for bodies in the ocean. In view of the rumours that one of the players, Alfredo Tomasini, had spoken with the pilot whilst they were both struggling to survive in the sea, his family had tried to rent a private boat, but they were not allowed to do so. In fact, the Navy prohibited all civilian vessels from entering the scene of the accident preferring to conduct the search and rescue operations on its own.

It is not surprising to note that this behaviour on the part of the Navy aroused suspicions amongst the people of Lima and beyond and gave rise to a number of interpretations of the circumstances surrounding the disaster that differed from the official standpoint. In this article, we sustain that the number and content of 'unofficial' stories that emerged reflect both the prevailing distrust and suspicion of the Armed Forces at that time, in the midst of a 'dirty war' that was gripping the country, and also deeper cultural differences present in contemporary Peru.

ALTERNATIVE STORIES OF THE DISASTER

Before examining the content and meaning of the alternative stories or explanations of the disaster, it is crucial to explain the political context that gave rise to them. The year 1987 was a dramatic one in the history of Peru. The political violence that began in 1980 with the emergence of the Shining Path, a Maoist-inspired armed movement, had spread throughout the country and finally reached the capital city Lima. The Shining Path was a small party that broke with the rest of the Left after the transition to democracy in 1980 and opted for armed action against the state. Based originally in the impoverished and largely indigenous region of Ayacucho, the Shining Path sought a 'true' agrarian and communist society under the authoritarian rule of its leader, Abimael Guzmán, who proclaimed himself the 'fourth sword of the world revolution' after Marx, Lenin and Mao. Their strategy was to take the horrors of war from the countryside to the city and included devastating terrorist actions. This campaign, ultimately designed to destabilize Peru was proving successful. The economic situation of the country as a whole was rapidly declining, and in 1987 the government attempted to nationalize the banking and financial system, which accelerated the loss of its credibility and legitimacy amongst the Peruvian populace.[12]

As the Shining Path took its war to Lima, it began to commit a series of assassinations of high-ranking Navy officers who had been in charge of combating the movement in the so-called Emergency Zones of the Peruvian highlands since 1982. In fact, Navy agents trained in the School of the Americas in Panama were assigned to Ayacucho, the original bastion of the Shining Path, during the opening years of political violence, and were responsible for the highest number of human rights violations during that period. By 1987 it was common knowledge that the security forces had also resorted to arbitrary detentions, torture, disappearances and extra judicial killings in their battle against this violent movement. According to the recent report of the national Truth and Reconciliation Commission, between 1980 and 2000 an estimated 69,280 people died or disappeared in this 'dirty war'. Of these figures, 46 per cent were victims of the Shining Path and 36 per cent were victims of the various armed forces (another 24 per cent died at the hands of peasant self-defence leagues and other paramilitary groups).[13] As a result, the civilian population was, in some cases, as fearful of the Navy agents as they were of the Shining Path.

What needs to be stressed here is that the massacres and extra-judicial executions began to spread to the capital city, where they had powerful resonance. In May 1986, a Shining Path death squad assassinated Rear-Admiral Carlos Ponce, a member of the Peruvian Navy Staff. This had a significant impact on the national conflict because it was the first killing of a high-rank military official. It is likely to have played a major part in the Peruvian government's harsh reaction to a mutiny in Lima's prisons a few months later. Taking advantage of the fact that the annual conference of Socialist International was being held in Lima, prisoners accused of terrorism rebelled in the different prisons, demanding various penitentiary benefits. President Alan García, a charismatic young social democrat with a following in Europe, ordered the Armed Forces to suppress the rebels, and this led to what became known as the Massacre of the Prisons, resulting in around 300 deaths. According to a report by Amnesty International,[14] members of the Navy shot many of the prisoners in the back of the head after they had surrendered.

It did not take long for the Shining Path to react to this event, and a new surge of assassinations of political and social leaders in the capital city quickly followed. In October, members of the Shining Path assassinated the former Commander-in-Chief of the Navy, Vice-Admiral Jeronimo Cafferata. Consequently, when the Alianza tragedy occurred in 1987, Peru was in the midst of a cycle of violence, political turmoil and social and economic instability. In this period, blackouts caused by blown up electricity pylons, regular 'car bombings', and selective assassinations were commonplace. As our research reveals, this context was crucial in the construction of a number of unofficial or alternative 'stories' that interpreted the disaster in new ways.

It is clear that the alternative accounts of the Alianza Lima disaster that were produced in 1987 were rooted in particular socio-economic and political circumstances. More specifically, they were based on both the prevailing distrust of the State and Armed Forces, and on longstanding fears and fantasies that form part of Peruvian popular culture. A traumatic event can lead to a number of fragmented images, including those that may have been latent and related to previous historical experiences. In the case of this tragedy, it is reasonable to assume that the 'truth' of these stories is not based on the facts themselves, but on the way individuals culturally process historical events experienced in their own lives. At the same time, these accounts emerged in the public sphere as challenges to the official story or explanation of the disaster and the power structures behind it.

In regard to the above, Gaytri Spivak notes that one of the principal means of subaltern communication is through rumour, which often serves to structure alternative interpretations of social reality. In effect, rumours may displace the authority of 'official' versions of reality and thus promote a space for resistance to social domination and new forms of praxis and social representation. For Spivak, rumour is the return of a fragment of historical memory and shows the staging of a social fantasy that persists in its pertinence. In Latin America, the study of rumour leads us to the margins of official rationality and the great breach between the popular world and dominant institutions. Thanks to rumour, the images of the past return politically to establish a critique of the present. Hence the positivist veracity of the stories told does not matter as much as the composition of their images, the possible meanings associated with them, and the need to transmit them in a specific time and place.[15]

As an example of the above, since colonial times a persistent rumour spread across the Andes about a personage destined to extract the fat from people in order to increase production and improve the sound of the Church bells. According to popular accounts, this ghost – known as 'Pishtaco' – attacked unsuspecting rural residents who walked about at night. The appearance of Pishtacos has been a constant in Peruvian history, generally coinciding with periods of great social crisis. When the armed conflict of the 1980s moved from the countryside to the city, this brought about the reappearance of the Pishtaco, albeit in a new form. Pishtacos were now described as tall 'gringos' or foreigners, armed with knives and pistols and wearing military uniforms, and seen as government envoys whose objective was to sell the fat of their victims in order to pay off the country's steep foreign debt. This example suggests that the generalization of the armed conflict in the 1980s not only produced death and destruction, but also stories that served as channels of expression that the population used to symbolize the horrors they were experiencing at the time. Human rights violations by both terrorist groups and the Armed Forces were recurrent and a general feeling of fear seized many Peruvians.

Social and political ghosts also rose from the dead and reappeared in what we have identified as three distinct types of stories or accounts of the Alianza Lima tragedy. In the first, special emphasis was placed on presenting the State (or specific agents of the state) as primarily responsible for the tragedy. In the second, greater emphasis is put on the role of the dead players as virtuous popular heroes, and hence exceptions in a society marked by racism and disdain for the subaltern classes. The third also stems from the multiethnic nature of Peruvian society, but emphasizes the possibility of overcoming underlying racial and social tensions through a shared tragedy.

In relation to the first alternative account, the most common story circulating at the time alleged that the Navy aircraft carrying the Alianza Lima party was transporting large quantities of cocaine hidden in its hold. It was said that the Alianza players had discovered this during the flight and had threatened to publicly report the navy officers to the appropriate authorities. The navy officers responded to this threat by shooting the Alianza soccer players. This, it was claimed, was what caused the accident prior to landing. This account of the disaster is evident in the testimonies below that are worth quoting at some length. The first is from Ofelia Bravo, the widow of the player Tomás 'Pechito' Farfán who lost his life in the disaster:

> It is quite clear to me: the airplane was carrying drugs and the marines shot the plane down. There is evidence. My husband's voter card was practically intact, only slightly damaged by water. Do you think it would have been in that state if it had been in salt water? No. With so many days in the sea, that card would have been destroyed. I am sure the marines dipped it in water so that they could go unnoticed. I am sure they abducted the boys with the intention of making them disappear, and that is what they did. Another piece of evidence was that Marcos Calderón's underpants had a bloodstain which, according to his wife, had been there before the accident. How is it possible for the bloodstain to continue there after so many days in the sea? On the other hand, the luggage and soccer boots had all burst. Strange, is it not? I believe that some of the players never appeared because they had been shot. In all likelihood they confronted the marines. My husband appeared eight days later, but I do not know how they killed him.[16]

María López, mother of another dead player, Francisco 'Pachito' Bustamante tells a similar story:

> No, no, my son is not dead, that is why I have never ordered a memorial mass but a healing mass. God's hand was not involved in this, only the hand of man. I still have hopes of seeing him again. He could not have drowned, because my son was a good Catholic, he always prayed in the María Auxiliadora chapel. Where are they? I don't know, perhaps they took him to some other place, or maybe they never travelled at all. There is something strange about all this. And I told this to Jaime Bayly once on TV after that Navy ship was busted in San Diego (USA) carrying drugs. I told him that the Navy was involved in drugs. That airplane was carrying drugs and it did not crash into the sea, but on the shore. Besides, what a coincidence that the pilot was the only one who survived. If I had that pilot in front of me, I would treat him like a coward. Why would he never meet with the mothers of the victims to tell them what happened? Because he knows the truth. Now I can speak the truth, after all, what could happen to me? I am old and not afraid of anything.[17]

Guido de Lucio, founder of the fan group *Cabezas Azules* (Blue Heads)[18] concurs with this view:

> The plane was loaded with cocaine and the marines shot it down. It was part of the war on the drug trade. The fact that some of the bodies were never

found is because they were riddled with bullets, so they had to disappear so that nobody could see the evidence. Even the sides of the aircraft were not found. A neighbour of mine who is in the navy told me they had been cut off with a blowtorch. That is very possible, considering the relationship between the government – particularly Mantilla, Minister of the Interior at the time – and the drug trade. The pilot was discharged and went to the United States. He never made any statements, nor did he ever come face to face with the relatives. That is further proof of their collusion with the drug traffickers.[19]

Tito Navarro, a sports reporter with a popular radio program, also airs this particular explanation of the disaster:

Some people in the Navy told us that this was the third time this airplane was coming from Pucallpa and that on the two previous occasions it had carried cocaine. When the reporters went to investigate the next day, they were shot at. Where is the pilot? Why did he not make a statement? Nobody could say anything in those days, everyone was scared of speaking out. According to hearsay, Dr Orestes Rodríguez had a bullet hole in the back of his head, Caico had been shot and some of Marcos Calderón's clothes were not even wet. Surely the airplane was carrying cocaine and someone was waiting for it, therefore it tried to turn around and it was shot down. That is what happened.[20]

As mentioned above, we must stress that stories of this nature were created in an attempt to make sense of an incident that seemed incomprehensible and traumatic. Zizek argues that the creation of narratives characterized by fantasy provides meaning when there is much more chaos than sense.[21] Vico adds that fantasy or 'poetic imagination' is capable of allowing individuals to comprehend deep emotional truths that cannot be understood by simple reasoning.[22] The creation of the fantasies and alternative stories surrounding the air crash was clearly an attempt by those strongly affected by the disaster to make some sense of the events that led to the tragedy. They did this by drawing on their understanding of the disaster and incorporating it into the prevailing social context of the time. In this alternative story, for example, two performers face one another in antagonistic roles. On the one hand are the players of the Alianza Lima team, and on the other the Navy officers representing the Peruvian State. The former uncover evidence not only of the corrupt nature of a leading state institution, but also the more general abuse of power evident in Peru at that time, and the latter have no hesitation in abducting, executing and making them disappear to prevent the truth from being revealed. As far as this story is concerned, the accident was not the result of a technical failure or an unfortunate incident, but a political conspiracy. Implicit within this account was public criticism and condemnation of the way the country was being run.

We would like to dwell on the representation of 'truth' and concealment thereof that this story represents. According to this narrative, the State will not allow the 'truth' to come to light, because to do so would undermine the basic foundations of its authority, and of community life itself. If we accept that the State is the main guarantor of social life, and we discover that the State is corrupt, then corruption itself may become the basis upon which community life occurs. From this point of view, revealing the corruption of the State becomes incompatible with social order and must therefore be repressed. Thus, it can be suggested that social order is founded on an illusion or fantasy that ensures the neutralization of antagonisms and creates a sense of unity. With the truth concealed, society will continue functioning as though nothing ever happened. As long as society is divided and opaque, such fantasies are needed to prop it up.[23] In this story, it is the Alianza Lima players who 'discover' the corruption of the State on this ill-fated flight, and that is why they died – to avoid revealing that the apparent guarantor of social life was corrupt, and that social life was founded on a lie or illusion. Zizek states that 'fantasy gives an account of how things appear to the subject', which is why the relatives made every effort to produce evidence that suggests the persistence of identity, of life, and also of foul play (the voter's card, the blood-stained garment, the burst luggage).[24]

The second scenario or alternative representation of the crash produced a group of stories aimed at emphasizing the heroism and endurance of the Alianza players in the face of adversity. The most prominent of these alleges that when the mechanical failure occurred on board the Fokker, the Alianza players, fearing that the plane would plunge into a nearby shanty town, decided to sacrifice themselves and forced the pilot to crash into the sea rather than attempt a landing. In doing so the players prevented numerous deaths.[25] Such stories were produced and encouraged by the daily press in the days immediately following the accident and transformed the Alianza players into heroes in the popular imagination of the nation. In line with Fenn's depiction of heroes, the players were clearly represented as virtuous and as individuals who demonstrated extraordinary acts of sacrifice and selflessness.[26] Faced with the possibility of a far greater tragedy, the heroes expressed inordinate human generosity, far beyond the limits of ordinary individuals. This allowed them to change the course of the disaster and prevent further loss of life. According to these accounts, with their sacrifice, the Alianza team gave the tragedy a sense of heroism that was contrasted against the role that the state is alleged to have played in the disaster.

In the aftermath of the crash, the Peruvian population needed to create heroes to help them come to terms with what happened. The Alianza players fulfilled all the characteristics required: they were young, mostly poor and of black or mixed race; they had a brilliant future and – according to the first alternative story – were committed to the truth. It is therefore not difficult to sustain the theory that the need for heroism is consistent with the symbolic support that socially excluded and underprivileged groups need in order to legitimize their place in society. In the midst of Peruvian culture, in which racism is structural and a culture of disdain is commonplace,[27] the Alianza colts represented a new image in the popular world, which at the crucial time of the tragedy, was a symbol of honesty and virtue.

The third representation of the disaster is also bound up with racial and social differences in Peruvian society, and portrays a scenario in which these can be overcome. This is best illustrated by the story surrounding the pilot Ediberto Villar and the Alianza striker Alfredo Tomasini, who are alleged to have survived the impact of the crash. According to the pilot's testimony, they had both survived the accident and had been swimming for hours, holding on to parts of the plane as they waited for someone to come to their rescue. These accounts stress Tomasini's courageous struggle to keep afloat, with a broken leg, while he confessed his undying love for his mother to the pilot. The navy pilot had encouraged this conversation to prevent the soccer player from surrendering to fatigue. However, just when a rescue helicopter was preparing to save him, Tomasini could hang on no longer and disappeared into the Ocean of Ventanilla.[28]

The accounts of Tomasini's fate are notable for two reasons. First of all, they stress that unlike the other young colts, he had not been born in the 'Alianza cradle'. In other words, he did not come up from the Club's minor divisions, which was a crucial factor in the community and family-minded focus of the Alianza identity, and he had a different social origin. Tomasini was a 'white' (European descent) son of an upper-class family who had attended an elite British school. This meant that unlike the others he had had a comfortable upbringing and had a world of possibilities other than football ahead of him. Yet despite these objective differences, what is most interesting about the Tomasini stories is their emphasis on his assimilation into the Alianza family. Tomasini had declared himself a fan of Alianza since childhood, and even when he was recruited by another team in the minors division he continued to dream of being part of Alianza. A worker at the club reported that Tomasini's beloved mother had supported her son's desire to play for Alianza, and within a short time after joining he became successfully integrated into a group that was mostly comprised of black or mixed race players from poorer socio-economic backgrounds. His strong and powerful style of playing became the ideal complement to the technical skills of his teammates. Consequently, although Tomasini survived a few hours, as a member of Alianza he could not be saved, for (as the stories go) he was destined to share the same fate as his friends and spiritual brothers, *los Potrillos*.

In general terms, it must be said that Tomasini's integration into Alianza was consistent with the expansion of Alianza's fans beyond the boundaries of class and race that marked the creation of the club at the beginning of the twentieth century. The story of Alianza Lima's original foundation indicates that it was a team created in a poor neighbourhood, comprised mainly of textile and civil construction workers, most of whom were black. For decades, Alianza Lima was one of the few symbols of prestige and acknowledgement of Afro Peruvians. Nevertheless, the successes of the *Potrillos* weakened the racial and class boundaries around the team, in favour of emotional and cultural factors that had a greater appeal to individuals of all social groups. Thus, Alianza Lima had moved from being the people's club to being 'everyone's club', with heroism and community spirit at the base of the cheers for 'Alianza Corazón!!'

CONCLUSION

What are the desires and experiences that gave rise to these alternative accounts of the disaster? What is the relationship between the images represented here and the social history of a country plagued by political instability, racism and conflict? Our argument here is that these stories, while clearly fantasies, are culturally and politically determined accounts that combine real experiences with unconscious desires. On the one hand, these accounts express a deep and understandable distrust of the State, and particularly of the Armed Forces. The search for another guilty party (beyond the Alianza Club itself) is a characteristic reaction to episodes of this kind, and in this case the military in the 1980s was an easy target. In the popular imagination, the alleged complicity of the military in extra-judicial violence and drug trafficking, which was the stuff of daily news during this period, was transferred to this case and became the 'real' or hidden factor behind the tragedy. Such allegations not only allowed the population to understand a traumatic incident that initially seemed confusing, but may also be read as a broader comment on the exercise of power in Peru.

On the other hand, the desire to transform the victims into heroes and martyrs is also a characteristic reaction to events of this kind. It is evident that in all of these stories there is an implicit account of heroism. The tragic death of such promising young people has the virtue of restoring values and ideals in a corrupt and unjust social order. Through these stories, the young colts remain in the popular imagination as symbols of strength in adversity, and as individuals who will always loom large in the public consciousness. In this process, as Bauza has said, heroes break the narrow cultural and historic framework in which they were born and become popular idols.[29]

Ultimately, we believe that these accounts express both the fantasy that people need to explain tragic and unjust events, and the capacity to 'cross the boundaries of fantasy' into aspects of reality. As Ubilluz has noted, this implies an identification with real antagonisms that survive in real circumstances.[30] Although these stories circulated mainly in socially underprivileged environments, and were catalogued as absurd by the political and intellectual establishment, they imply an underlying distrust and critique of that establishment which remains to this day.

172

NOTES

1. We would like to thank Jose Carlos Rojas for helping us conduct the interviews, and Cynthia Sanborn and our friends in TEMPO (Taller de Estudio de Mentalidades Populares) from the Catholic University of Peru for their valuable comments on an earlier version of this text.
2. *El Gráfico* (weekly magazine), 15 June 1978, pp.8–9.
3. In popular memory, the greatest moments of Peruvian football on the international scene have been associated with the presence of excellent players from Alianza Lima. This was the case with Alejandro Villanueva and Juan Valdivieso in the Berlin Olympics of 1936, as well as with Cubillas and Julio Baylón in the World Cup 1970, and Cubillas, Cueto and Velásquez in 1978 and 1982. Peru did not qualify for the World Cup in 1986, and this generation of veteran players had retired, hence the new *Potrillos* of Alianza became the hope of the entire country. See Orlando Duarte, *Todas las Copas del Mundo* (Madrid: McGraw-Hill, 1990).
4. Liz Mineo, 'La Ultima Tarde', *SI* (weekly magazine), 14 Dec. 1987, pp.68–73.
5. Mario Campos, 'El Vuelo de la Muerte' (interview with Juan Parra), *Caretas* (weekly magazine), 14 Dec. 1987, pp.22–6.
6. Aldo Panfichi, 'El Alianza: todos los colores', *Quehacer* (bi-monthly magazine), 51 (March–April 1988), 86–90.
7. *La Crónica* (newspaper), 9 Dec., 1987. Also see Gavin Mellor's study in this collection.
8. *La Republica* (newspaper), 12 Dec. 1987.
9. See 'El Campeonato Absurdo', *SI*, 43 (12 Dec. 1987).
10. *El Nacional* (newspaper), 13 Dec. 1987.
11. Authors' interviews with Alex Berrocal, Lima, 1 March 2003; Ricardo Correa, Lima, 15 March 2003; Tito Navarro, Lima, 8 April 2003.
12. See Gustavo Gorriti, *The Shining Path: A History of the Millenarian War in Peru* (Chapell Hill, Carolina del Norte: The University of North Carolina Press, 1999).
13. Comisión de la Verdad y Reconciliación, *Informe Final de la Comisión de la Verdad y Reconciliación* (Lima: CVR, 2003).
14. Amnesty International, *Caught Between Two Fires* (New York: Amnesty International, 1989).
15. See Gayatri Spivak, 'Estudios de la subalternidad. Deconstruyendo la historiografía', in Silvia Rivera and Rossana Barragan, *Debates Post Coloniales. Una introduccion a los estudios de la subalternidad* (La Paz: Sephis-Arawiyiri, 1997), pp.247–78.
16. Interview with Ofelia Bravo, Lima, 1 April 2003.
17. See *OJO* (daily newspaper), 14 Jan. 2004; interview with María López.
18. The Cabezas Azules was a group of fans from different tough neighbourhoods that disputed with other groups the leadership of the 'barra brava' of Alianza Lima. See Aldo Panfichi and Jorge Thieroldt, 'Barras Bravas: Representation and Crowd Violence in Peruvian Football', in E. Dunning, P. Murphy, I. Waddington and A. Astrinakis, *Fighting Fans: Football Hooliganism as a World Phenomenon* (Dublin: University College Dublin Press, 2002), pp.143–75.
19. Interview with Guido de Lucio (chief of the 'Cabezas Azules' fans), Lima, 24 Feb. 2003.
20. Interview with Tito Navarro, Lima, 8 April 2003.
21. Slavoj Zizek, *El acoso de las fantasías* (México: Siglo XXI, 1999), p.17.
22. Cited by Hugo Bauza, *El Mito del Heroe. Morfologia y Semantica de la Figura Heroica* (México D.F.: FCE, 1998), p.160. Giambattista Vico (1668–1744), prominent Italian Political Philosopher.
23. Ernesto Laclau and Chantal Mouffe, *Hegemonía y estrategia socialista. Hacia una radicalización de la democracia* (México D.F.: Siglo XXI, 1987).
24. Zizek, *El acoso de las fantasías*, pp.17–18.
25. *El Nacional*, 10 Dec. 1987; *La Crónica*, 10 Dec. 1987.
26. Richard Fenn, *Beyond Idols: The Shape of Secular Society* (New York: Oxford University Press, 2001).
27. See Nelson Manrique, *La Piel y la Pluma: Escritos sobre Literatura, Etnicidad y Racismo* (Lima: SUR, 1999); Aldo Panfichi and Felipe Portocarrero (eds), *Mundos Interiores de Lima: 1850–1950* (Lima: CIUP, 1995); Gonzalo Portocarrero, *Racismo y Mestizaje en el Peru* (Lima: SER, 1993); and Francois Bourricaud, 'Indian, Mestizo and Cholo as Symbols in the Peruvian System of Stratification' in E. Glazer (ed.), *Ethnicity – Theory and Experience* (Cambridge: Harvard University Press, 1975).
28. *La Crónica*, 10 Dec. 1987.
29. Hugo Bauza, *El mito del héroe. Morfología y semántica de la figura heroica* (México D.F: Fondo de Cultura Económica, 1998).
30. Juan Carlos Ubillus, *El sujeto criollo y el monte*cinismo (Unpublished manuscript, 2003).

173

11

The Superga Disaster and the Death of the 'great Torino'

PAUL DIETSCHY

THE TRAGEDY ON SUPERGA HILL

In the late afternoon of 4 May 1949, Sauro Tomà, the Torino full-back, discovered a crowd of neighbours, some known and others unknown, in front of the building where he was living. Tomà was at home because he had been injured and was unable to fly with his teammates to play a friendly match against Benfica in Lisbon. The crowd had come to his house not to congratulate him on Torino's victory in Lisbon but rather to convey the tragic news that his teammates had been killed in a plane crash on their way back from Portugal.[1] The plane, a FIAT G-212 belonging to the Italian company Aeritalia, had made its descent in heavy fog resulting in the pilot, Captain Pier Luigi Meroni, missing his approach to the airport. At 5.03 p.m. the plane crashed at the foot of the Royal Basilica of the Savoy family, located on the Superga hill, a few kilometres from Turin. There were no survivors. Along with the flight crew, 18 Torino players as well as the trainers Erbstein and Lievesley, the club official Agnisetta and the journalists Tosatti, Cavallero and Casalbore, lost their lives in the accident.[2]

Not only did the crash affect Sauro Tomà's life profoundly,[3] but it also impacted on the lives of millions of others. Like all disasters involving famous individuals or celebrities, and accidents that raise questions about the safety of modern forms of transport, interest in the tragedy extended well beyond the sports media and, indeed, Italy's borders. Even though the sense of loss was felt most strongly in Turin, the identity of the victims of the tragedy became known throughout the country and beyond. The players of this Torino team are still remembered today. The main reason for this is because of the status of the team at that time. The players that died in the disaster had dominated club football in Italy since the early 1940s, winning the *Scudetto*, the national championship, in 1943, 1946, 1947 and 1948. The club also dominated the *squadra azzurra*, Italy's national team, in this period. For example, for the game between Italy and Hungary played in Turin on 11 May 1947, ten of the 11 Italian players played for Torino.[4] The club's profile and success not only embodied excellence, but also the reconstruction and recovery of Italy and Turin in the aftermath of the Second World War. However, the disaster, symbolically at least, halted both Italy and Turin's recovery. Of course, the tragedy had huge ramifications for the progress of Torino. In particular, it highlighted and deepened the financial difficulties that the club had been experiencing since the 1930s and illustrated the weakness of its economic base. The disaster also demonstrated the strength of the emotional bond between the club and its supporters. This bond deepened in the aftermath of the crash and Torino's fans, the *grenat tifosi,* became football activists intent on preserving the memory of the '*caduti di Superga*', the players who died on the hill.

MOURNING 'NATIONAL' HEROES

It was up to Vittorio Pozzo, the old selector of the Italian national team, and Roberto Copernico, member of the board of the club, to identify the remains of the victims. The funeral took place two days after the tragedy on 6 May 1949. More than 500,000 people converged on the centre of the Piedmont's capital, in particular on piazza Castello, to pay their respects to the deceased. A chapel of rest had been set up for the mourners in the Madame palace in the centre of the piazza Castello. According to reports by the *questore* of Turin, the pressure of the crowd wanting to get close to the coffins was such that the *Celere*, the police force, had to turn back fans and other onlookers on several occasions.[5] Following speeches by the mayor, sports authorities and Giulio Andreotti, assistant Secretary of State at the Council Presidency representing Alcide De Gasperi, the funeral procession progressed to the *Duomo*, Turin's cathedral, where the archbishop of Turin celebrated the funeral mass. The dead were then buried in the city's general cemetery.

As a mark of respect, the Italian FA (FIGC), in agreement with the other Italian clubs, awarded the *Scudetto* to Torino. The club responded by seeing out the remainder of the season by playing their junior team in front of mourning crowds. Although this was a hugely symbolic gesture and demonstrated a sense of solidarity with Torino, it was not as big a sacrifice for the other clubs as it might appear. Before the team travelled to Lisbon, Torino had secured a draw in the San Siro stadium against Inter Milan, a result that kept them five points clear at the top of the league table. With only four matches remaining, three of which were at home, this draw had all but secured the title anyway.

As might have been anticipated, Italy's media covered the disaster for more than a week in exhaustive detail and it joined with the Italian people and football authorities in mourning, remembering and eulogizing the football 'martyrs' who had lost their lives. However, the effect of the disaster was felt far beyond Italy's borders and its reach extended across the Atlantic Ocean. When news of the tragedy reached South America, the Football Associations there 'agreed to keep' the date of the disaster as 'a day of football'. Other acts of remembrance in South America included the decision by the Argentine club, River Plate, to organize a benefit match to raise funds for the families of the deceased. Torino, led by

Ferruccio Novo, also undertook a short tour of Argentina in June 1951 and, whilst there, were met by General Peron in person.[6] The outpouring of empathy from South America can be partially explained by the numbers of Italian immigrants living there. In addition, Torino's tours of Brazil and Argentina on the eve of the First World War ensured that their reputation was known throughout these countries.[7] Indeed, their 2-0 success over the Argentine national team in Buenos Aires did much to generate interest amongst the local population. This link with Argentina was strengthened when Torino's President, Enrico Marone, bought Argentinean players such as Libonatti in the inter-war period. On the international front, the Executive Committee of the Fédération Internationale de Football Association (FIFA), acting on the recommendation of Jules Rimet, its president at the time, decided 'that all international matches and matches played by first division clubs on Sunday 7th May 1950 shall be interrupted and one minute of silence will be observed in memory of the disaster of Torino'.[8]

The Superga disaster and the deaths of the Torino players and officials were felt strongly among its contemporaries because the tragedy had involved a group of individuals who incarnated sporting excellence. As mentioned previously, Torino had dominated the Italian Championship in the immediate post-war years. Their successes in the *Scudetto* were comprehensive. They won the 1946–47 championship, ten points clear of local rivals Juventus, who had dominated Italian football in a similar fashion in the early 1930s.[9] The gap was even greater the following season when they secured the title with 16 points to spare over the second-placed club, Inter Milan. The team also beat its opponents soundly that year as Franco Ossola and Renato Tavella emphasize: 'It's enough to remember for example that among the numerous victories that season the records show: Roma-Torino 1-7, Torino-Salernitana 7-1, Torino-Inter 5-0, Torino-Triestina 6-0, Torino-Fiorentina 6-0 and even, Torino-Alessandria 10-0!'[10] Torino's success in this period was due in no small part to their adoption of the WM system of play at the end of 1941.[11] They were amongst the first Italian clubs, along with Genoa, to introduce *il sistema*, as the WM formation came to be known in Italy. Once the team had adapted to this tactical formation under the guidance of its trainer, the Hungarian Erbi Erbstein, Torino acquired a balance between individual virtuosity and collective cohesion and success quickly followed.[12]

Torino's innovative style of play and the league titles that this brought led the club to obtain the admiration of sports fans all the way into the Mezzogiorno. That this was the case had much to do with what their success represented outside the context of sport. Torino's adoption of such an innovative and rational system of play echoed the modernization of an economy in Turin that had FIAT at its forefront. The victories that followed symbolized the hopes and aspirations of both the Turinese and Italian people to rise up from the destruction of the Second World War and to reconstruct and modernize their city and their nation. Since the end of the war the club had effectively served as an ambassador for an Italy that had been marginalized by its diplomatic choices during the war and its murderous fascist past.[13] For example, as early as September 1945, Torino's 3-1 victory over Lausanne was interpreted by the press as 'a very satisfying day for the Italian sports and morals'.[14] As Aurelio Lepre pointed out, the popularity and success of the team was due to the national and international context where 'the only field where national pride (for Italians) could be freely expressed, was that of sports'.[15]

The respect that the team was held in was very much in evidence in January 1949 when, according to Erbstein, groups of *tifosi* converged on the stations where the train bringing the team from Salerno to Palermo was scheduled to stop so that they could greet the team, get an autograph or exchange a few words. The enthusiasm of the fans was such that in the Sicilian capital, the team's hotel was surrounded by supporters, and the *Celere* had to intervene to disperse the 'fanatics'.[16] When travelling in the North of the country Torino used a coach that came to be known as '*Il conte Rosso*', the Red Count, and when it passed through different communities on its way to games it regularly created scenes of excitement. It should be noted though that there were occasions when traditional forms of antagonistic football rivalry typified the response of opposition supporters to Torino. For example, following a victory over Livorno in Tuscany in January 1948, applause for the Torino players was followed by chants of 'England! England!'[17] This was a reference to a forthcoming match between the Torino-dominated *squadra azzurra* and England which was being played to mark the fiftieth anniversary of the Italian Football Federation. The actions of the Tuscan *tifosi* demonstrated that, while Torino had acquired a level of respect that cut across historical regional differences in the Italian domestic game, the club had not managed to establish a solid, organized nation-wide *tifosi*. Nonetheless, the national reputation of the team and the respect for what it had achieved and represented in both a sporting and wider sense, ensured that the Superga disaster was experienced as a national loss.

AN URBAN LOSS

Whilst the disaster resonated nationally, the loss of the team took on a much deeper sense in the Piedmontese capital, particularly within the context of the rivalry between Juventus and Torino, the clubs of the 'two cities' within Turin.[18] The first of these 'cities' comprised the aristocratic and bourgeois centre of Turin, which was traditionally a Juventus 'stronghold', at least until immigration from Southern Italy from 1955. The working class suburbs on the other hand were firmly behind Torino. Derby games between the two clubs saw a confrontation between the tasteful black and white football shirts of Juventus, representing the Turinese bourgeois classes, and the *grenat*, almost blood red shirts, of Torino which symbolized the working class of the city. Since the 1930s the habits and behaviour of the two sets of supporters created stereotypes rooted in the class-based antagonisms between both clubs. In the central stands of the *Corso Marsiglia* stadium and later in *stadio Mussolini*, the Juventus fans expressed their support for the club with restraint and style. This contrasted heavily with the atmosphere in Torino's *stadio Filadelfia* not far from the FIAT Lingotto plant, where the atmosphere was considerably more raucous and loud. These differences in fandom were encapsulated in *La Stampa Sportiva's* coverage of the derby in 1931. The typical Juventus fan was described in the following terms: 'Even when he's in the parterre or in the popular benches he knows how to keep his style; from the parting of his hair to the stripe on his trousers, it's one single line.' The nature of the fandom expressed in Torino's home stadium was very different: 'The Torino supporter doesn't hide his passions, on the contrary he shows them to the whole world. Refusing to comply with the Juventus chic he wore the colours or the emblem (the bull) of his team on various items such as flags or papier-mâché statues at the stadium in the street, in the tram, in the café.'[19] Since the 1920s the *grenat* supporters had formalized this type of behaviour into an early form of organized *tifo*. At a derby played in 1927, for example, the police confiscated 'a thousand red hats with a white paper band that were supposed to identify the Torino supporters' from the *grenat tifosi* and prohibited 'the use of various trumpets to make noise as well as fifty megaphones'.[20] These differences in style and behaviour reflected real social antagonisms. Indeed, the successes of Torino in the derby matches were celebrated as victories of the working class over the Juve 'aristocrats'.

The rivalry between the two sets of fans was intensified because both clubs were often in direct competition for the *Scudetto*. Juventus's titles in the 1930s would have been difficult for the *grenat* to live with. However, prior to their successes in the 1940s, Torino won the Italian championship on two occasions. Whilst its 1927 title was withdrawn by the Italian Football Federation following allegations of corruption,[21] the club secured the league the following year. These feats were not repeated until the arrival of the new club President, the industrialist Ferruccio Novo, in the autumn of 1939. Novo invested significant funds in the team, both in terms of buying players and paying large salaries. For example, he acquired the centre-forward Gabetto from Juventus for 330,000 liras in 1941,[22] and Mazzola and Loik from Venice for 1,200,000 liras, the following year.[23] Novo's investment and his acquisitions were key to Torino's dominance of Italian football until the Superga accident.

Novo did much more than bankroll the club in this period. The context in which the club soon operated needed to be carefully charted. Turin was particularly hard-hit during the Second World War. The densely populated and industrial suburbs had been badly damaged by Anglo-American bombings. The building where Valentino Mazzola lived had been hit, as had the Filadelfia stadium.[24] From September 1943, partisan organizations and civilians in the city had also been subject to the terror, tortures and massacres at the hands of the Republican Fascists and the Nazis. In that context Ferruccio Novo handled the club as any company owner would, with much caution and a hope for better days. His most pressing concern was to protect his 'player capital' from two threats. The first was the risk of the youngest players being conscripted into the republican troops. The exemption to conscription that had applied to elite level Italian sportsmen no longer applied with the Italian National Olympic Committee (CONI), which had relocated to the north of Italy having decided that 'any participation in sports events was prohibited for men declared unfit for military service'.[25] The second danger was the enrolment of football players in the enforced labour teams in Italy or Germany. To guard against these threats, Novo decided to seek a solution by drawing on the help of FIAT, the company that had provided the economic backing for Torino's local rival. Novo managed to fashion an agreement that led to the players being deemed employees of FIAT, representing the company in its sports activities.[26] In doing so, they were exempted from military service. As a consequence of this trend of players obtaining employment with companies like FIAT and experiencing the same difficult circumstances of war torn Italy, the working class fans of Torino could more readily identify with the Torino team of the 1940s. Thus, a close bond formed between the fans and the team. Players such as Valentino Mazzola and Sauro Tomà were identified as coming from identical backgrounds to the fans, having worked at the Alfa Romeo factory in Milan and the La Spezia Arsenal respectively. The centre-forward Gabetto was also born in the workers' stronghold of Borgo San Paolo in Turin, thereby strengthening the working-class roots of the whole club. In these circumstances, it is no surprise to learn that the first people to pay their respect to the victims of the Superga disaster on the day of the funeral were the workers who 'before going to work – it was hardly daylight yet – walked by silently in the Madame palace and then at the end of their day's work, filled the streets where the funeral procession had passed to be with them once more'.[27]

Whilst the club's close affinity with the workers was a factor in the grief and respect expressed following the disaster, the sense of loss felt at the passing of the 'great Torino' was not limited to Torino's working-class fan base. An understanding of those who mourned victims highlights another view of the club's success in the 1940s. This view was regionalist in character and portrayed Torino's league titles as a form of compensation for Turin and the Piedmont's status as the birthplace of Italy's unity. It was felt that this had not been appropriately rewarded and that Torino had brought the city the recognition that it deserved. This was the view of Massimo Caputo, director of *La Gazzetta del Popolo*'s, who asserted, a year after the disaster, that the team was one of 'the numerous creations by which [...] Turin, that had sacrificed all its privileges on the altar of Italian unity, had been able to maintain its prestige and an important position in the life of the nation and in the eyes of the world. It was another sign of its vitality.'[28] Thus, the loss of the Torino team awoke a sense of belonging to the city that, for a few days at least, made the population forget their social and political differences. 'There were those who just looked, silent and sorrowful, those who let their tears run, those who crossed themselves, those who raised their clenched fist. The catastrophe brought everybody together, rich and poor, and for a day the antagonisms were forgotten.'

One year after the disaster this sense of unity was still in evidence. For example, Gianni Agnelli, owner of Juventus, and the Juve players attended a memorial ceremony on Superga hill on the first anniversary of the tragedy.[29] However, the intense rivalry between the clubs re-emerged in the 1951–52 season, and the derby played at Filadelfia in December 1951 marked a return to types of fandom evident in previous Torino-Juventus encounters. As one observer remarked, the 'stadium was dressed for a feast' and 'hundreds of flags and writing ordered a win'. Perhaps the clearest example that the Juventus-Torino rivalry had returned to pre-1949 levels became evident in the 1970s when Juve fans began to incorporate the Superga disaster into their attempts to antagonize and insult the Torino fans. This manifested itself in the form of the chant, 'Grande Toro, we pray you: if you take plane, we pay the ticket'.[30]

THE 'GREAT TORINO': THE IDOL WITH CLAY FEET

The titles won by Torino during the Second World War might appear to be attributable to the financial backing of Ferruccio Novo and the other directors of the club. However, after liberation such expenditure was not seen at Torino,[31] and the club began to operate in economic conditions similar to the 1930s. Novo did not have the finances to invest in the club, and certainly could not match the investment that Gianni Agnelli, the President of Juventus from the summer of 1947, was making in Torino's rivals.[32] The club also lacked the type of fan base that sustained Roma or Milan. The number of spectators at Torino's matches could not compare with the crowds that filled the San Siro stadium in Milan. From 1946 to 1949 the average number of spectators varied between 15,800 and 21,300. Although this figure was 3,000 more than Juventus regularly attracted, the average gate at Inter or AC Milan games exceeded Torino's by at least 10,000.[33] Even though the number of spectators increased during this immediate post-war period, attendances subsequently reached a plateau. The *grenat* leaders rented the renamed *stadio comunale* (formerly the *stadio Mussolini*) for derby matches, where attendances reached 60,000, but the *Filadelfia*, with a capacity 40,000, was rarely full. Torino's successes were largely followed in the press, the radio or in the cafés, rather than in the stadium. When negotiating a reduction of the taxes on the entrance fees from 5 to 4 per cent with the City of Turin in March 1949, the board of Torino hinted that that it might play all of the following season's matches at the *stadio comunale* and thus optimize the use of the city's biggest stadium. In doing so it revealed a harsh reality: that Torino lacked funds.

Even before the Superga disaster decimated the player assets of Torino, the club was suffering from financial difficulties. From September 1948, in agreement with the board, the president Ferruccio Novo had taken a back seat at the club and had given full administrative powers to the Secretary General Arnaldo Agnisetta. With the new title of General Director, Agnisetta was tasked with preparing a range of reforms for the club and easing its financial difficulties.[34]

This was a difficult task because despite the fact that the popular success of the club had brought in an average 100 million liras (80 million from the home matches, 20 million as a part of the visiting teams' contribution), the budget was constantly at a deficit with annual expenditure often reaching 200 million liras. According to Sauro Tomà, on the eve of the Superga disaster, Torino's deficit was running at about 100 million liras.[35] Nevertheless, losses at the end of the season seem to have been common for Italian clubs. Bari, for instance, finished the 1947–48 season with a deficit of 40 million liras, which forced it to sell three of its best players.[36] The best that many clubs could hope for was to balance their accounts.

Aside from the relatively low numbers of spectators mentioned above, the weak financial plight of Torino was compounded by two further issues. Firstly, the game was subject to increased taxation in the immediate post-war period. According to *La Gazzetta dello Sport* in September 1945, out of every 100 liras paid through the turnstile, Serie A clubs only retained 56.10 liras. The remainder went to the National Solidarity Fund (13 liras), indirect taxes (21.90 liras), the Italian Football Federation (5 liras) and to the municipality as rent for the stadium (3 liras).[37] The taxes, both federal and local, had thus increased from 25 per cent before the war, to more than 46 per cent afterwards. Secondly, the players' salaries seem to have weighed particularly heavily on Torino's budget. At the time, many Italian clubs paid a 're-employment' bonus to their 'best players', which, added to salary and match bonuses, meant that the total package reached 6 million liras per player per year. As far as transfers were concerned, Torino did not spend the types of money that it did in the early 1940s and the maximum paid for a player was 5,200,000 liras for Martelli from Brescia in 1946. Although there are few details regarding Agnisetta's project to turn the club's finances around, it is clear that it was not implemented or that it did not have the expected results because in the 1950s, as we shall see below, Torino's finances still depended heavily on a small number of sponsors. Only a drastic reduction of its expenditure and thus a lowering of its sporting ambitions would allow Torino to balance its accounts.

In terms of the fiscal health of the club, the Superga disaster could not have happened at a worse time, and Torino might not have survived had it not been for the support that they received in the aftermath of the crash. For example, the Comitato Olimpico Nazionale Italiano (CONI) lent the club 200 million liras to rebuild the team. In addition to this support, 16 million liras were donated by both well-known and unknown donors to a fund called 'Torino-simbolo'.[38] Finally a committee led by Giulio Andreotti, and consisting of the Italian Football Federation and CONI presidents Barassi and Onesti, was set up to supervise the dissemination of funds amounting to 30,187,896 liras collected for the victims' families.[39]

These monies were crucial in terms of the immediate survival of the club, but Torino was still living beyond its means and if the club was to have a financially viable future then it had to find new sources of financing. To this end, in May

1953 the club created the limited company 'Torino-Sport'. This non-profit organization had as its mission 'principally to assist the Association Calcio Torino in
all its activities and sports and economic endeavours'.[40] Lacking a major sponsor
since Novo retired from the presidency to become honorary president in 1955, it
was really a question of attracting as many well-heeled sympathizers as possible
who could together contribute large sums of money to the club. The 'Torino-
Sport' company showed how useful it was from the summer of 1954. At the end
1953–54 season the debts had actually reached the level of 180 millions liras.[41] The
sale of players and some other assets reduced it to 80 million. Torino-Sport came
in at that stage with a contribution of 50 million, further reducing the deficit. The
municipality of Turin gave a further 500,000 liras to the Torino-Sport company
in order to, according to the Christian-Democrat counsellor Torretta, 'reinforce
the CALCIO Torino team that the Turin population had already wanted to help
at a particularly difficult and painful time'.[42]

Torino's financial plight was still not resolved though, and three years later
the club faced an economic crisis. In May 1957 the club owed 274,751,000 liras.[43]
From a financial point of view, the Superga disaster had clearly not been overcome. Not only were the usual solutions proposed, new ones had to be found. In
that spirit, the new president, the industrialist Mario Rubatto, presented a plan to
reduce the deficit based on the normal income of the club. Firstly, 94 million liras
had to be found to pay the most urgent creditors (in particular 58 million to the
banks). Rubatto proposed that a new loan of 80 million liras be secured and
guaranteed by the 'Torino-Sport' company and another of 40 million guaranteed
by the Municipality of Turin. The Municipality also gave an annual subsidy of 15
million liras under the condition that Torino agree to play its matches at Juventus's home ground, the *stadio comunale*.[44] The club was then required to save 180
million through a rigorous budget policy. Considering that, on average, the club
brought in 120 million liras per season from ticket sales and from their percentage
of the gate from away matches, Rubatto insisted that the club should not spend
more than 100 million a year. This would have created a surplus of 80 million
over a period of four years. By including a projected annual contribution of 25
million from the members of the Board, the debts should have been cleared in
four years.

As well as using traditional means of financing football clubs, Rubatto demonstrated himself to be an innovator when he decided to turn to a new form of fund-
raising: shirt sponsoring. Rubatto negotiated an agreement with the president of
the food-company Venchi-Unica for 55 million per season, which represented
about 45 per cent of the club's own revenues.[45] The deal was proposed for three
years and stipulated that the club was to be called Talmone-Torino and that all
players would wear a white T on their shirts.[46] The club's financial recovery in the
aftermath of Superga was a slow one. The disaster revealed and deepened structural difficulties that were apparent within Torino in the 1930s and that were
inherent to the fragile economics of professional football in Italy. Ultimately, it

took an event as catastrophic as the tragedy of 4 May 1949 for the club's managers to implement the type of financial procedures and plan that might allow Torino to establish a sound financial footing in the decades to come.

TIFOSI ACTIVISM AND MEMORY

Whilst Rubatto's financial prudence saw the club recover economically, this did not translate on to the playing field. In the first and, indeed, only year of this plan, Torino's results declined. In December 1958 the Piedmontese journalist Carlin lamented: 'Everything has been taken away from the old Torino; its house, its name and its best players.'[47] Even though the sale of some players and the financial support of Venchi Unica had reduced the deficit considerably and financially saved the club according to *Tuttosport*, the team was relegated to Serie B for the first time in its history. In addition, many Torino fans felt that the club had lost its soul, firstly by leaving its historic home stadium and secondly by changing its name. The response to this from the club's fans was vociferous. On 31 December 1958 the *cavaliere* Cillario, representing the Torino *tifosi*, called for the 'the immediate return to *campo Filadelfia*'.[48] At the same time, during a debate of the Municipal Council on the subsidy to the club, the Christian-Democrat councillor Giuseppe Grosso stated: 'The Torino-Talmone is a commercial enterprise. The heart and the feelings are no part of it. The Torino-Talmone can win or lose; it's no longer the Torino.'[49] These sentiments echoed the protests that were raised when Gianni Agnelli proposed to unite Juventus and Torino at the end of the season 1956–57 following equally poor results at the rival clubs.

The expression of such sentiments illustrates that the Superga disaster, far from discouraging the *grenat* fans, made them unite and become much more actively involved in voicing their views on how the club should be moved forward. This new activist *tifosi* was motivated by a desire to defend the memory of the lost ones, and they felt that this could be best achieved by getting behind the new team on the one hand and closely monitoring the way that the club was being run on the other. This is why some *tifosi* decided to formalize the expression of their support from the early 1950s onwards. According to this group 'the *tifosi* don't [live] alone, on the contrary they [feel] the need to meet frequently, in the cafés in the centre or in the outskirts of the city to express their passion freely'. In short, these fans wanted to be recognized by the club as 'a representative force'.[50] In some sense, the disaster made the *tifosi* much more expressive and willing to participate more actively in the life of the club and make it much more democratic.

Although this activist fan group began to make its voice heard in the early 1950s,[51] it was not until the second half of the 1950s that this *tifosi* began to really make its presence felt and acquire some recognition from the club. This was largely due to the fact that in August 1956, the association of *sostenitori* established itself as a 'sports group' and christened itself as the *Fedelisimi Granata*. Its goal was to 'unite in a single association all the real *tifosi* of Torino to prepare all possible travelling to accompany the team and to defend the existence of the company against any threat of fusion'.[52] The group lost no time in making its presence felt and in January 1957, the vice-president of the *Fedelissimi*, Ignazio Tedesco, interviewed by *Tuttosport*, requested the departure of those directors that were frequently absent from the club.[53] The group was formally recognized by the club hierarchy and Rubatto who, before the start of the Torino-Roma match, addressed those in the stadium via a loudspeaker and asked for 'the traditional support of the fans' whilst making reference to 'the enlargement of the social structure (of the fans)'.[54] From then on, facing united and autonomous fans, the president of Torino had to take into account their views and act almost as a 'tribune' for the people of the Toro, and not as a senator, insensitive to their voice. This was a dramatic departure from the way that the fans expressed themselves in the 1940s and earlier. Indeed, in the days of the 'great Toro' the fans simply focused their attention on what was happening on the field of play and creating a raucous and colourful atmosphere in the stadium. They left the club's officials to get on with the task of managing the club.

In the late 1950s it became increasingly evident that the *tifosi* was motivated largely by a desire to ensure that the club developed in a way that honoured the memory of those lost on Superga hill. On the 10th anniversary of the tragedy the *fedelissimi* published an article in their newsletter or 'fanzine', the *Toro*, which stressed this desire: 'we only ask you to go into the field with the memory of your great predecessors in mind and one single will in your hearts, one single firm intention: the Toro can't die, it must live, long live the Toro!'[55] The disaster had clearly mobilized this group and allowed them to distinguish themselves as 'real *tifosi*' as opposed to 'occasional fans' who would not follow their club in hard times as well as good. These hard times were not far away and by the spring of 1959 Torino were threatened with relegation. In March the *fedelissimi* booked a special train for 400 people to support their team at an away match in Bologna as a way of demonstrating their loyalty and translating their words into actions. Despite their support, the team lost and was relegated to Serie B.[56] Relegation did not discourage those who saw themselves as '*supertifosi*', and during the following season in Serie B the *fedelissimi* sent representatives to all away matches. In doing so they made a contribution to Torino's promotion back to Serie A.

Thus, a special form of *tifo* was born from the Superga disaster, based on activism and memory. This *tifo* has persisted and has manifested itself in recent years. For example, when Torino won the *Scudetto* in the 1975–76 season, its president, Orfeo Pianelli, and the trainer Gigi Radice led a celebratory but respectful procession of more than 20,000 *tifosi* to the Royal Basilica and the site of the crash. More recently on 4 May 2003, tens of thousands of fans marched from the *Filadelfia* stadium to the piazza San Carlo.[57] Although Torino had been relegated to Serie B for a fourth time in 14 years, this demonstration of support for the club illustrated the pride that was felt at being a Torino fan. Given that demographic changes in Turin had led to an influx of people from the Mezzogiorno, most of whom started to support Juventus,[58] this march was also a way of affirming a sense of pride of being from the Piedmontese and being the 'true' representatives of Turin.

Aside from inspiring the formation of an activist fan group, the victims of the disaster were remembered and honoured in other ways. For example, since the beginning of the 1950s the cult of the great players such as Loik and Mazzola who lost their lives was regularly celebrated in *Tuttosport*.[59] Picture postcards were also printed in the aftermath of the crash and these allowed the fans to remember and celebrate the achievement of the dead players. Indeed, even today these reminders of the 'martyrs of 1949' can still be found in many tobacco shops in Turin.[60] Also, from the 1980s literature and commemorative material was published for old and new fans which has ensured that the 'great Torino' remain at the forefront of the club's history and that the Superga disaster continues to be embedded in what it means to be a Torino fan.[61]

NOTES

1. Sauro Tomà, *Vecchio Cuore Granata* (Turin: Graphot, 1997), p.74.
2. The names of the dead players were as follows: Bacigalupo, Ballarin I, Ballarin II, Bongiorni, Castigliano, Fadini, Gabetto, Grava, Grezar, Loik, Martelli, Menti, Maroso, Mazzola, Operto, Ossola, Rigamonti and Subert.
3. As he said during our interview on 11 Feb. 1997.
4. 'Italia-Ungheria', *La Stampa*, 13 May 1947.
5. Archivio di Stato di Torino, gabinetto della prefettura (hereafter AST gb), busta n. 404, telegram 6 May 1949 from the *questore* (superintendent) Brunetti to the prefect of Turin.
6. 'Il Torino-Simbolo ha ricambiato la solidarietà al River Plate festeggiante il cinquantenario', *Il Calcio Illustrato*, 5 July 1951.
7. Vittorio Pozzo, *Campioni del mondo* (Rome: CEN, 1960), pp.32–3.
8. FIFA Archive, FIFA Executive Committee, Agenda Minutes 1947–1950, Meeting held in Paris on 17 Dec. 1949 in the office of the Fédération Française de Football.
9. The Juventus team led by Edoardo Agnelli, the son of FIATS's founder and its owner, won five championships in a row from 1931–35.
10. Franco Ossola and Renato Tavella, *Breve storia del Torino calcio* (Rome: Newton, 1995), p.26.
11. 'L'attività dei calciatori torinesi. Il granata e il "sistema"', *La Stampa*, 25 Dec. 1941.
12. 'Il Segreto del Torino', *La Gazzetta dello Sport*, 13 June 1944.
13. After the Ethiopian war and the British and French opposition to it, Mussolini signed the Axe agreement with Hitler in November 1936 that led Italy into the war against France, England and USA. After the fall of fascism and the American landing, in summer 1943, Mussolini was reinstalled by the Germans in northern Italy at the head of a fascist Republic. Then began a civil war between fascist troops and the Italian Resistance. During the fighting, fascists tortured and massacred partisans and the general population.
14. 'Granata in Svizzera si affermano brillantemente', *La Stampa*, 18 Sept. 1945.
15. Aurelio Lepre, *Storia della prima Repubblica* (Bologne: Il Mulino, 1993), p.146.
16. 'Avventure del Torino da Palermo a Busto', *Tuttosport*, 9 Jan. 1949.
17. 'Livorno-Torino (1-3)', *Tuttosport*, 12 Jan. 1948.
18. The term 'two cities' is taken from the title of Mario Soldati's novel published in 1964.
19. 'Introduzione al match Juventus-Torino', *La Stampa Sportiva*, 17 Dec. 1931.
20. AST gb, busta n. 405, telegram from *questore* Chiaravellotti to Turin's prefect, 5 June 1927.
21. 'Il Torino privato del titolo di campione d'Italie. La grave deliberazione del Direttorio Federale', *La Stampa*, 4 Nov. 1927.
22. Gianmaria De Pauli, *Il Barone Volante. Vita e carriera di Guglielmo Gabetto* (Turin: Editrice Press, 2003), p.59.

23. This deal also saw two Torino players move in the opposite direction. Gabriele Chiuminatto and Alberto Mangiantini, *90 anni Torino Calcio* (Turin: Editrice Triedi, 1996), p.42.
24. 'Torino-Ambrosiana 6-2', *La Gazzetta dello Sport*, 5 June 1944.
25. 'Una nota del CONI. Gli atleti e il servizio militare', *La Gazzetta dello Sport*, 22 Jan. 1944.
26. 'Novità nel Torino', *La Gazzetta dello Sport*, 24 May 1944.
27. 'Il popolo in ginocchio gettava fiori sulle bare', *Tuttosport*, 5 May 1949.
28. 'A un anno dalla sciagura di Superga', *La Gazzetta del Popolo*, 4 May 1950.
29. 'Superga', *Tuttosport*, 6 May 1950.
30. Christian Bromberger, *Le match de football. Ethnologie d'une passion partisane à Marseille, Naples et Turin* (Paris: Editions de la Maison des sciences de l'homme, 1995), p.66.
31. *Il film del Campionato di calcio 1942–1943.*
32. Renato Tavella, *Il romanzo della grande Juventus* (Rome: Newton, 1997), p.128.
33. Figures from Paul Dietschy, 'Football et société à Turin 1920–1960', unpublished PhD thesis, (Lyon: University Lyon II, 1997) pp.464–5.
34. 'Il Torino vuole un "sistema" anche amministrativo', *Tuttosport*, 6 Sept. 1948.
35. Tomà, *Vecchio Cuore Granata*, p.81.
36. 'Il Bari vende per sanare il bilancio', *La Gazzetta dello Sport*, 13 July 1948.
37. 'Budget di un club di serie A', *La Gazzetta dello Sport*, 13 Sept. 1945.
38. 'Raccolti 18 milioni da 'Torino-Simbolo', *La Gazzetta del Popolo*, 21 Sept. 1949.
39. 'I fondi provittime di Superga nelle dichiarazioni di Barassi', *La Stampa*, 7 Feb. 1950.
40. 'E stata costituita la Società Torino-Sport', *Tuttosport*, 22 May 1953.
41. 'Necessità sociali e techniche nella base del Nuovo Torino' *Tuttosport*, 22 July 1954.
42. 'Il contributo del Commune alla squadra del Torino scatena una vivace discussione sulla situazione dello sport italiano', *La Gazzetta del Popolo*, 7 July 1954.
43. 'La situazione patrimoniale del Torino e il plano quadrienale di risanamento', *Tuttosport*, 19 May 1957.
44. Atti Municipali del Comune di Torino (hereafter AMCT), 1958, deliberazione del 21 gennaro 1958, § 9, 'Erogazione di un contributo da parte della Città. Revoca della deliberazione del Consiglio Communale in data 4 settembre 1957' and AMCT, 1958, deliberazione del 14 luglio 1958, § 48, 'Stadio civico concessione per l'uso del campo di calcio dall'AC Torino, approvazione dello schema di convenzione'.
45. 'Talmone-Torino: firmato l'accordo', *Tuttosport*, 13 April 1958.
46. Talmone was the name of a chocolate brand from Turin and its advertising had been common in the Juventus and Torino stadiums in the 1920s.
47. 'Torino-Inter 0-5', *Tuttosport*, 29 Dec. 1958.
48. 'Dopo le demissioni del presidente e dei consiglieri', *Tuttospor*t, 1 Jan. 1959.
49. *La Stampa*, 21 Jan. 1959.
50. 'Gli attivisti del tifo granata si presentono con un comunicato', *Tuttosport*, 10 Nov. 1951.
51. For example, in an open letter to the managers of Torino published by *Tuttosport* on 10 Nov. 1951, a section of the *tifosi* requested a meeting with representatives of the club to discuss its future.
52. 'Il Gruppo Fedelissimi Granata si è costituito in Associazione Sportiva', *Tuttosport*, 25 Aug. 1956.
53. 'La crisi del Torino', *Tuttosport*, 23 Jan. 1957.
54. 'Torino-Roma 1-0', *Tuttosport*, 11 March 1957.
55. 'Due parole ai vivi', *Il Toro*, 4 May 1959, a single issue.
56. 'Treno speciale di tifosi granata a Bologna', *Tuttosport*, 19 March 1959.
57. 50,000 according to *La Repubblica* on line. See 'In piazza l'orgoglio granata', 4 May 2003, www.repubblica.it.
58. Goffredo Fofi, *L'immigrazione meridionale a Torino* (Milan: Feltrinelli, 1975), p.76.
59. 'Ricordiamo I caduti di Superga. Un passato che indica un avvenire', *Tuttosport*, 4 May 1951.
60. The most representative examples have been reproduced in Luca Giannelli (ed.), *100 Anni del Campionato di Calcio* (Florence: Scramasax edizioni, 1997), p.72.
61. See for instance Franco Ossola, *Grande Torino per sempre!* (Turin: Il Punto, 1998); Renato Tavella, *Valentino Mazzola. Un uomo, un calciatore, un mito* (Turin: Graphot, 1998); the 11 short stories by Fabrizio Calzia, *Le nuvole di Superga. Il racconto in favole del Grande Torino* (Turin: Sagep, 2002); and Stefano Bovero, *Un sogno granata … E se il grande Torino fosse sopravvissuto a Superga?* (Turin: Il Punto, 1999).

INDEX

191

press. In the week after the disaster, the *Manchester Evening Chronicle* described how commercial and retail organizations in Manchester that had refused to fly flags at half mast in recognition of the Munich Disaster were being criticized for showing 'a disregard for public feeling'. In response to this report, a number of letters were published that strongly refused to accept the homogeneous response to the air crash that the discourse of unity demanded. A Manchester reader wrote:

> Business people whom [your newspaper] accuses of showing a lack of respect by not flying flags ... to half-mast ... and indeed with the same ... lives in debt ... can 'the sheep' in the very act of setting better. No doubt ... on Old Trafford terraces on Saturdays were both deeply ... ... the sad death of the United players and the management. But can the ... be made public in ... when the football crazy ... could be the ...

In the ... by most of ... recorded ... of ... cautious ... against the unity of ... and ... despite of ... ... a ... this ... the ... the ... were met with a lively response ... ... if not only in readers letters. After Alberta series of letters in March 1958, responding to ... ... it was apparently for the people of Manchester ... acceptance, to write to the *Manchester Munich*, Arthur Walmsley, the *Manchester Evening Chronicle*'s sports editor, wrote:

> Manchester, ruled by ... and ... ... the ... in ... the ... ... and WITHIN ... over ... ... remembering ... Manchester ... other ... ... and ... ... and ... in this ... ... of an ... ... if we ... to ... ... for ... ... which ... ... the ... of ... and ... in ... in behalf ... greater of ... civilise world. If only we are accused of ... ... most of ... Munich ... disaster in carrying it on through the ... and ...

Walmsley defended these criticisms by stating that they were 'inspired by some genius and even an eternal form of envy at the tremendous loyalty display of by the Manchester public to the United club'. He went on ... arguing by a number of letters to the *Chronicle*. Under the title 'Stop ... these furious criticism of United' one reader claimed that any decline in the cruder sympathy than had previously existed for United in the press was inherent ... personalities that, with specific reference to newspaper reporting of football. Manchester United's disaster over West Bromwich Albion in a 'cautious round' of the FA Cup, the sports editor:

> 'Babbling' 'cautious' ... 'nothing pitiful' ... these are among the highly coloured descriptions of Old Trafford times seen since the defeat of Wolves ...